Katharina Hansen Löve

THE EVOLUTION OF SPACE IN RUSSIAN LITERATURE
A SPATIAL READING OF 19-TH AND 20-TH CENTURY NARRATIVE LITERATURE

Amsterdam - Atlanta, GA 1994

ISBN: 90-5183-669-4 (CIP)
©Editions Rodopi B.V., Amsterdam - Atlanta, GA 1994
Printed in the Netherlands

"Like every living creature, a writer is a universe unto himself, only more so. There is always more in him that separates him from his colleagues than vice versa. To talk about his pedigree, trying to fit him into this or that tradition of literature is, essentially, to move in a direction exactly opposite to the one in which he himself was moving. In general, this temptation of seeing literature as a coherent whole is always stronger when it's viewed very much from the outside. In this sense, perhaps, literary criticism indeed resembles astronomy; one wonders, though, if this resemblance is really flattering."
(Joseph Brodsky, 1986: 291)

voor mijn ouders

Contents

Preface

The analyses in the second part of this book are all modified versions of previously published articles. Chapters 1, 3 and 4 were published in *Russian Literature* (XXXIV-I pp. 37-59, 1993, XXVIII-II pp. 175-211, 1990, XXX-II pp. 109-135, 1991), Chapter 2 in *Semantic Analysis of Literary Texts* (Eds. E. de Haard, Th. Langerak, W.G. Weststeijn), 1990, Amsterdam, and Chapter 5 in *Dutch Contributions to the Eleventh International Congress of Slavists in Bratislava 1993*, 1994, Amsterdam (forthcoming).

Translations of quotations from literary texts are taken from existing English translations, as indicated in the annotations that accompany them. Unless mentioned otherwise, all remaining translations of Russian fragments are mine. Transliterations of the Russian language are in accordance with the system of scholarly transliteration. However, I decided to omit the apostrophe in the spelling of Gogol's name, because of the somewhat strange appearance of the possessive case (Gogol''s). Transliterations in English quotations may, of course, differ from the system I used.

Acknowledgements

This study would never have been completed without the constant support of a number of people to whom I would like to express my heartfelt thanks. Above all, I am grately indebted to my promotor, professor Willem G. Weststeijn, who invited me to work on this thesis. I thank him for his confidence, his patience and his useful suggestions and advice. I am also grateful to professor Jan van der Eng for his stimulating remarks during the early stages of my work. I thank my colleagues at the University of Amsterdam for their critical reading and often useful comments on the various chapters of this book. I am especially grateful to my dear friend Emilie Gordenker for her careful reading of the manuscript and her corrections of the English language. I also thank the persons who helped correcting the manuscript. I thank my husband Stefan Woudenberg for editing and designing the lay out. Last but most important, I wish to thank my friends and family for their moral support, their encouragement and their help with solving all kinds of practical problems.

Introduction

The subject of this thesis is a comparative study of the function, structure and meaning of space in a number of successive periods in Russian literature, i.e. Romanticism, Realism, Symbolism and Modernism. The central question is whether it is possible to discern a development, or at least change in the way space expresses itself in literary form. What are the differences and the similarities between the spatial categories of the narrative texts in these periods?

The study consists of a theoretical section and an analytical section. In a third, concluding section, the outcome of the analyses will be compared with current theories on literary space and literary evolution.

Ever since Tynjanov and Jakobson's 1928 adagio "История системы есть в свою очередь система" [The history of a system is in turn a system] (Striedter 1972, II: 388) scholars have been studying the process of literary history as the continuous change of a system. Their fascination for the changes of the literary system in the course of its evolution has resulted in a number of different theories[1]. Each of these theories shows an apparent eagerness for arranging the literary phenomena into consistent groups. This has resulted in the formulation of, so called, literary typologies, some of which will be discussed in the following chapter.

The search for the systematic character of literary evolution, initiated by the Russian Formalists, in particular by Tynjanov and Jakobson in the above quoted article, was continued in the first place by the Czech Structuralists. In more recent years, scholars such as D.S. Lichačev, I.P. Smirnov and J.R. Döring-Smirnov have resumed these theoretical activities, the latter two as representatives of the Semiotic approach to literature, but with an obvious kinship to Formalism and Structuralism.

Literary, or stylistic typologies in general, are in effect the reconstruction of the system of rules governing a certain period of (literary) history. This system is then regarded as the aesthetic code of that period. Smirnov and Döring-Smirnov have drawn up a whole catalogue, or cluster, of sub-codes, that together represent a certain style-period. From one period to the next this cluster of sub-codes changes, which ultimately results in an entirely new aesthetic system. Of all the sub-codes, I am in the first place interested in those which determine literary space.

However, changes of one system to the next are always gradual and characterized by the existence of transitional forms. The dominance of one of these forms ultimately determines the course of literary development.

For my analysis, I have selected a number of representative texts from the periods under discussion. As "representative" I consider well-known texts by important authors, texts which furthermore must contain sufficient spatial details to justify an extensive investigation of this form of literary expression. Each analysis might be considered, therefore, a "spatial reading" - чтение сквозь призму пространственности - of the text.

In my discussion of the function of spatial elements in literature I have put into practice the theories on literary space, as they were developed by Jurij Lotman and

Vladimir Toporov in the late sixties, seventies and early eighties. A first attempt at a typological description of Russian literature based on spatial features of the text was made by the Dutch slavist Joost van Baak (1984, 1988). All these theories are the subject of the second part of the theoretical section.

The period of Russian Romanticism was analysed on the basis of two texts. The important romantic genre of the exotic tale, in Russian literature mainly situated in the Caucasus, is represented by Ju.M. Lermontov's poema "Mcyri" ["The Novice"]. That this text has been written in verse and not in prose, was not considered a handicap, in view of the presence of the traditional narrative categories of plot, hero and setting in this narrative poem. In N.V. Gogol's short story "Nevskij prospekt", it was the combination of the fantastic theme with the St. Petersburg-location that attracted me. Both texts are rather late examples of Romanticism, which explains some transitory features, and which makes them all the more interesting in the light of my investigation of literary development.

The behaviour of the spatial category during Russian Realism was analysed in I.A. Gončarov's novel *Oblomov*. It was a challenging task to detect the importance of the spatial category in a novel where the main emphasis is on the hero of the story and which is dominated by the principle of characterization and psychologization.

Notwithstanding the fact that Russian Symbolism was very much dominated by the lyrical genre, some excellent prose has been written by the Symbolists. My choice fell on the story "V tolpe" ["In the Crowd"] by F. Sologub. Owing to its preoccupation with an illusory world of symbols, judged to be more "real" than the physically tangible world of things, Symbolism created a strongly dualistic model of the world, permeating the text on all levels. Space is seen to play an important function in creating this bipolarity, as I have tried to demonstrate in the case of Sologub's story.

As an example of Modernist space, I have analysed Andrej Platonov's novel *Kotlovan* [*The Foundation Pit*]. Space is connected with the major issues in this story - man's place in this world - and therefore plays a key role in the establishing of meaning of the text. Modernism can, to a certain extent, be considered as the culminating point of a development in which the spatial category reaches unprecedented importance.

For my analysis of the function of space in Russian literature, I not only based myself on the theories of Lotman, Toporov and Van Baak, but was also stimulated by their own analyses. Lotman's work on Gogol' (1968) and Bulgakov's *Master i Margerita* (1986), Toporov's extensive discussion of Dostoevskij's *Prestuplenie i nakazanie* [*Crime and Punishment*] (1973) and Van Baak's analyses of Zamjatin's story "Peščera" ["The Cave"] (1981), and Babel's cycle *Konarmija* [*The Red Cavalry*] (1983) deserve special mention.

2

Part I

CHAPTER I

Continuity and change in literary evolution

1.0 introduction

Just as literature can be perceived as a system of continuous changes against a background of continuity, so literary theory can be regarded as a system in flux. This holds true in particular for the theories concerning the phenomenon of literary history, or, as it is generally known today, according to Formalist terminology, literary evolution. Theoretical movements as Formalism, Structuralism and Semiotics can therefore be considered as an evolutionary array[2], comparable to, e.g., Romanticism, Realism, Symbolism. Certain concepts become "automatic", prompting the reconsideration of the theoretical model and thus provoking new theories. But at the same time, old concepts and theories may reappear in subsequent phases of theoretical thinking.

1.1 Russian Formalism

During the 1920s, the Russian Formalists initiated the theoretical debate about the systematic research of literary history. In a number of programmatic articles they lay down the rules and methods of research of the immanent laws of literary history in its development, or, as it became known ever since, its "evolution".

With their "model of evolution" these scholars distanced themselves from the more traditional ways of approaching the phenomenon of literary history, where a causal, deductionist view prevailed. It was especially the harmonious, peaceful way in which literary history was described in biographical, sociological, economic and other empirical terms, that deeply dissatisfied them[3]. According to Formalist understanding, literary evolution is an extremely dynamic matter, dominated by the principles of conflict and struggle.

I will restrict myself here to the articles that deal explicitly with the problems of literary evolution, i.e. Tynjanov 1924 and 1927, and Tynjanov & Jakobson 1928, all of which could easily be called programmatic for different phases of Formalist theoretical thinking[4].

Early Formalism, with its emphasis on devices of defamiliarization, automatization, estrangement and impeded perception, terms coined by Viktor Šklovskij in his programmatic essay "Iskusstvo kak priem" ["Art as device"] (1916), concentrated primarily on literary innovations. The theory failed to account for the other, more conservative, phenomena in literature, the so-called constants necessary for the preservation of the identity of the system, and as the guarantee for its continuity. At this point, literary evolution was understood as a seesawing between canonization and decanonization of forms and genres, a literary perpetuum mobile. However, it would be erroneous to identify this cyclical model of evolution with Formalist understanding of literary development in general, for Formalism itself was in state of constant evolution.

The Formalist's early, extreme position was attenuated in the following, more mature and subtle period, with Tynjanov as the most outspoken theoretician on problems concerning literary history. In this phase of Formalism, the work of art, as well as the literary system, became seen as a system of interrelated, structural elements, each element having its specific function.

As for literary history, the Formalists were mainly interested in the evolution of literary genres and the concomitant change of literary devices. This, however, does not preclude the application of their theories and terminology to other aspects of the literary text and to other fields of literary research. In view of the problems under discussion in this study, i.e. the function and meaning of literary space in various periods in Russian literature, I would like to consider the traditional narrative categories, such as plot, hero, and the time-space continuum (or setting), the so-called constituent elements of the text, from a Formalist point of view. This means that these categories or elements also undergo functional changes in the course of literary history. Each evolutionary stage implements a recasting and refunctioning of all the components of the system, structural, constituent and stylistical elements alike, in which some elements will show a tendency toward change and rejuvenation, whereas others will manifest a more conservative nature.

The function of each narrative category is thereby determined by the code of the stylistic period to which the work of art belongs. This function, understood as the functional relation of a particular narrative category with the other blocks, is therefore to a certain extent restricted. Space, for instance, may play a more or less important role. A change of codes from one period to the next bears influence on the nature of the mutual relation between dominant and subjected functions and categories.

This restriction, of course, takes place on a supra-individual level, whereas the artist in pursuit of creative freedom, consciously or unconsciously, has to struggle with these limitations. As a matter of fact, the possibilities for the individual author to depict and describe the various narrative elements are virtually unlimited.

An important difference between a literary work and norm is that a literary work undergoes constant rejuvenation in the historical process while manifesting latent, hitherto unknown, possibilities against a background of new realities. On the other hand, a norm, once it has fulfilled its historical mission, disappears from literary consciousness and becomes historical past. (M. Grygar 1982: 191-2)

With the distinction between synfunction and autofunction in "O literaturnoj èvoljucii" ["On literary evolution"] (1927), Tynjanov, for the first time, revealed the dual orientation of each structural element, its correlation, on the one hand, with the other elements in the same system (text), and on the other hand its correlation with similar elements from other systems.

Авто-функция, т.е. соотнесенность какого-либо элемента с рядом подобных элементов других систем и других рядов, является условием син-функции, конструктивной функции данного элемента. (Tynjanov 1927: 440)
[The autofunction, that is, the correlation of any element to the series of analogous elements in other systems and other series [..] is the condition for the synfunction, the constructive function of that element in the given, concrete work.]

The synfunction is, therefore, subordinate to the autofunction:

Die konstruktive Funktion (="Synfunktion") resultiert aus der gegebenen Korrelation der Werkfaktoren zum Werkganzen und - aufgrund der Dynamik der Form - aus der übergeordneten literarischen Funktion (="Autofunktion") die von der "Korrelation der Werkelemente zu anderen Werksystemen und sogar zu anderen Reihen" bestimmt wird.
(A.A. Hansen-Löve 1978: 378)

Although the autofunction applies to the correlation with all sorts of "other series", not necessarily only literary ones, it was soon understood as a specifically diachronic function. The terms synchrony and diachrony appear in point 4. of Tynjanov and Jakobson's "Problemy izučenija literatury i jazyka" ["Problems in the Study of Language and Literature"] (1928), where they are used in a specific literary theoretical (and not linguistic) meaning. According to Tynjanov, the elucidation of an element's relation to the literary tradition of that element is the condition for understanding its function and significance within the system itself, for every element in the text is the result of a selection from a repertoire of possible applications.

Because each given synchronic function, specific to a given work, can be realized only as a diachronic function, directly or indirectly related to a handed-down repertoire of possible applications, a tension results between these two dimensions of every work as a whole. This tension makes the work's structure dynamic, as, conversely, every concrete work, by its specific selection and combination of elements and devices, actualizes the tradition and makes it dynamic.
(Striedter 1989: 91-92)

In the specific case of literary space as a structural element of the text, the "repertoire" of possible applications is restricted, owing to the ultimate limitations of human biophysical nature. Like time, space is less liable to changes than other aspects of the literary text. This aspect manifests itself in recurrent elements, also designated as "archetypes", such as for instance the road, the river, the wood, the border, that have preserved their ancient, archaic connotations of meaning from mythological times onward. As a result of their anchoring in primeval culture, such archetypical images may serve as a vehicle for the preservation of the identity of literature as a system.

On the other hand, the norms and values connected with space and spatial details may vary in the course of literary evolution, owing to cultural, ideological and other historical changes. This will be discussed more thoroughly in the second chapter of the theoretical part of this study, which will deal specifically with problems of literary space and its evaluation.

That the elements of space and time were factors responsible for literary continuity, was acknowledged by a contemporary of the Formalist movement, Michail Bachtin, who, at the time, was also one of its more important critics[5]. In "Formy vremeni i chronotopa v romane. Očerki po istoričeskoj poètike" ["Forms of Time and the Chronotope in the Novel] (1937-8, first published 1975) Bachtin introduced the term chronotope, to designate the specific correlation of the temporal and spatial categories of the literary text. He acknowledged the dual nature of this literary category, its evaluative connotations and its function as a carrier of literary memory[6], which Bachtin understood as specific genre memory.

Жанр живет настоящим, но всегда помнит свое прошлое, свое начало.
(Bachtin 1963: 179)
[A genre lives in the present but always remembers its past, its beginnings.]

Хронотоп определяет художественное единство литературного произведения в его отношении к реальной действительности. Поэтому хронотоп в произведении всегда включает в себя ценностный момент.
(Bachtin, 1975: 391)
[A literary work's artistic unity in relationship to an actual reality is defined by its chronotope. Therefore the chronotope in a work always contains an evaluating aspect.]

A more thorough discussion of Bachtin's concept of the chronotope and its relation to contemporary theoretical discussion on literary space, will be given in the second chapter of the theoretical first part of this study.

Furthermore, according to Formalist theories in the latter period, the elements within a system manifest a certain arrangement. This internal organization of the structural elements is marked by dominance, in which one particular principle of construction subordinates all other elements of the text. As a result of this dominance deformation takes place on the level of subordination. Naturally, this leads to a certain tension within the system, which is a source of a permanent struggle between dominant and subordinate factors. This struggle is responsible for the "dynamics of the form" and thus one of the motors of the system's evolution, (cf. also A.A. Hansen-Löve 1978: 318).

I take the position that the functional changes of literary space must be understood in the light of this mechanism of dominance and deformation, as a shift within the hierarchy of the system.

At this point, the Formalist model of evolution may still be depicted cyclically, as a scheme in four stages, with a basically dialectical mechanism of canonization and decanonization[7], with the principle of opposition and the struggle between dominant and subordinate factors as driving forces. One must not forget, however, that Tynjanov did modify this cyclical scheme, by introducing the idea that the alternation of movements, the alternation of systems, is never a complete substitution but always only a partial shift of dominance:

В литературе существуют явления разных пластов, в этом смысле нет полной смены одного литературного течения другим. Но эта смена есть в другом смысле - сменяются главенствующие течения, главенствующие жанры.
(Tynjanov: 430)
[Literature consists of heterogeneous phenomena. In this respect there is no complete substitution of one literary movement by another. This substitution, however, exists in another sense, the change between dominating movements, and dominating genres.]

This statement offers the possibility to escape the black-and-white way of thinking that is characteristic of most theories of literary history. The shift takes place only on a certain level, the level of dominance, whereas other layers of the text, for the time being, preserve the old structures. For this reason, the cyclical understanding of the evolutionary process must be replaced by a spiralic one. This seems a more adequate approximation of the process in which change, replacement, and innovation go hand in hand with permanence, durability and preservation[8].

In subsequent years, it was Jakobson who developed this theory of the dominant:

Inquiry into the dominant had important consequences for Formalist views of literary evolution. In the evolution of poetic form it is not so much a question of the disappearance of certain elements and the emergence of others as it is the question of shifts in the mutual relationship among the diverse components of the system, in other words, a question of the shifting dominant.
(Jakobson, 1981: 753-4)

Despite Tynjanov's modification of the cyclical scheme, the dialectical understanding (in the more stricter sense) of the evolutionary process continues to play an important role in many subsequent theories on literary development[9]. This is seen, for instance, in the models proposed by Žirmunskij, Lichačev and, especially, Smirnov and Döring-Smirnov. All these scholars maintain that literary evolution is characterized by a kind of swing-mechanism, by a continuous alternation of two opposite principles. This form of dialectical thinking seems to be typical for a certain branch of modern Russian literary theory, notably Structuralism and Semiotics. The more subtle, least rigid models of evolution were proposed by Lichačev and Smirnov, who drew up a kind of "catalogue of conventions" for a number of cultural, and literary periods. These typologies seem to be rooted in Mukařovský's idea of the aesthetic norm.

I will focus on these theories in the sections below. These theories will subsequently serve as an orientational standard in my analysis of literary space in various periods of Russian literature, as the background against which literary innovations as well as preservation of old structures can be perceived.

1.2 Czech Structuralism

Czech literary Structuralism, which in many respects continued from where Tynjanov left off[10], elaborated the concept of literary evolution by taking extra-literary circumstances into consideration. This renewed commitment to extraliterary circumstances was principally caused by the recognition of the ultimate limitations of purely immanent models of evolution. This new phase in the theoretical debate on literary history was heralded by Tynjanov and Jakobson's 1928 article, notably in the recommendation phrased in point 8., on the correlation between literary and other historical series:

Вопрос о конкретном выборе пути, или по крайней мере доминанты, может быть решен только путем анализа соотнесенности литературного ряда с прочими историческими рядами.
(Tynjanov & Jakobson 1928: 390)
[The question of a specific choice of path, or at least of the dominant, can be solved only through an analysis of the correlation between the literary series and other historical series.]

The Structuralist preoccupation with aesthetic value and reception resulted in the description of the aesthetic conventions of a particular period against which a work of art must be perceived and understood. The investigation of the aesthetic evolution and the history of the reception of a work of art led to the disclosure of the norms and rules governing the taste of a certain period.

As far as the object of interest in this thesis is concerned, the knowledge of the currently prevailing aesthetic norms, the literary code of the period in question, is the precondition for determining whether and how literary space, and the spatial details of the text, their presentation and evaluation, are perceived as deviating or not, and how they contribute to the construction of the meaning of the text.

> The specific character of the aesthetic norm consists in the fact that it tends to be violated rather than to be observed. It has less than any other norm the character of an inviolable law. It is rather a point of orientation serving to make felt the degree of deformation of the artistic tradition by new tendencies.
> (Mukařovský, 1978: 52)

The concept of the aesthetic norm is therefore seen as an orientational standard, rather than as a strict rule, such as for instance the grammatical norm of a language. Furthermore, Mukařovský sees a permanent tension between this supra-individual structure and its individual application.

The concept of a system of aesthetic norms and the concept of aesthetic typologies remain two distinct approaches, however close they may be. Typologies are not normative, they describe the typical from a certain distance in time; the historical perspective is in this case a precondition for seeing what is typical for a stylistic and literary period. Aesthetic systems of norms, on the other hand, are a "reconstruction" of the rules and standards that governed the literary convention of a certain period[11]. Both concepts, however, may be understood as a "code" and be taken as a point of orientation.

Typologies are closely linked to the concept of the dominant, which we came across in our discussion of Formalism, and which Jakobson elaborated in his Prague-years:

> The dominant may be defined as the focusing component of a work of art: it rules, determines, and transforms the remaining components. It is the dominant which guarantees the integrity of the structure.
> (1981: 751)

> We may seek a dominant not only in the poetic work of an individual artist and not only in the poetic canon, the set of norms of a given poetic school, but also in the art of a given epoch, viewed as a particular whole.
> (ibid., 752)

Jakobson's theory of dominance, offers an alternative to the oppositional model of mutually exclusive systems. As he understands it, the literary system, or for that matter, any value system, is understood as the interaction between dominant and dominated functions, qualities, or components.

2.0 cultural, stylistic and literary typologies

2.1 Lichačev's typology of styles

In spite of Lichačev's brevity on the subject, his ideas on literary evolution have proven to be of great influence. Moreover, these ideas can be considered a crucial link between the Formalist model of evolution and present-day, notably soviet-semiotic, understanding of literary development and cultural development in general.

I shall, therefore, discuss at some length the chapter "Velikie stili i stil' barokko" ["The Great Styles and the Baroque Style"] from the book *Razvitie russkoj literatury X-XVII vv. Epochi i stili* , [*The Development of Russian Literature from the 10th-17th Century. Epochs and Styles*] (1973: 172-183) in which Lichačev expands his theories, especially since his theory of styles is not very well known outside the circle of Russian literary scholars.

First of all, Lichačev dismisses the ideas of scholars like Žirmunskij, Tschižewskij, or Curtius, whom he quotes explicitly. He is particularly opposed to the idea that all "great" styles (Gothic, Renaissance, Baroque, Classicism, Romanticism etc.) are equal and of equal significance, "ravnopravnymi i ravnoznačitel'nymi". Instead, he argues:

> Исторические стили разнообразны и разнозначительны по своей архитектонике и по своей исторической роли.
> (172)
> [Historical styles are heterogeneous and of different significance, not only by their structure, but also by their historical role.]

According to Lichačev the formation and further development of various styles, is of a fundamental asymmetrical character. Within this process it is possible to distinguish two types of motion. The first is of a gradual nature, whereby a certain style develops from simplicity into complexity, as it were "evolutionary", the other movement is a more sudden, even abrupt - "revolutionary" - leap from complexity back to[12] simplicity.

> Каждый стиль постепенно изменяется от простого к сложному, однако от сложного к простому он возвращается только в результате скачка.
> (172)
> [Every style gradually shifts from simplicity to complexity, however, it returns from complexity to simplicity only as result of a jump.]

The simple variant thereby acquires the status of *primary* style, whereas the complex one is alloted only *secondary* status. As a result, the history of culture consists of so-called megaperiods[13], each of which is composed of a pair of such styles. Thus, a phased system of development comes into being, consisting of two stages, in which the second stage depends on the first. On a formal level, the secondary style period owes its existence to the preceding primary one, from which it emerged. The relation between both styles could be designated as "genetical-immanent". On the level of content, the two phases of a megaperiod are also interrelated. In his explanation of the process of a style becoming more complicated Lichačev states:

> Что же такое усложнение стиля [...]? Это постепенное рождение нового стиля, противоположного по своему характеру, но при котором новый стиль все же является вторичным.
> (176)
> [What exactly is the complication of a style? [...] It is the gradual birth of a new, style, opposite in its nature, that is nevertheless secondary.]

Lichačev's typology of styles is remarkable for the idea that literary development consists of two different, essentially unequal, types of motion. There is one basic motion, directing the evolution from one megaperiod to the next. Within this motion, other, merely relative and subordinate, developments take place.

В развитии искусств мы видим два движения. Одно движение - главное; другое - относительное.
(178).
[In the development of art we see two movements. One movement is the main one, the other is relative.]

In order to verify his thesis, Lichačev discusses at length the transition from the Romanesque style period to the Gothic (and the subsequent emergence of the Renaissance). The traditional strict caesura between these two styles is not in accordance with the actual historical situation. Both periods are rather very much interrelated. During the first phase of the Romanesque/Gothic megaperiod, man was extremely ingenious and productive in all fields of culture, religion, technique and especially architecture. This period was therefore the most creative, innovating and original of the two. The secondary - Gothic - period that followed, benefited from this fecundity but did not contribute anything fundamentally new. The Gothic age therefore was a continuation of the Romanesque culture. It superficially extended and refined it by adding all kinds of ornaments. An example of this ornamentalism, this so-called "usložnenie stilja" is seen in the flamboyant Gothic decoration that was added to the Romanesque basic structure.

Within a megaperiod, it is the continuous line of development - "nepreryvnost' razvitija"(175) - that counts, argues Lichačev. In his elaboration of Lichačev's ideas Smirnov (1977) subsequently puts forward the idea of continuous movement - "ideja nepreryvnogo dviženija". Whereas Lichačev assesses continuity only within one megaperiod, Smirnov views the whole of literary history as one big coherent totality. Obviously, here we touch upon a development within the thinking on literary development itself. Whereas the theories of the first half of the century prefer to distinguish discrete entities, more recently the credo of continuity has become popular with scholars of literary history[14].

In Lichačev's view, the transition from one megaperiod to the next, i.e. from secondary style "back to" primary, takes the form of a complete rupture with the old system. The "jump" from Gothic to Renaissance, to continue our discussion of Lichačev's example, was indeed a clear break with the existing movement. It is interesting to note that, according to Lichačev, this is not so much a stylistic development but rather a socio-ideological one.

Появление каждой новой пары стилей обусловлено не внутренней закономерностью «саморазвития» стилей, а радикальными социальными изменениями.
(181)
[The emergence of each new pair of styles is not determined by the immanent laws of the "self-development" of styles, but by radical social changes.]

The emergence of a new style presupposes and involves the rise of a new ideology, in this case: Humanism. Such a revolutionary change takes place because the old forms are not able to express the new meanings in an adequate way:

Новое содержание взорвало старую форму и вызвало к жизни новый стиль - ренессанс.
(175)
[The new content disrupted the old form and gave birth to a new style: Renaissance.]

During the twilight of the secondary style, new ideas ripen which eventually give birth to a new form. It means that the new content requires a period of incubation. Such a period, however, implies a more or less gradual transition, whereas, paradoxically, Lichačev has indicated the change as quick, abrupt and radical. Probably the image of the "jump" does not concern the speed of the change but rather its nature. "Jump", therefore, does not preclude a preparatory period of some length before the new primary style period[15].

The Renaissance marks the beginning of a new megaperiod in cultural history, developing via Manierism into the Baroque and eventually Rococo, the latter one being a clear example of a style completely preoccupied by ornamentality and outward appearance. As early as the Baroque yet another megaperiod makes itself known, reaching from Classicism - correlated ideology: Enlightenment - to Romanticism, via transitional stages such as Sentimentalism and Pre-romanticism.

Lichačev's evolutionary model can be visualized as follows:

primary style: *secondary style:*

primary style:	secondary style:
Romanesque	Gothic
Renaissance	Baroque
Classicism	Romanticism

According to Smirnov it is possible to add two more megaperiods to Lichačev's model:

Realism	Symbolism
Modernism	Postmodernism

As far as the latter megaperiod is concerned, Smirnov speaks about Avant-garde and the secondary styleforms of contemporary art.

Each new style in this evolutionary sequence takes its bearings from preceding styles of the same type. Lichačev speaks of kinship, "rodstvennaja svjaz'", that accounts for the correspondences within each category and explains similarities between styles that are separated in time. Examples are the orientation of both Renaissance and Classicism towards classical antiquity, or the parallels between Symbolism and Romanticism.

Curiously enough, Lichačev is able to name all sorts of characteristics typical of the secondary style, whereas he deals only roughly with the primary one. Primary styles are usually connected with a distinct ideology (e.g. Renaissance with Humanism or Realism with Positivism) whereas the situation with secondary styles is a more complicated one. These styles often serve several, even contradictory, ideologies at the same time. Romanticism, for one, combines a historical interest, an orientation towards the past, sometimes even glorification of bygone years, a "reactionary" ideology, with more progressive ideals, such as national liberation, emancipation and the awakening of a national consciousness.

Apart from being connected with a distinct ideology, a primary style is designated in very general terms as "concentrated, conceptual and intense in its simplicity" (179-180). A style of the primary type develops into the secondary one because it undergoes an inevitable process of increasing complexity and formalization[16]. Secondary styles, on the contrary, distinguish themselves not only by their complexity, but also by a greater conventionality, an emphasis on the code-character of art, and a shift from content to form, i.e. by a focus on ornament.

In his book, Lichačev explicitly warns not to misunderstand his descriptive model as a purely mechanistic system:

Надо особенно подчеркнуть, что развитие стилей не следует строгой схеме, оно не уходит в «дурную бесконечность» однообразных повторений: постепенного усложнения первоначальной простоты и резкого обращения к новой идеологической ее основой. (177-8)
[It must be stressed explicitly, that the development of styles does not follow a strict scheme, and it is not a "foolish and endless" monotonous repetition of a gradual complication of the primeval simplicity and a sudden turn toward a new ideological basis.]

Contrary to the presupposition that the process of literary development implies a "foolish" repetition of similar styles, an idea typical of the various "pendulum theories" which he rejects, Lichačev points out that we are dealing with a *one way* motion - "odnonapravlennoe razvitie". In his book, Lichačev makes an original attempt to answer one of the crucial questions of evolutionary concepts in general: in what direction is cultural history actually moving, where does evolution lead to?

According to Lichačev, one may detect, in the first place, an acceleration in the alternation of styles. The various stylistic periods are becoming shorter and shorter, which is especially apparent in the development of the last century, which shows a quick succession of a great variety of movements.

Another argument why culture, and for that matter literature, is a *developing* system and not an endless replay, is the gradual simplification of art, what Lichačev calls the "oslablenie uslovnosti iskusstva" - the attenuation of art's normativeness. If one would juxtapose all primary style periods, that represent the development's actual mainstream, chronologically: Romanesque, Renaissance, Classicism, Realism, we may conclude that art has to meet less and less (artistic) conditions. In Lichačev's own words: while developing, art is slowly moving in the direction of reality. Regarding secondary styles, Lichačev discerns, on the contrary, a growing complexity in the course of history, a fine contemporary example would be Postmodernism, with its eclecticism of styles. This, of course, is in agreement with the idea that the secondary style system is an inversion of the primary one.

Lichačev's third argument for purposeful and goal-oriented development is the fact that initially the styles still embrace all fields of human activity (cf. the Romanesque as sketched briefly above). In the course of history, however, their "sphere of influence" diminishes, they become more and more restricted to certain art forms and aspects of culture. Simultaneously, artists among themselves show increasing individual stylistic differences. In other words, in art there is a growing individuality and growing aesthetic freedom. Realism - according to Lichačev - is both the climax and finale of the line of development he describes, and he hesitates whether Realism should be treated as a style equal to previous stylistic periods.

Реализм - саморазвивающееся направление в искусстве. Он возможен благодаря гибкости эстетического сознания современного общества, которое может пользоваться разными «эстетическими кодами». (182)
[Realism is a self-developing movement in art. It exists, owing to the flexibility of the modern aesthetic mind, which is able to use several "aesthetic codes" at the same time.]

14

In Lichačev's view, Realism represents the end of the monopoly of one style. It is the concluding piece in a certain line of development in western European cultural history. This radical statement, neglecting or even denying all post-realist artforms, is, of course, unacceptable. Smirnov, fortunately, is less radical in his views on recent developments in the process of literary evolution, and discusses Realism and subsequent styles in the same way as preceding ones, thus placing them in one, as yet unending, line of development. This scholar's theories will be examined in the following section.

2.2 the Smirnov model

In the late seventies Smirnov, later joined by Döring-Smirnov, developed Lichačev's rather schematic theory of styles. In a number of publications, notably Smirnov's book *Chudožestvennyj smysl i èvoljucija poètičeskich sistem* [*Literary Meaning and the Evolution of Poetic Systems*] (1977) and Smirnov's and Döring-Smirnov's article "Realizm: diachroničeskij podchod" ["Realism: a diachronic approach"] (1980), the two scholars drew up catalogues of the conventions of the various style periods in literary history. Furthermore, they provide the reader with a rich variety of examples from Russian literature to illustrate their theories on literary development. This is by far the most stimulating aspect of Smirnov's and Döring-Smirnov's work, which otherwise is characterised by a rather complicated theoretical approach. In his 1977 book, Smirnov attempts to find a logical balance between a) the synchronous aspect of a literary work, b) the aspect that is the result of diachronous transformations, and c) the work of art as the carrier of achronous, universal (archetypical) categories of conscience (Smirnov, 1977: 200).

In order to accomplish this rather ambitious task, he takes a number of heterogeneous contemporary literary theories into consideration, such as semantics, Formalist and structuralist theories on literary evolution, archetypology, cultural semiotics and even structural anthropology, (cf. also A.A. Hansen-Löve: 1980, who provides a clarifying summary of these theories in a critical survey of Smirnov's writings until 1980). In my discussion of Smirnov's views I will concentrate on his ideas concerning the typology of literature and the related theories on literary evolution.

Like most of his fellow cultural semioticians of the Moscow-Tartu school, such as Lotman and Toporov, Smirnov believes that every work of art forms a world in itself. Each work of art, each text, represents a certain model of the world, or world-picture[17]. Each picture of the world is a conglomerate of semantic categories, i.e. spatial, temporal, causal and other (axiological, social) categories. The categories of meaning are universal for all literary systems, independent of the period or the author's personality. They represent the, so-called, achronic and supraindividual forms of thinking.

The specific character of a certain literary period is determined by the laws according to which writers at a particular time transform universal meaning in order to obtain the concrete meaning of a literary text. Smirnov distinguishes world-pictures on two levels. First of all, the individual world-pictures of the actual works of literature, which are the result of the procedures of transformation a concrete author performs on the universal categories of meaning. Thus individual variants of world-pictures emerge - so-called "personal'nye varianty". The combination of all the personal variants within one period of style results in interindividual - "mežindividual'nye" - semantic systems.

15

Из частных моделей мира вырастает общая картина реальности, свойственная той или иной литературной эпохе.
(1977: 3)
[Out of the personal world-pictures, a general picture of reality emerges that is typical of this or that literary period.]

Thus, Smirnov is able to account for the individual characteristics of each work of art, as well as for the distinguishing characteristics of a certain period or style. In the English survey at the end of the book, this reads as follows:

> Diachronous transformations producing change of artistic systems are subject to retransformation due to which individual semantic universes (the synchronous aspect of study of literary texts) appear within these systems. [...] In other words, simultaneously existing universes vary in the same way as historically changing systems do.
> (Smirnov 1977: 202)

The dynamics of literary evolution consist of so called "deep-level transformations" - "glubinnaja, bazisnaja transformacija" (1977: 21). From one period to the next, the interrelation of the constituents of the system changes fundamentally. This takes place at the basis of the system, and is not consciously perceived by contemporaries. What is perceived on the surface, are the derivatives of these transformations, the so called "proizvodnye prevraščenija". Furthermore, the "basic transformation" with the ensuing emergence of a new style, is the result of "surface transformations" (Smirnov 1977: 25). The system itself is in a state of constant flux, transformations take place all the time and on all levels (thematical, semantical, functional, stylistical etc.).

> Разного рода внутрисистемные трансформации будут отличаться друг от друга, в частности, тем, на каком из уровней художественной структуры они протекают. Ввиду того что каждый слой литературной структуры относительно самостоятелен, вполне реальны ситуации, когда трансформационные истории разных уровней не совпадут между собой и уровни будут расходиться по степени их эволюционной продвинутости (отсталости).
> (1977: 22)
> [Heterogeneous transformations within the system will depend, partly, on which level of the system they take place. In view of the fact that each layer of the literary structure is more or less independent, situations of incongruence of transformational histories are very likely to occur. And the levels will differ as a result of their evolutionary anticipation (retardation).]

These internal transformations accumulate and culminate in a transformation at the base. At a certain point, the old system is no longer recognizable, and as a whole converts into something new.

> БТ (Базисная Трансмормация) застает систему на таком этапе, когда та уже достаточно насыщена результатами трансформаций, имеющих обратные знаки в сравнении с отправными свойствами литературного ансамбля.
> (1977: 25)
> [The basic transformation finds the system at a stage, when it is already sufficiently satisfied by the results of such transformations, that carry inverse signs with respect to the initial characteristics of the literary whole.]

Smirnov therefore believes literary evolution to be of a gradual nature, with many transitory, intermediary forms in between two (dialectically opposed) stylistic periods. In my opinion this concept represents an excellent proposal for a subtle and phased model of evolution. It can be very well combined with the idea of a gradual shift in dominance between the various constituents and functions of the system. It is therefore regrettable that in his 1980 article Smirnov appears to have returned to a more purely dialectical model of evolution, without however explicitly renouncing the existence of transitory stages from one period to the next.

Smirnov's view on literary evolution as a coherent system, the "ideja nepreryvnogo dviženija" (1977: 17), suggests a radical shift in theoretical thinking, which was hitherto dominated by the Formalist concept of discontinuity. Smirnov seeks to account for the pluriformity of works of art belonging to the same cultural period, and the coexistence of heterogeneous movements, as for instance Futurism and Acmeism as two very distinct postsymbolist stylistic formations.

Another important point in Smirnov's theory of transformation, at least as far as the 1977 version is concerned, is the hypothesis that diachronous transformations are irreversible. Although he agrees with Lichačev's idea of typological similarity between all primary styles on the one hand, and all secondary styles on the other, and up to a certain point it is therefore possible to speak of a primary and a secondary style-code, typologically related styles never become completely identical.

> Каждая система обретает значение в соотношении с предыдущей. Противостоя ближайшему литературному ансамблю новосозданная система тем не менее не дублирует ту, которая отдалена от нее на два трансформационных шага, [...] это только опора, а не возвратное движение.
> (1977: 27-8)
> [Each system acquires meaning in relation to the preceding one. While being contrary to the nearest literary ensemble, the newly created system at the same time does not repeat the one from which it is separated by two transformational steps [...] it is only a point of support, not a backward movement.]

Notwithstanding his use of purely semiotic language to describe the system of literary evolution as such, Smirnov from the very beginning reveals his kinship with Russian Formalism:

> Передвижку от одной семантической системы к другой целесообразно объяснить как диалектическое изменение соотношений между теми компонентами, из которых слагается структура всякаго смысла, а именно как изменение соотношений между означающими, означаемыми и обозначаемыми.
> (1977: 4)
> [It is useful to explain the shift from one semantical system to the next as a dialectical change in the interrelation of those components, that constitute the structure of significance in general, namely as a change between signifiant, signifié and denotation.]

Reaching back to Lichačev's definition of primary and secondary styles, Smirnov again effects a semiotic re-translation:

Суть этой дихотомии в том, что все "вторичные" художественные системы ("стили") отождествляют фактическую реальность с семантическим универсумом, т.е. сообщают ей черты текста, членят ее на план выражения и план содержания, на наблюдаемую и умопостигаемую области, тогда как все "первичные" художественные системы, наоборот, понимают мир смыслов как продолжение фактической действительности, сливают воедино изображение с изображаемым.
(Döring & Smirnov 1980: 1-2)
[The essence of this dichotomy lies in the fact, that "secondary" artistic systems ("styles") identify actual reality with the semantic universe, i.e. they ascribe to it features of a text, and divide it into a level of expression and a level of content, into a sphere of perception and a sphere accessible to the mind, whereas all "primary" artistic systems, on the contrary, understand the world of meaning as an extension of actual reality, where the depiction and the depicted become one.]

Many ideas from the 1977 publication no longer figure in Döring & Smirnov's 1980 article. Especially the notion of continuity, the idea of a gradual development in the course of literary evolution, is conspicuously missing. Instead, the reader encounters a dichotomous model of development, offering less room for subtle distinctions. The major part of the 1980 article is devoted to a detailed description of the style code of Realism. Moreover, Smirnov and Döring-Smirnov here extend Lichačev's typology of styles, by adding a great number of distinctive features of both primary and secondary styles.

2.2.1 secondary styles

One of the merits of Smirnov's typology of styles is his attempt to clarify the difference between similar style-types.

Эти литературные направления, на первый взгляд близкие, в действительности не совпадают между собой в области глубинных семиотических программ.
(1977: 28)
[These literary movements, at first sight similar, actually do not correspond in the field of their deep-level semiotic programs.]

He juxtaposes two secondary style periods, Romanticism and Symbolism (and also Futurism and Baroque). The difference in attitude towards the world, life and reality, as it is demonstrated by the art of these two distinct periods, should elucidate the dissimilarity of the seemingly similar:

Если один факт не может замещать другой факт в качестве знака синхронно, то они должны быть связаны между собой генетически, следованием во времени. Вот почему романтизм строил сугубо историзованную картину мира; смысл явления раскрывался его генезисом, определялся тем, что ему предшествует; «прочесть» событие значило выяснить его причину на хроногенетической оси. Даже сверхъестественные события обычно становились в романтической литературе детерминированными.
(1977: 29)
[If one fact is unable to replace another fact in the capacity of a sign synchronically, they will have to be interrelated genetically, through succession in time. This is why Romanticism built a deeply historified picture of the world; a phenomenon's meaning was explained by its genesis, and was determined by what preceded it; to "read" an event meant to elucidate its cause on the chronogenetical axis. Even supernatural phenomena used to become predetermined ones in romantic literature.]

and:

(Символисты) - особенно на первых этапах движения - отрицают какое бы то ни было иконическое сходство между явным и тайным мирами: между планами выражения и содержания, усмотренными в области естественных фактов. Поскольку высшая реальность не имела физического обличия [...] ей придавался сугубо мыслительный характер.
(1977: 30)
[(The Symbolists) - especially in the first period of the movement - deny any iconic identity whatsoever between the real and the hidden world: between the level of expression and content found in the field of natural facts. Since the highest reality had no physical covering [...] it was ascribed a distinct illusory character.]

Both Romanticism and Symbolism design a bipartite picture of the world, resulting from a logic on two levels. According to this way of thinking, man, and the artist in particular, perceives one world directly, through the senses, whereas the other world is accessible to the mind - rational comprehension - only. In spite of this apparent similarity, the nature of both styles is in fact asymmetrical, each of them interprets the "text of being" (Z. Minc 1974) in its own, unique way. Semiotically speaking, according to Smirnov, this difference stems from the circumstance that Romanticists were interested in the relation between denotation (the word) and designation (thing, deed, fact), the relation between content and expression being irrelevant in their eyes. In fact, they ignored the possibility that certain phenomena can replace others.

Furthermore, the "other" world according to the romantic concept, is ruled by comprehensible laws, be it the world of the nation's heroic past, or a fantastic construction of the poet's imagination, or perhaps the marvellous world of nature. The point is to penetrate to the very essence of the other world's "language", which is pre-eminently the task of the romantic poet[18]. It is important to note that in the romanticist concept of two worlds, "understanding" the other language is not impossible. With the help of the mind - i.e. rational capacities, and/or intuition, one can penetrate into the other world.

Symbolism in its turn is deprived of this latter capacity. According to their world-view, a true understanding of the "other" reality is impossible. Even though the Symbolists, contrary to the Romantics, accept, even postulate, the possibility of substitution of one phenomenon for another, the other world remains mysterious and impenetrable till the very end. In order to illustrate this difference between Romanticism and Symbolism, I quote two poems, by Puškin and Blok.

The last couplet of Puškin's poem "Stichi sočinennye noč'ju vo vremja bessonnicy" ["Verses composed during a night of insomnia"] is typical of the romantic poets' attitude towards a mysterious, hidden other world:

Мне не спится, нет огня;
Всюду мрак и сон докучный.
Ход часов лишь однозвучный
Раздается близ меня.
Парки бабье лепетанье,
Спящей ночи трепетанье,
Жизни мышья беготня...
Что тревожишь ты меня?
Что ты значишь, скучный шепот?
Укоризна или ропот
Мной утраченного дня?
От меня чего ты хочешь?
Ты зовешь или пророчишь?
Я понять тебя хочу,
Смысла я в тебе ищу...
(A.S.Puškin Sobr.Soč. v 10-ti tomach, tom III: 186)

Unlike his romantic colleague, Aleksandr Blok in principle excludes the possibility of true knowledge of "the other world", though both poets have a desire for understanding, a longing to grasp the meaning of the "text of life".

Небесное умом не измеримо,
Лазурное сокрыто от умов.
Лишь изредка приносят серафимы
Священный сон избранникам миров.
(A.Blok Sobr.Soč. v 6-ti tomach, tom I: 141)

Despite Smirnov's emphasis on the divergence between similar style-types, the overall typological feature of a bipartite picture of the world remains a general characteristic of both these secondary style periods. However, "dvumirie" as such is not exclusively restricted to this style type alone, as I will show in the analytical part of this study. The evocation of an alternative world may take place in primary style periods such as Realism and Modernism as well. It may happen in dreams (cf. *Oblomov*), in recollections of the past (Proust's *A la recherche de temps perdu*) or in texts with utopian or apocalyptic themes.

The presence of a bipartite world-picture alone is not enough evidence for ranking a work among the secondary style types. Additional typological features must be present as well. Van Baak (1990), however, regards this feature as a distinct characteristic of secondary styles, thereby ranking Avant-garde (and therefore Modernism) among this style-type. An important criterium according to this scholar is that the two juxtaposed worlds must be heterogeneous, i.e. incompatible, and that this circumstance must serve as a source of the conflict of the story.

2.2.2 primary versus secondary styles

An overall characteristic of the difference between primary and secondary styles is the tendency of secondary styles to intensify the conventionality of art as much as possible, whereas primary styles tend, on the whole, to avoid any form of convention. Cf. my discussion of Lichačev's stylistic typology, who characterizes the two stylistic formations as "simple" vs. "complicated, ornamental, encoded".

Döring & Smirnov 1980 greatly extend the few characteristics Lichačev mentions, and draw up an exhaustive typology of styles. According to A.A. Hansen-Löve (1980) they consider no less than 22 different characteristics, 22 for each style, both primary and secondary, cf. pp. 138-140. I will not repeat Hansen-Löve's enumeration, but only point at some main conclusions.

In general, according to the two authors, primary styles tend to consider the "alien" or "other" as belonging to the "self", whereas secondary styles, on the contrary, experience the "self" as being of "another", as something totally "strange" (Döring and Smirnov, 1980: 3). This implies that in texts of the former type, the reader may encounter situations in which the "I" (the hero, the narrator) tends to indentify himself with the other, which results, for instance, in themes like compassion and social injustice - Dostoevskij's *Bednye ljudi* [*Poor Folk*] is a strong exponent of this type - or stylistically in the use of free indirect speech (the penetration of the speech of the character in the author's speech). In both cases the boundary between the "I" and the "other" is blurred.

Texts of the second type, on the other hand, are inclined to mask, sometimes even to mystify the identity of the narrator or author. Such is, for instance, the case in Puškin's "Povesti Belkiña" ["Tales of Belkin"] with its deliberately complicated narrative structure.

During primary style periods, plagiarism is seen as a very serious offence, whereas in periods of the other type all sorts of literary imitation, falsification and parody flourish and enjoy popularity.

Another distinguishing feature between the two style-types are the different ways of communication between man and the world. However paradoxical this may sound, sensory perception of the natural world plays an important role in primary style periods, *sentio ergo sum* could very well serve as a motto here, whereas a rational approach of reality is typical of secondary style periods, for which *cogito ergo sum* would be the appropriate maxim (cf. ibid. p. 6). The description of landscapes in realist literature, for instance, are often characterised by "direct" communication with the surrounding world via the senses: sight, hearing, smell. We see this, for instance, very clearly in I.A. Turgenev's *Zapiski ochotnika* [*A Sportsman's Sketches*]. A famous example in which the faculties of smell and taste play the intermediary role, is to be found in the first book of Marcel Proust's *A la recherche du temps perdu*, where eating of a *madeleine*, soaked in lime-blossom tea evokes a whole range of recollections, images of childhood as vivid as if they were tangible reality.

Van Baak (1984) gives a fine example of the contrast between mental and sensory perception and communication with the world in a comparative analysis of the role of the Caucasus in Russian Romanticism and Realism respectively. He ascertains that romantic descriptions of the landscape are strongly metaphoric, mountains and the climate are ascribed all kinds of human features, emotions and passions. Furthermore, the romantic poet attributes all sorts of moral values to natural phenomena. This results in a so called aesthetization of reality, i.e. a process of semiotization in which it is the poet's task to understand the "language" of nature and to "translate" it in order to make it accessible for the reader. The realist text, on the other hand, prefers empirical knowledge of the world, to which the senses are the perfect instrument. The "eye"-witness narrator will always try to render his impressions as accurately and authentically as possible, by means of exact details such as shapes, colours, smell, distance etc.

What is remarkable about Döring & Smirnov's model, as described in their 1980 article, is its explicit binarity and oppositionality. They formulate the relation between the secondary and the primary kind of style as follows:

"Первичные" и "вторичные стили" утверждают взаимоисключающие принципы, которыми определяется связь литературного произведения с предшествующим ему художественным сообщением.
(1980: 13)
["Primary" and "secondary styles" maintain mutually exclusive principles, principles that determine the relation of the literary work with the literary message that preceded it.]

"Вторичные стили" инверсируют логические связи, которые господствуют в "первичных стилях".
(1980: 17)
["Secondary styles" invert the logical relations, that dominated the "primary styles".]

Owing to their concepts of "mutually exclusive principles" and an "inversion of logical links", concerning the relationship between the two systems of styles, the conclusion can be reached that the authors have in fact returned to the strict binary model of evolution, the Formalist "opposite principle of construction", and Lichačev's "opposite character of the new style, that emanates from the old one". All Döring & Smirnov do is to accentuate this particular point a little more strongly. It should also be noted, that in each case they only refer to the relation between a secondary style and the preceding primary one. The secondary character of the "secondary style", according to Döring & Smirnov, lies in the fact that these artistic formations represent nothing but a negative parallel to the preceding semantic system. The authors do not answer the question of the relation between primary styles and secondary ones, or how new megaperiods come into existence.

2.2.3 primary style

In the third part of their 1980 article, under the title "Realizm kak sistema tranzitivnych otnošenij" ["Realism as a System of Transitive Relations"], Smirnov and Döring-Smirnov illustrate their thesis concerning the nature of Realism as a primary style period. They make some very useful general remarks about this stylistic formation. The most important statement touches upon the overall principle of transitivity. This means: .

Реализм был поглощен поиском посредующих звеньев между различающимися элементами мирового целого.
(1980: 18)
[Realism was absorbed by the search for the intermediary links between the differing elements of the world's totality.]

Again, the authors profess their belief in the dialectical nature of literary history:

В качестве системы, в которой доминировала транзитивность, реализм составил один "мегапериод" вместе с отрицающим его фундаментальную предпосылку символизмом.
(1980: 18)
[As a system that was dominated by transitivity, Realism represents a "megaperiod" together with Symbolism, that in its turn denied this fundamental principle.]

The typically realist notion of the social environment, the milieu, serves as a connecting link between elements, which are in principle separated from each other. Such a typical surrounding neutralises all sorts of existing contrasts, most prominently the one between the "self" and the "other" - "svoe vs. čužoe". This is exactly the kind of contrast which is so omnipresent in Romanticism and Symbolism, although it takes on different appearances in each of these periods.

Another typical feature of Realism is the "прием проведения единого через разное" [the device of demonstrating one and the same in different ways]:

> Такой способ организации словесной картины мира предполагал среди прочего, что разные семантические категории, из которых она складывается, должны находиться в отношении взаимозаменимости, связываться друг с другом с помощью одного и того же многоместного предиката.
> (1980: 29)
> [This way of organising the verbal picture of the world assumed, among others, that the various semantic categories that constituted this picture, were interchangeable, and related to each other by one and the same multifunctional concept.]

This implies that the various semantic categories of the text have to harmonise. A certain hero with a certain kind of background (birth, family) is therefore situated in an environment, which is consistent with this background. (If this is not the case, this fact may serve as a source of the realist conflict). In other words, the milieu or environment - in the sociological as well as spatial sense of the word (the setting) - and the hero and his actions, are carefully attuned to each other. I think that Smirnov at this point speaks about the so-called naturalist tendencies in Realism.

Another characteristic of this period, related to the preceding one, is the fact that the writers at that time tended to make their work correspond as closely as possible with the "text of being"[19]:

> Писатели воспринимают текст как модель внетекстовой действительности и стремятся организовать его по законам, подобным этой действительности.
> (Z. Minc, 1974: 134)
> [Writers regard the text as a model of extratextual reality and strive to organize it according to the rules of this reality.]

Smirnov's postulate of transitive relations is, in fact, not far removed from Roman Jakobson's idea of the principle of contiguity, lying at the basis of realist art.

> Following the path of contiguous relationship, the realistic author metonymically digresses from the plot to the atmosphere and from the characters to the setting in space and time.
> (R. Jakobson, 1956: 78)

According to Jakobson, both processes, the metaphorical and the metonymical, are continually operative in art (as they are in language). However, from one style-period to the next, one may discern the prevalence of one of the two. Therefore, even during Realism, metaphoric, or symbolic descriptions can be found besides the more important metonymic ones, as will be shown below in the analysis of *Oblomov*.

At the end of this section on stylistic typologies, the conclusion may be reached that literary evolution can be regarded as a change in the literary system which leads to a

23

different hierarchy of elements in this system. It is possible to describe the various distinctive features of a certain period as a code system. From one period to the next a recasting of the mutual relationships between the various functions takes place under the influence of a modulation of this code-system. This "evolution" is, in my opinion, not so much a question of the disappearance of the old and the emergence of new style-codes as of a new, different, emphasis. With respect to the metaphorical and metonymical processes in language, Jakobson has remarked that both these processes are continually operative. As a result of various influences (culture, the behaviour of social groups, personal taste etc.), either of the two may prevail. However, only in pathological cases, such as aphasic disturbances, one of the two poles may be blocked, up to the point of the "fixation of one of the poles to the exclusion of the other" (Jakobson, 1956: 78).

These remarks about the nature of language may be extended to the literary system. During primary style periods, the literary system is dominated mainly by primary style codes. However, the other codes may retain their influence, be it less pronounced. Most works of literature can therefore better be designated as "predominantly" realist, or "predominantly" romantic, rather than as "pure" realist or "pure" romantic.

3.0 summary

The clear and systematic character of all the models discussed so far is obviously very attractive. What disturbs me about all of them is, however subtle the various formulations may be, the recurring idea that the system of development should consist of two alternating basic types of an opposite nature. A fundamental objection against this bipolarity can be made, especially against the idea that secondary systems represent an inversion of the primary one. This shuts the door on differentiation and subtle distinction, notions which are of primary importance for literary analysis. The above discussed theories pigeon-hole every work of literature. As a result of the notion of inversion, ambivalent situations are, as a matter of fact, nonexistent. After all, a certain phenomenon can not be A and not-A simultaneously. None of the mentioned theories takes into account the possibility that a work of art may belong to two adjoining, overlapping periods of literature. None of them reckon with the possibility of inconclusiveness of styles[20]. Each typology as such takes the model as the starting point and classifies all the phenomena of literary reality according to this model. As a result, the concrete, individual work of art is reduced to mere illustration of the general regularity of the evolutionary process, which, consequently, more often than not acquires a mechanistic character.

One of the aims of this study, is a confrontation between existing models of literary development and a number of literary texts. In this confrontation I shall have to deal with ambivalent situations of style, in which both dominant and affiliated style-codes and functions are involved in the creation of meaning.

An important circumstance in literary evolution is the twofold nature of each literary element. Each shows a tendency toward innovation but has stable aspects as well. The changes take place on the level of semiotization, a process that is strongly dependent of the cultural circumstances of the text, the writer, and the reader. The meaning assigned to any literary detail, the norms and values communicated through literature are manifold. However, the literary forms, the vehicles for the artistic message, are drawn from a limited "reservoir" that has come to be designated as the repertoire of archetypical images. These achronic forms assure the continuity of the system. However, in some literary periods archetypical images will be more or less prominent, just as the semiotization of specific literary elements may fluctuate more or less strongly from one period to the next.

Furthermore, I would like to argue that it is not at all necessary for all semantic categories and functions to modify at the same time. Some functions (and related categories) appear to behave more conservative than others. What we mainly perceive is the shifting of the dominant category, in most cases this is either the action or the hero, whereas other categories such as time, space, causality show a much slower pace of evolution. The shifting of these latter categories takes place in the course of a much longer period of time, they may remain constant during a number of subsequent stylistic periods.

I would therefore like to advocate a so called phased model of evolution, which should be able to account for the changes as well as the immobility of the system in an adequate way. The scope of this study is too narrow to test the evolutionary behaviour of all narrative categories. I will restrict myself to an examination of one narrative category only - the spatial component of literary texts. I thereby take space as the central narrative category, without letting out of sight its interaction with the other blocks, such as heroes and plot.

It should be noted that it seems possible indeed to draw more general conclusions concerning the world-picture of a given text, and implicitly of the stylistic period to which it belongs, based on spatial analysis only. This is related to the fact that the category of space plays an important and decisive role in the creation of meaning, as has been demonstrated by Lotman, Toporov and Van Baak. The various theories concerning the function of space in literature, will be discussed in the next chapter.

1. Cf. Jauss 1967 who surveys the most important theories, and also Striedter 1989.

2. Cf. Striedter's 1989 approach at these matters.

3. Cf. Tynjanov's "Literaturnyj fakt" (1924) in: Striedter 1969, I: 392-430.

4. There are several current classifications of the formalist theoretical movement. Victor Erlich (1955) bases himself on pure historical development, from a polemical first phase (1916-1920), via a productive main period in the first half of the second decennium, until the period of decline, as a result of internal crisis and growing pressure from without, at the end of the twenties.

A.A. Hansen-Löve (1978) bases his classification on theoretical criteria, thus distinguishing a first phase of the so called "Paradigmatisches Reduktionsmodell", designated as FI, a second phase "Syntagmatisches Funktionsmodell" (FII), and third a pragmatic model during FIII.

Jurij Striedter (1989) includes the subsequent Structuralist movement into his evolutionary model. The first phase viewed the introduction of the key-notions of Formalism, such as device, function, defamiliarization. The second phase was concerned with problems of syn- and diachrony. Finally, in the third phase, when Formalism continued to exist under the name of Czech Structuralism (of course without disregarding the typical and originally Czech aspects of this movement) the work of art became to be seen as a sign with an aesthetic function.

5. In his 1928 book, *Formal'nyj metod v literaturovedenii* [*The Formal Method in Literary Scholarship*], by some scholars ascribed to Michail Bachtin, Medvedev criticizes the term "evolution", which Tynjanov c.s. use in order to designate their concept of development. According to him this term even represents a logical error, for basic formalist assumptions like struggle and replacement are incompatible with the notion of evolution. What is important in an evolutionary process is to prove that two phenomena are correlated in such a way, that the earlier fact essentially determines the latter, subsequent one, to such an extent that one could even speak of predetermination, cf. P. Medvedev, 1976: 213.

6. Bachtin can be considered as a forerunner of the cultural semiotic and post-structuralist discussion about the mechanism of cultural memory. I do not wish to enter into a detailed account of these ideas, and will restrict myself to the following quotation, as an illustration of the theoretical approach at these matters:

> Wenn die Kultursemiotik davon ausgeht, dasz die Kultur als genetisch nicht vererbbares Gedächtnis (eines Volkes) über einen Speicher- und Transformationsmechanismus verfügt, der zum einen Stilinvarianz (Identitätsbewahrung einer Kultur) - vermittels bestimmter konstanter Texte, konstanter Kodes, einer bestimmten Gesetzmäszigkeit in der Transformation kultureller Information - garantiert, zum andern aber einen generativen Apparat zuläszt, der neue Mechanismen der Transformation anzeigt, so stellt die Konkurrens von Texten, die als Akkumulatoren, und Texten, die als Generatoren funktionieren, ein Problem kultureller Beschreibung dar.
> (Lachmann, 1990: 46)

It is, however, in the field of folklore-studies, that this type of literary research has proven especially productive, notably in the works of Vladimir Propp, cf. his book *Istoričeskie korni volšebnoj skazki* [*The historical roots of the fairy-tale*]. Cf. also the following statement by V.V. Ivanov and V.N. Toporov in their article "Invariant i transformacii v mifologičeskich i fol'klornych tekstach" ["Invariances and transformations in mythological and folklore texts"] (1975):

> Предтечей такого подхода в своих ранних работах был В.Я. Пропп, описавший не только трансформации отдельных элементов, но и наметивший универсальные пути замен «основных форм» в ходе эволюции.
> (48).
> [A forerunner of such an approach was V.Ja. Propp in his early works. Propp described not only the

transformations of individual elements, but also pointed out universal rules of the changes of "basical forms" in the course of evolution.]

7. Stage 1. entails the automatization of a certain, prevailing principle of construction, which dialectically provokes an opposite principle of construction. This stage occurs especially during transitory literary periods. Stage 2. sees the application of the new principle of construction, its "impregnation", whereas during stage 3. it expands until it embraces a maximum of phenomena, this is the phase of "imperialism". Finally in, stage 4. this principlel of construction becomes itself automatic and thus, in its turn, provokes a new, antithetical principle of construction, which brings us back to where we started. (Striedter 1969: 412).

8. There are other reasons as well why the image of the spiral seems more appropriate for the description of the evolutionary system, cf. a.o. A.A. Hansen-Löve 1978: 384.

9. Various literary and other aesthetic typologies have appeared since. More or less wellknown theories on literary development are, for instance, those of Žirmunskij (1928), Tschižewskij (1968), Curtius (1969). I propose to regard the German art-historian Wörringer as an early exponent of the typological approach. He published his views on the development of the visual arts in 1908. The theories of these scholars are typical examples of the "theory of the pendulum", an idea according to which the development of artistic systems swings to and fro between two basic stylistic formations. The latter are indicated by more or less conditional names, not to be identified or confused with historical formations of the same name, such as "classic" vs. "romantic" (Žirmunskij) or "classicist" vs. "romantic" (Tschižewskij), Curtius' typological opposition between "classicism" and "mannerism" or Wörringer's "mimetic" vs. "non-mimetic" art .
    All stylistic movements occuring in the course of cultural or literary history can be arranged and classified according to one of the two alternating basic types. What is not touched upon in any of the mentioned theories is the problem of coherence between the periods, the question of the connection and transition from one typological variant to another.
    As a matter of fact, all these style-theories with their "pendulum" are based only on the early formalist ideas about the evolutionary process, according to which the nature of the new form is essentially opposed to the preceding one. This implies that the process of development would consist of only two - opposite - basical principles between which literary history is merely seesawing. This is precisely the aberration that was inherent to the early formalist theories of evolution, the, so-called, cyclical model. However, the Formalists themselves did modify this model in subsequent years. It is striking that those scholars who were familiar with these modifications did not take them over.

10. After 1928 Formalism virtually ceased to exist inside the Soviet Union. Jakobson had already emigrated to Prague, Tynjanov took up writing of historical novels.

11. This aspect of Structuralism represents in fact a rupture with Formalism: "Tynjanov's heftige Kritik an einem Traditionsbegriff, der normativ oder typologisch einen Standard historisch-genetisch ableitet (als Folge) und gleichzeitig wieder auf die Geschichte selbst (als Ursache) überträgt" (A.A. Hansen-Löve 1978: 390).

12. Lichačev's idea of a return to an earlier situation indicates an affinity with formalist thinking. Compare, for instance, the transition from phase 4 back to phase 1 in Tynjanov's model of evolution.

13. Smirnov 1977: 156 ascribes this term to Panofsky, alas without specifying his source. Megaperiods, as far as I know, do not have names of their own. They could be designated as follows: Romanesque/Gothic, Renaissance/Baroque, Classicism/Romanticism, Realism/Symbolism and Modernism/Postmodernism.

14. Cf. on the evolution of theoretical thinking A.A. Hansen-Löve 1980: 133-4 and Smirnov 1977: 17 + note 14.

15. An obvious example is the transition from Romanticism to Realism during the twenties, thirties and even forties of the 19th century.

16. Lichačev's concept of the alternation of styles is not so far removed from Tynjanov's ideas on literary processes in a general sense. According to the formalist theoretician, during the process of literary development it is pluriformity and heterogeneity on one hand, taking turns with simplicity (uniformity) on the other hand.

Неизбежны моменты, когда казалось бы бесконечно-разнообразное течение мелеет и когда ему на смену приходят явления, в начале мелкие, мало заметные. Бесконечно-разнообразно «слияние конструктивного принципа с материалом» [...] совершается в массе разнообразных форм, но неминуем для каждого литературного течения час исторической централизации и приведения к простому и несложному.
(Striedter 1969: 430)
[Moments, when a seemingly infinitely multifaced movement gets bogged down and is replaced by phenomena, that seem insignificant and inconspicuous at first, are inevitable. The ways in which the principle of construction and the material merge is infinitely various [...] and takes on countless different forms. However, for each literary movement the hour of historical centralisation and simplification is inescapable.]

Contradictory to Lichačev, Tynjanov views formalisation as simplification. I do not think that this implies crucial difference between both points of view.

17. This idea is related to the theory that works of art are secondary modelling systems - a theory that will be discussed in chapter 2 of the first part of this study.

18. Cf. the typically romantic concept of the poet as a prophet.

19. This is also how Smirnov explains the rise and popularity of photography in the nineteenth century, as the medium to render visual reality in its most authentic form, notably at that time.

20. Cf. on the problem of typological inconclusiveness Van Baak 1989.

CHAPTER II

On the notion of space in literature

1.0 introduction

A survey of the most important theories concerning the phenomenon of space in literature, can be found in Van Baak's *The Place of Space in Narration* (1983), where the author in his introduction outlines many of the older theories and more thoroughly discusses recent ones. This is why I will restrict myself to a brief mention of the most important traditional concepts of space in general and literary space in particular, before plunging into a detailed account of the approache(s) the Moscow-Tartu semiotics school takes at these matters.

Many scholars of literary theory, in studying the problem of space, show an apparent urge to define this notion in philosophical, psychological or anthropological terms. One may distinguish at least two, fundamentally different, philosophical interpretations of the concept of space: a Newtonian one, and a view based on the philosophy of Leibniz. According to Newton, space has to be seen as something absolute, a completely separate and self-sufficient entity, independent of matter and substance, and in no way determined by objects or things. Leibniz, on the contrary, views space as something relative, that derives its identity only from the objects with which it is filled. One could therefore designate these two basical concepts of space as "empty" and "filled" space, respectively[1]. Hereafter literary space will be considered as materially filled space. Space is in the first place understood as the container of elements whose interrelation is determined by their position in space, (cf. a.o. Lotman, 1968: 30).

In 1766 G.E. Lessing in *Laokoon* introduced a bipartition of the arts into, so called, "spatial" arts (visual art, architecture) and art forms dominated by the notion of time (literature, music), a classification that has been persistent ever since. In our century, it was Joseph Frank who critically took up Lessing's ideas, in his famous and influencial article *Spatial Form in the Narrative* [(1945) 1963]. In this article, Frank proposes that one of the distinctive characteristics of modern, i.e. modernist literature, is a shift in dominance within the literary system from the category of time to the category of space. This idea is of importance with regard to the present study, because it establishes a link between the literary category of space and the phenomenon of literary development and change, drawing into consideration the notion of dominance[2].

The purest theoretical approach of problems of space in narrative art can be found in a number of articles of the scholars of the Moscow-Tartu school of semiotics. Lotman and Toporov, the most prominent scholars of the group, are in search of the immanent laws of the literary system as an integral part of culture, and the unique character of *literary space* (as differing from other kinds of space, such as philosophical, mathematical etc.). Furthermore, over the years they have elaborated an analytical method, which, owing to its highly systematic character, is most attractive for literary criticism, Finally, it seems that literary critics have reached a consensus about these theories - the arguments have come to a conclusion, and are no longer in need of any fundamental revision. Lotman's theories on literary space and the function of spatial language for modelling cultural world-views, have remained unchanged up till the present day. They figure almost unaltered in his 1990 book *Universe of the Mind*, in which the author attempts a synthesis of his most important literary and cultural-historical theories. Problems concerning literary space are still very much prominent in this book, being embedded in an overall theory of the "semiosphere", understood as the cultural pendant of the biosphere in nature[3].

According to the Moscow-Tartu semiotics school, space in works of literature is in the first place *literary space*, i.e. the continuum in which the literary heroes appear and where the action or conflict takes place.

> Художественное пространство в литературном произведении - это континуум, в котором размещаются персонажи и совершается действие.
> (Lotman 1968: 12)
> [Space in a literary work is the continuum on which the heroes are situated and where the action takes place.]

From the very start, the members of the school each displayed their own specific approach. The different theoretical background and traditions from which Moscow and Tartu respectively emerged, with their own distinct heritage, may account for the theoretical diversities between them. The Moscow branch shows a predominant interest in linguistic problems, whereas Tartu's primary focus is on literature. Both schools have common roots in Russian Formalism. This movement was equally characterized by a geographical and thematic "bipartition", with the Moscow Linguistic Circle on the one hand and the Petrograd Society for Research of Poetic Language, on the other. The difference between the Moscow and the Tartu school comes to the fore especially in the investigation of literary space. Therefore, in the following sections, the Tartu (Lotman) and the Moscow (Toporov) school will be treated as separate movements[4]. I can not overemphasize, however, that both schools do not preclude or refute each other - polemics between both are, as far as I know, nonexistent - on the contrary, they even show great resemblances and are of complementary nature.

1.1 Bachtin's chronotope

The concept of the chronotope, introduced by Michail Bachtin in his long article "Formy vremeni i chronotopa v romane", conceived during the thirties, but published only in 1975, must be regarded as the most important forerunner and source of inspiration for the subsequent research of the Moscow-Tartu semiotics circle on literary space.

> Существенная взаимосвязь временных и пространственных отношений художественно освоенных в литературе, мы будем называть хронотопом (это значит в дословном переводе «время пространсвто»).
> (Bachtin 1975: 234)
>
> [The essential correlation between the temporary and spatial relations that have been accepted into literature, we shall designate as the *chronotope* (which literally means time-space).]

Bachtin adapted this notion, originally derived from physics, for literary criticism. In the first place, space and time are indissoluble, they interact and mutually influence each other (Einstein). In the second place, the categories of space and time are the decorum, the indispensable background against which heroes and actions are perceived. They are always there, even when not mentioned or described explicitly (Kant). And thirdly, the chronotope is understood as the most important link between literature and reality.

Bachtin's interest is in the first place directed at the function of the chronotope as a carrier of information about the identity of the genre - "žanrovaja pamjat'", the genre's memory - and his research concentrates mainly on the "hybrid" genre of the novel. The chronotope determines which rules and norms transform (deform) the natural categories of time and space into a time-space category, adequate for the genre in question. In Bachtin's view, the genre is even determined by the chronotope (cf. 1975: 235). Examples of typical novel-chronotopes are, for instance: the road, the marketplace, the crossroad, the threshold, the "salon", or the railway station. The chronotope, according to Bachtin, has an important function as a vehicle for cultural memory. Owing to the chronotope, genres (and for that matter literature as such, I would argue) are able to preserve their identity over time.

This touches upon the thesis put forward in the introductory part of the previous chapter on literary evolution. In my opinion, the category of space has a double identity. On a supra-individual level spatial elements and the possibilities for expressing space are limited in number. The artist unwillingly and often unconsciously makes a selection from a finite set of spatial "archetypes", the road, the landscape, the house, the river, the boundary, inside or outside space etc. Bachtin's chronotope may be associated notably with this aspect of continuity of literary space. However, one may also find allusions to the other, more dynamic and evaluative, aspect of literary space in Bachtin's article, concerning the semiotization of space, that differs and is new and original in every work of art and in every literary period. A more detailed discussion of this question will be given later.

1.2 literature as a modelling system

In order to outline the problem of space within the framework of the theories of the Moscow Tartu semiotics school, I will have to discuss one of their fundamental principles first, concerning the presumption about the modelling function of literature. An important, even famous, thesis of this group of scholars is the idea that works of literature, like all works of art, represent "models of reality" (Lotman 1964, reprint 1968: 14-15). According to Lotman, each work of art is, in principle, of an "ambivalent" nature. On the one hand, it is strongly rooted in extra-literary reality, because it makes use of the means and possibilities reality has to offer, such as images, language, shapes, tones etc., thereby approximating reality itself (mimetic vs. non-mimetic art). On the other hand, each work of art constitutes an independent world unto itself, with its own laws and with its own "reality". The more the object and its representation resemble each other, the more the differences between them become apparent (the preciser a painting of, e.g., an apple, the more obvious the fact that this apple has no flavour and that you can't eat it etc.). Apart from the metaphorical relation between art and reality, Lotman is therefore especially concerned with the metonymical one, whereby the picture is seen as part of a whole (namely reality) (Lotman 1964: 19-20).

Furthermore, according to Lotman, abstract, modernist, avant-garde art forms show a higher degree of resemblance to the original, than, e.g., so-called "realist" art, owing to the circumstance that all attention has shifted from the superficial outward resemblance, and is now focussed on an internal likeness. This idea implies that the inner similarity is more essential than the external, thus ranking content above form. Here, there appears to be a link with Viktor Šklovskij's concept of "zatrudnennaja forma" [difficult form], (cf. "Iskusstvo kak priem" ["Art as device"] in: Striedter 1969: 14). Besides the device of estrangement, it is this other device of "impeded perception", "making difficult", through which art, according to the Formalists, may accomplish its most important task: the deautomatization of the perception of the recipient, or impeded perception. In the case of such art forms as anti-representational painting, atonalist music or stream-of consciousness narration, the artist, as it were, puts into play all his resources to prolong the perception, to make it as complex as possible, less "natural" and less obvious, but thereby stressing art's essence.

Lotman, in his first theoretical study of some length, the 1964 *Lekcii po struktural'noj poètike* [Lectures on Structural Poetics] more than once stresses the dual nature of art. A work of art is simultaneously a sign and a model, cf. "двойная сущность художественного произведения - моделирующая и знаковая", (Lotman 1964: 37). The *theory of the model*, in this case, concerns the relation between work of art and reality (art as a way to knowledge and understanding, the, so called, cognitive function, or "poznavatel'naja funkcija"), whereas the *theory of the sign* touches upon the relation between the work of art and the reader (art as a form of transmitting information, related with the communicative function, or "kommunikativnaja funkcija"). Although both functions are closely related - "tesno svjazany" - they still belong to different spheres - "raznye voprosy".

Lotman views the reciprocal status of model and sign as follows. An object is converted into a sign at the very moment the original is replaced by its picture (cf. the simple example, where a pair of scissors on a board on the front of a house designate a barbershop). This sign is subject to the same processes as all models: notwithstanding the fact that it represents only part of the features of the original, the representation is still a model of the whole, the totality. This also implies that *all non-present aspects of the original are represented*.

This implies that a work of art, a literary work, always models reality. It is therefore possible for the reader or critic to speak about the world-view underlying the structure of a text, basing himself or herself solely on textual details.

These problems may also be understood in the broader and more general context of the process of literary communication, as it was described by Jakobson (1960). Like Jakobson, be it in slightly modified terms, Lotman distinguishes several participants or elements in the process of communication, such as, the work of art (in Jakobson's model this does not figure explicitly), reality and reader. This parallel can be demonstrated by considering Jakobson's famous scheme of communication. I would suggest that Lotman's theories concerning the model relate to the upper part of the scheme (especially the referential function), whereas theories of the sign involve the lower half (with code and receiver as main participants)[5].

When working with Lotman's theories, it is important to realize which elements of the process of communication are involved. Depending on the point of view, either reality or the reader, either the model- or the sign character of art are implied. Each concerns simply a different function of the same work of art, it is not a question of major and minor importance, respectively.

2.0 Lotman's theory on literary space, spatial language and his analytical method

It was actually Lotman[6] who initiated the investigation of literary space from a semiotic point of view, with his 1968 article on space in Gogol's prose, "Problema chudožestvennogo prostranstva v proze Gogolja" ["Problems of Literary Space in Gogol's Prose"]. In this "pilot study", he introduces various terms and concepts and experiments upon their practicability. In later years some of these concepts have been modified, others have disappeared, but most of his central ideas have proven to be persistent and have become generally accepted notions in literary research. Lotman is primarily interested in *space as such*, what we could designate as pure space. Space's correlate time is of minor, almost no, importance in his theory[7].

Lotman's articles, in which he deals explicitly with matters concerning literary space, and the terminology he uses reveal a rather abstract understanding of the role of space in literature. His interest in spatial structures is above all an interest in literary and, more in general, cultural world-views, pictures or models of the world, that are supposed to lie at the root of these spatial structures. Spatial concepts are primarily seen as a tool for "decoding" such worldpictures.

Художественное пространство представляет собой модель мира данного автора, выраженную на языке его пространственных представлений.
(Lotman 1968: 6)
[Literary space represents an author's model of the world, expressed in the language of spatial representation.]

Пространство в художественном произведении моделирует разные связи картины мира: временные, социальные, этические и т.п. [...] в художественном модели мира «пространство» подчас метафорически принимает на себя выражение совсем не пространственных отношений в моделирующей структуре мира.
(1968: 6)
[In a literary work, space models different relations of the world-picture: temporary, social, ethical and others. [...] in the literary model of the world "space" sometimes metaphorically adopts meanings of relations in the modelled world-structure, that are themselves not spatial at all.]

Язык пространственных отношений оказывается одним из основных средств осмысления действительности.
(Lotman 1971: 267)
[The language of spatial relations appears to be one of the fundamental means to make sense of reality.]

Lotman takes the view that space and the spatial relations or structures in a literary text must be regarded as a special kind of "language", a language very much appropriate for the modelling of meaning in general. Owing to this special faculty, literary space is the most appropriate literary category for expressing and representing cultural world-pictures. One may conclude therefore, that Lotman accords space a more or less "privileged" status among the narrative categories.

In his literary analysis, Lotman departs from the presupposition that the most fundamental organizing element of literary space is the boundary. An exploration of the literary universe must start with the detection of this dividing line. As a result, spatial oppositions will emerge, oppositions polarized by that same boundary. It must be notified that borders, in general, have a separating as well as a connecting function - they do not only divide but also bring together what is different - and are therefore of extremely ambivalent nature. Lotman, however, exclusively emphasizes the separating function of borders, as the point of orientation for his semantic oppositions.

Lotman designates the cultural bipartition that is the result of these divisions as the typological opposition between: "свой [svoj]" and "чужой [čužoj]" - which can be read as follows: this side of the boundary, this part of space is "ours", "my own", "cultured", "safe", "harmoniously organized" , whereas the other, opposite side, "their" space, is "alien", "other", "unknown", or even "hostile", "dangerous", and "chaotic".

More concrete examples of the dividing line within the cultural-literary universe, are spatial details such as the door, the window, or the threshold, all boundaries between inside and outside, or open and closed spaces. As a result of the spatial bipartition, meaning is ascribed to the respective poles, inside space is seen as safe or, on the contrary, as stuffy and cramped. What is of importance, is the fact that the other spatial member takes on the inverse significance, i.e. is seen as hostile or free. Between the two worlds there is a "mirror-like relationship" (Lotman, 1990: 132).

Which member of the opposition acquires which of the two contrary significances, depends, according to Lotman, on the world-view that is represented by the text at hand. "How this binary division is interpreted depends on the typology of the culture" (1990: 131). For the literary scholar, it is of crucial importance to realize that the evaluation of various parts of space that make up the universe of the narration is strictly relative.

The use of semantic oppositions is, as such, a typical feature of the analytical methods of the Moscow-Tartu school of semiotics. The whole concept of binary oppositions as the basic mechanism of human thought derives, of course, from structural anthropology (a.o. Lévi-Strauss' *La pensée sauvage*). In this discipline, semantic oppositions, or binary logics, are believed to be typical of the logical mechanism of myth, the "primitive" form of human thought. Basically, the semantics of every universe are determined by binary opposition. They are probably a primeval form of thinking, cultural constants, which each culture and cultural phase reactivates anew and in its own way.

There are a number of possible classifications of spatial parameters. They may be embedded in a general system of logical oppositions, as proposed by the cultural semioticians Ivanov and Toporov (1965: 63 ff). From a pragmatic point of view, the basic logical opposition is the one between "positive" and "negative", that is divisible into a number of subgroups or categories. From the point of view of the ritual (anthropology), the same oppositions may, again, be subdivided according to a general opposition, the one between "sacred" and "profane".

Lotman stresses spatial oppositions, owing to their capacity of modelling and transmitting various, non-spatial, messages as well. Joint concepts such as "high - low", "left - right", "close - distant", "open - closed" thereby establish cultural models, that in themselves are not exclusively spatial. Other possible values linked to spatial oppositions are notions such as "familiar - alien", "safe - hostile", "known - unknown", "order - chaos", "proper - improper", "true - false", "freedom - confinement", "valuable - valueless", "good - bad", "own - alien" ["svoj-čužoj"], "holy - sinful"[8].

Spatial metaphors are by their very nature not completely arbitrary, but rooted in the physical and cultural experience of human kind. The evaluative meanings connected with the opposition "high - low" are almost the same in every human community, because of the fact that the head and brain are on top of the body and we live on a planet ruled by the force of gravity. Hence metaphorical expressions such as "to rise to the top", "to feel down", "to cheer up". This probably also explains the circumstance that in almost all religious systems the gods are situated up high on top of a mountain (the Olympus) or in heaven, and the forces of evil and the realm of death down below, underground. It is, however, not impossible to imagine a culture (the community of birds, fishes or inhabitants of Mars) in which physical conditions differ to such an extent that this same opposition would acquire interpretations and semantic values of completely different nature.

As far as everyday speech is concerned, there are countless expressions based on a metaphorical use of space. Think of the sociological connotation in "marginalized social groups" reminding of the opposition between "centre" and "periphery" where the elite usually lives in the centre (of town), the less significant members of society on the outskirts. Interesting examples are those expressions in which spatial metaphors are used for the description of temporal relations, as, for instance, "to leave the past behind" and "her whole life lay still in front of her". (It should be noted that situating the past behind and the future in front is not universal for all human cultures). Time may be viewed as linear or cyclical - "the road of life", "the year has come full circle". Apparently the category of space is felt to be illustrative of the more abstract category of time.

According to Lotman, the metaphorical potential of spatial notions is of great importance with respect to the modelling function of literature, for space may model social, religious and political (i.e. ideological) or moral aspects of a world-view. What, then, is exactly meant by the modelling capacity of space? According to Lotman, this may be detected by ascertaining in which type of locations a certain story, novel, conflict, or episode may take place and where absolutely not. The question is, whether the meaning of a text would change fundamentally, if the conflict were transferred to another location.

Текст развертывается в пространстве А, но моделирует Б. А поскольку столь неравные пространства как А и Б, объявляются идентичными, то обнаруживается, что общность их имеет не вещественно-протяженный, а топологический характер. Именно топологические свойства пространства создают возможность превращения его в модель непространственных отношений.
(Lotman 1968: 12 note 10)

[The text is situated in space A, but models B. In so far as unequal spaces such as A and B appear to be identical, we find that their similarity is not of material-extensive but of topological nature. The topological characteristics of space enable it to become a model for non-spatial relations.]

The transition from the real, geographically defined, materially tangible location to a more or less abstract topological one reveals the oppositions relevant for understanding the world-views in a certain story, cf. for instance, the crucial oppositions "centre - periphery", and "city - countryside" in the novel *Oblomov*. Part of the novel, set in the Vyborg district, could also take place in any other remote outskirt of St. Petersburg, but never in the very centre or the countryside, let alone in Moscow or abroad. The story of *Robinson Crusoe* is unthinkable in a location other than an island.

Furthermore, in his theory, Lotman gives special importance to the road, the hero has to travel, both elements of the plot having a connecting function and joining together the two parts of the literary universe. In his 1968 article, Lotman distinguishes two types of road, a differentiation not explicitly mentioned in latter publications. Owing to the circumstance that the Russian language knows two words for "road", one is understood as merely spatial element - "дорога", the other as the metaphorical "road of life", "path", or "destiny" - "путь":

«Дорога» - некоторый тип художественного пространства, «путь» - движение литературного персонажа в этом пространстве. «Путь» есть реализация (полная или неполная) или не-реализация «дороги».
(Lotman 1968: 47)
["The road" is a specific type of literary space, whereas "the path" is the movement of the literary character in that space. "Path" is the (complete or incomplete) effectuation or non-effectuation of the "road".]

Lotman regards as true heroes only those characters in the story who possess the capacity to cross the fundamental boundary of the textual universe. In my analysis of *Oblomov*, in the second part of this thesis, there will be a critical discussion of this idea.

In his analysis of Gogol's prose, Lotman identifies a recurrent clashing of two different types of space, also designated as a clashing or confrontation of two worlds. From this point of view, the literary conflict amounts to a confrontation of two types of culture, with ensuing fundamentally different values and organizations of space. In each of the analysed stories, the spatial universe appears to be divided into at least two constrasting types of space, one of which is, for instance, marked by distinct enclosure, fences and barriers, whereas these features are notably absent in the other type of space.

In some of Gogol's stories, the demarcation of space is carried ad absurdum, as for example, in "Povest' o tom, kak possorilis' Ivan Ivanovič s Ivanom Nikiforovičem" ["The Tale of how Ivan Ivanovich quarreled with Ivan Nikiforovich"]. Extreme forms of closing off may lead to human isolation and a breakdown in communication among people with sometimes disastrous consequences, seems to be Gogol's message in this tale, a message predominantly encoded in spatial language, according to Lotman's reading. "Starosvetskie pomeščiki" ["Old-world Land-owners"] creates an archaic-mythic picture of the world, whereby the protecting, pleasant and comfortable, cosy "own" space of the house - with a strong emphasis on the delimitation by concentrically wrapped, protecting layers between inside and outside world - is contrasted with a threatening, cold and unknown "alien" world outside.

Another, radically different, evaluation of the opposition "open vs. closed" space, is to be found in "Taras Bulba". In this story, Gogol portrays the nomadic world of the Cossack comunity. He explains the destructive behaviour of these people as a natural aversion to all hindrances, all obstacles against free movement in space. Not only permanent dwellings are seen as such, even material belongings like furniture - the entire contents of the house - are destroyed.

At this point it must be noted that the representation of the plot as a clashing of two worlds is often only a more or less schematical model of the literary conflict. In practice, any number of world-views may be involved in the literary conflict. This was demonstrated by Van Baak in his analysis of the conflict-space and correlated models of culture in Babel's *Konarmija*, (Van Baak 1983), where several types of (sub) space are identified.

Lotman is well aware that his method carries the risk of simple and rigid interpretations (1968: 34). Spatial categories with similar structures always carry new and essentially different messages. The process of semiotization as such depends on the specific character of a given culture, be it a literary period, an individual writer or the movement to which he belongs, or the specific cultural background of the reader, especially in those cases when the recipient is not a contemporary of the work of art. Different types of culture, subcultures, individuals will evaluate one and the same detail of the text in different ways.

In this, Lotman is a true follower of Bachtin's doctrine on the emotional and evaluative colouration of all temporal and spatial details in verbal art:

> Хронотоп в произведении всегда включает в себя ценностный момент [...] Все временно-пространственные определения в искусстве и литературе не отделимы друг от друга и всегда эмоционально-ценностно окрашены.
> (1975: 391)
> [The chronotope in a work always contains within it an evaluating aspect [...] In literature and art itself, temporal and spatial determinations are inseparable from one another, and always coloured by emotions and values.]

The fundamental ambivalence of semiosis accounts for the fact that on the level of literary space no location in a literary text possesses an absolute, final, and constant meaning. To illustrate this once more, we take as an example the divergent evaluation of the opposition "own country - foreign land" , "svoj - čužoj" in Old Russian culture and utopian stories respectively. In the eyes of the medieval Russian, his own land was known, and therefore good and right, whereas the unknown and strange was sinful and bad. The utopian, and therefore alien country is in a similar way antithetically joined with one's own world, but is, on the contrary regarded as valuable, desirable, and the focal point of all sorts of ideals, whereas the own land acquires negative features as a consequence.

3.0 Toporov's mythopoetic space

The other member of the Moscow-Tartu semiotics school who is also an important spokesman on literary space is Toporov. In his literary analysis, Toporov explicitly departs from an integral model of the world, which is composed of many different categories of meaning, among these, time and space as constitutive elements:

> Модель мира - сокращенное и упрощенное отображение всей суммы представлений о мире внутри данной традиции, взятых в их системном и операционном аспектах.
> (Mify, I: 161)
> [The model of the world is an abridged and simplified account of the sum of all the ideas about the world within a given cultural tradition, from the point of view of their systematical and operational aspects.]

Toporov revives the philosophical discussion on the nature of space, and introduces the concept of "mythopoetic" space as an alternative for the "rationalized" concepts of space, as they are generally accepted in the realm of science. In an exceptionally detailed analysis of Dostoevskij's novel *Prestuplenie i nakazanie* [*Crime and Punishment*] (1973), Toporov examines archaic structures of thought and, so-called, mythopoetic models of the world, manifest in modern literature. On all semantic levels of the text - the characters, the time-space continuum, ethic values, causality (logics), etc. - Toporov establishes connections between Dostoevskij's text and the Eurasian mythopoetic tradition. He designates these remainders of archaic thinking as archetypes. These primeval images are held responsible for the preservation of the archaic model of the world in cultural memory[9].

As far as the temporal and spatial aspects of archaic forms of thought in *Prestuplenie i nakazanie* are concerned, these manifest themselves in the fact that time and space constitute not merely the passive background, or setting, of the action, they are more than the framework of the story, they are active participants of the plot - elementary forces of nature, "stichija" - and as such they are able to influence or even manipulate the action itself (Toporov 1973: 238)[10].

Whereas Toporov at first handles space as one of several semantic categories that constitute the literary universum of the text, in a lengthy 1983 essay, he more specifically discusses the spatial category on its own terms, without ever forgetting the correlated category of time, in the tradition of Bachtin's chronotope.

As an alternative for the dead and dull concepts of space, as defined by mathematicians and certain philosophers, Toporov offers humanism the much broader concept of mythopoetic space (1983: 227-231). On reading Toporov, one is reminded of Ernst Cassirer's 1924 *Philosophie der symbolischen Formen*, notably part II, entitled "Das mythische Denken" where this German scholar describes the mythological sense of space as a prominent and constitutive part of mythological thinking:

> Die Anschauung des Raumes erwies sich insofern als ein Grundmoment des mythischen Denkens, als die sich von der Tendenz beherrscht zeigte, alle Unterschiede, die es setzt und ergreift, in räumliche Unterschiede zu verwandeln und sie in dieser Form unmittelbar zu vergegenwärtigen.
> (Cassirer 1977: 116)

In connection with many of the ideas that where to be elaborated by Lotman and Toporov in later years, another article by Cassirer deserves mention, in which the author clearly anticipates the research-methods of the Moscow-Tartu semiotics school in matters of literary space. I quote at length, in order to demonstrate the striking parallels with Lotman's, and especially Toporov's, mythopoetic, understanding of literary space. Not only the fact that Cassirer uses semantic oppositions, but also his evaluation of space as transmitter of in itself non-spatial meaning is conspicuously actual:

> Wenn der Mythos das Rechts und Links, das Oben und Unten, wenn er die verschiedenen Gegenden des Himmels, Osten und Westen, Nord und Süd voneinander scheidet - so hat er es hier nicht mit Orten und Stellen im Sinne unseres empirisch-physikalischen Raumes, noch mit Punkten und Richtungen im Sinne unseres geometrischen Raumes zu tun.
> Jeder Ort und jede Richtung ist vielmehr mit einer bestimmten mythische Qualität behaftet und mit ihr gewissermaszen geladen.
> Ihr ganzer Gehalt, ihr Sinn, ihr spezifischer Unterschied hängt von dieser Qualität ab. Was hier gesucht und was hier festgehalten wird - das sind nicht geometrische Bestimmungen, noch sind es physikalische "Eigenschaften", es sind bestimmte magische Züge.
> Heiligkeit oder Unheiligkeit, Zugänglichkeit oder Unzugänglichkeit, Segen oder Fluch, Vertrautheit oder Fremdheit, Glücksverheiszung oder drohende Gefahr, - das sind die Merkmale, nach denen der Mythos die Orte im Raume gegeneinander absondert und nach denen er die Richtungen im Raume unterscheidet.
> Jeder Ort steht hier in einer eigentümlichen Atmosphäre und bildet gewissermaszen einen eigenen magisch-mythische Dunstkreis um sich her.
> Denn er ist nur dadurch, dasz an ihm bestimmte Wirkungen haften, dasz Heil oder Unheil, göttliche oder dämonische Kräfte von ihm ausgehen. Nach diesen magische Kraftlinien gliedert und strukturiert sich das Ganze des mythischen Raumes und mit ihm das Ganze der mythische Welt.
> (Cassirer 1975: 27)

Cassirer is concerned with the "osmyslenie dejstvitel'nosti" [giving meaning to, or, semiotization of reality], as is Lotman. Toporov, in his turn, shares his conviction that time must be regarded as an inseparable correlate of space.

> Der echte Mythos beginnt erst dort, wo nicht nur die Anschauung des Universums und seiner einzelnen Teile und Kräfte sich zu bestimmten Bildern [...] formt, sondern wo diesen Gestalten ein Hervorgehen, ein Werden, ein Leben in der Zeit zugesprochen wird.
> (Cassirer 1977: 129).

Cf. Toporov:

> Прежде всего в архаичной модели мира пространство не противопоставлено времени как внешняя форма созерцания внутренней. [...] пространство и время, строго говоря, не отделимы друг от друга, они образуют единый пространственно-временой континуум.
> (Toporov, 1983: 231)
> [In the first place, in the archaic model of the world, space is *not* opposed to time as an *exterior* form of contemplation to an *interior* one. [...] time and space, strictly spoken, are inseparable and form one spatio-temporal continuum.]

In Toporov's conception of space, the road (destiny) is also accorded important organizing functions. But unlike Lotman, Toporov is in the first place interested in the uniting capacities of this spatial "mediator", rather than its dividing properties.

In *The Place of Space in Narration* Van Baak has elaborated on these issues (1983: 95 ff). "Several authors stress the archetypal nature of the journey as the fundamental model of the plot and thus of the spatial thematics connected with the road" (98). The author takes over Toporov's two basic forms of culturally perceiving space: *espace itinérant - espace rayonnant*[11]. These two types of space lie at the root of two distinct visions of the world, two types of culture, of which they express the world-view. Itinerant space thereby is understood to designate a nomadic world-view (of, *e.g.*, the migratory hunter), and is most prominently characterized by a conspicuous absence of boundaries and the road as the most fundamental archetype. Radial or concentric space reflects the vision of the world of sedentary man, of rural and subsequent urban communities. A connected archetype is the house, with its prominent demarcatory features.

In the mythopoetic world-view, as it is described by Toporov, the road connects the two poles of beginning and end, thereby neutralizing oppositions between "here - there", "own - alien", "inner - outer", "near - distant", "house - forest", "civilized - wild", "visible - invisible", "sacred - profane" (Mify 1982: 352). It is inherent that traveling on this type of road is extremely difficult.

Трудность пути - постоянное и неотъемлемое свойство, двигаться по пути, преодолевать его уже есть подвиг, подвижничество со стороны идущего подвижника, путника. (1983:259)
[The difficulty of the road is its constant and inseparable feature, *traveling* along the road, to overcome it, is in itself already a heroic deed, heroism of the *traveling hero*, wanderer.]

Простой смертный может реально вступить на горизонтальный путь и при особых усилиях проделать его, но вертикальный путь может быть проделан лишь фигурально - его душой.
(261)
[A simple mortal being may actually step unto the horizontal road and overcome it with great effort, but the vertical road may be traveled only figuratively speaking, by his soul.]

The above quotations bear witness to the fact that Toporov bases himself on archaic texts, ritual texts and texts belonging to folklore, such as fairy tales, in order to establish the nature of mythopoetic space. However, his ultimate concern is to trace the roots of archaic images in literature, of which the pivotal archetype of the road is a fine example ranging from Homer's *Odyssee* to Dante's *Divina Comedia*, and from Gogol's *Mertvye duši* [*Dead Souls*] to Belyj's *Peterburg*[12].

4.0 summary

In my opinion, Toporov's emphasis on the mythopoetic aspects of literary space on one hand and the more topologically oriented approach of Lotman on the other hand, form an excellent complementary relationship. The more or less constant spatial features and the recurrence of certain spatial elements and details throughout literary history may be interpreted as reactivated ancient images, rooted in mythological thinking. But the semiotization of space, connected with the problem of evaluation that differs not only from period to period and which may even shift within one work as I will prove in the subsequent section of my book, is best understood via a meticulous structural analysis with the help of semantic oppositions, as proposed by the Lotman-method.

An integral use of both approaches should ultimately result in a better understanding of the world-views modelled in the work of art.

5.0 the block of space in relation to other narrative categories

The category of space constitutes only one among several other blocks in a literary text. In the narrative model as it was suggested by Jan van der Eng 1978, the three categories of action, characterization and the geographical and social setting are distinguished. In other words, a literary text is constituted of three interrelated thematic blocks, the block of the story, the block of the characters and a spatio-temporal block. One of the aims of this study is to establish the position of the spatial category among the other narrative blocks of text, in successive periods of Russian literature. In the above section some issues connected with the problems of literary space, such as mobile versus immobile heroes and the road as an important organizing spatial principle have already come across. A few other topics as yet unmentioned will be briefly touched upon in this section. They concern the interrelation of the various narrative categories of the text, taking space as a point of orientation.

The following interrelations between space and other narrative categories, could be object of separate investigations:

a) The role of space in the construction of the plot, notably the crossing of the boundary.

b) The role of space for the characterization of the heroes, notably metaphoric or metonymic relations.

c) The point of view under which space is being perceived.

In my opinion, the interrelation between the various narrative blocks in the text may vary from period to period, and may also differ between the genres. Therefore, the dominance and subordination of heroes, plot and setting is not an absolute and static situation, but depends on the dynamics of diachrony.

During Realism there is a generally acknowledged emphasis on characterization. All other elements of the plot, setting, even thematics and structure are subordinate to the imperative of psychologization. Thereafter, the category of space is seen to play a more or less auxiliary role. Primarily as a result of the dominating principle of metonymic presentation, the surroundings are used for the description of the character of the hero. The description of the state of affairs in Oblomov's room is a good example of this typically realist function of space. However, this does not rule out the possibility of abundant spatial details, such as for instance descriptions of landscapes, that vary from period to period. Typically realist landscape features are, among others, "human" dimensions, in contrast to the extravagance of the Romantic landscape or the infinity of the Symbolist one.

The governing ideology of positivism and scientific thinking influences the way in which reality, i.e. the surrounding world, are being represented in Realist literature.

Topographical details, and agglomeration of details in general, serve as evidence for verisimilitude[13].

As a typical secondary style period, Romanticism exhibits a more diversified image. The general heterogeneity of this period applies also to the distribution of dominant and subordinate functions of the various narrative categories, that may vary from genre to genre. The overall tendency, however, is the emphasis on intrigue, whereby elements such as mystery, suspense, action and tension play an important role. In certain specific forms of the romantic tale, one may detect, however, the preeminent role of the setting, notably in the genre of the exotic, so-called Eastern tale, with the Caucasus as the most important location in Russian Romanticism. In a similar way, location and especially time influence all other categories in the genre of the historical tale, notably the category of the heroes and plot, that are subjected to the restricting demands of historical credibility.

Fin-de-siècle literature, of Russia as well as of Western Europe, undeniably reveals man's pessimistic attitude to life and his fundamental feeling of uncertainty in relation to reality around him. Man calls into question the familiar meaning of things, and sometimes even perceives the world as nothing but a grotesque play. Fiction written in this period reflects this pessimistic mood, not only thematically, but in some cases structurally as well. The literary hero's traditional position at the centre of the narration is called into question. And this, in turn, reflects the feeling that man has lost his central position in the world. The description of the chaos of the world is a recurrent theme. The depiction of the destruction of the hitherto familiar world-picture fundamentally affects the category of space in the text.

Traditional realist causality, i.e. the logical relation between behaviour and events on the one hand and milieu, circumstances, surroundings on the other hand, is challenged during the stylistic periods of Symbolism and Modernism alike. Suggestion replaces explanation. The level of action is reduced for the sake of atmosphere, mood and feelings. Space and time thereby gain importance, they even are seen to play a role unequalled in previous stylistic periods, cf. also Joseph Frank's thesis on modernist literature. State of mind, fantasy and perception are in constant interaction with the surrounding world, and we may even speak of a mutual influencing of characters and the spatio-temporal categories. Spatial and temporal structures at certain moments seem to depend on a character's perception, while on other occasions feelings and mood are manipulated by space and time.

The culmination of this emancipation of the spatial category from a subordinate to a more dominant position among the narrative categories may be seen in the French Noveau Roman where space at certain points of the narrative becomes the sole hero. This dominant role of space comes explicitly to the fore in the following statement by Michel Butor:

> [...] car l'ameublement dans le roman ne joue pas seulement un rôle "poétique" de proposition, mais de révélateur, car ces objets sont bien plus liés à notre existence que nous ne l'admettons communément. Décrire des meubles, des objets, c'est une façon de décrire des personnages, indispensable: il y a des choses que l'on ne peut faire sentir ou comprendre que si l'on ne met sous l'oeil du lecteur le décor et les accessoires.
> (1964: 53-54)

The significance of this statement could, however, be extended to metonymic relations in general, and therefore may also be applied to descriptions in Realist literature.

In the second part of this study, the above presented theories will be applied to a number of texts from Russian literature. In each story, the role, function, meaning and importance of space, and the way in which spatial language contributes to the establishment of meaning and world-views varies. In each analysis, I purposely took the work of art itself as a point of departure. It is the work that should guide the critic in selecting those aspects of the theory best suited to meet the peculiarities of the text.

1. "Innerhalb der mathematisch-mechanischen Naturbetrachtung gab es den Kampf zwischen der 1) eigentlichen Lehre Descartes' und der Kartesianer, die Materie und Raum einander gleichsetzen, und 2) den Anhängern der Atomistik (Demokrit, Epikur, Gassendi), die die Materie in starre, durch leeren Raum getrennte Einheiten zerlegten", (Aster, 1980:249).
A clear and concise discussion of other philosophical concepts of space (and time) can be found with Cassirer 1975. This scholar remarks that, depending on the kind of approach, space is <u>always something</u> <u>different</u>, thereby putting into perspective the use of philosophical concepts in respect to literary analysis, (Cassirer, 1975: 26).

2. Besides the classics on literary space named in this survey, Bachelard's highly original and very stimulating book *La poétique de l'espace* (1958) deserves special mention. In this book, the author connects philosophical ideas on the nature of space to presentations of space in literature.

3. Furthermore. it is the merit of Van Baak, to have elaborated and adapted many of Lotman's concepts on literary space, integrating them into an overall narratological model, cf. *The Place of Space in Narration*, 1983.

4. The existence of two approaches has been pointed out, briefly, by Lotman 1986 en Koschmal 1987.

5. This famous scheme of literary communication can be found in: Jakobson 1960: 353 and 357.

6. According to Lotman himself, it was his colleague, the specialist on Russian folklore, S.Ju. Nekljudov who inspired him (Lotman 1968: 7).

7. This fact marks an important difference between Lotman's concept and Toporov's.

8. In his thesis Van Baak embarks on a lenghty and very detailed enumeration of spatial parameters and orientations (1983: 55-78). He distinguishes five basic types:
a) verticality - horizontality
b) inside - outside
c) open - closed
d) near - distant
e) left - right and before - behind

9. The term "archtetype", which seems to be rather popular among cultural semioticians, is at present being used independent of its "spiritual father" C.G. Jung, cf.:
[...] для обозначения наиболее общих, фундаментальных и общечеловеческих мифологических мотивов, изначальных схем представлений, лежащих в основе любых художественных, и в т.ч. мифологических структур уже без обязательной связи с юнгианством.
(Toporov, in: Mify, I: 110)
[...to designate the most universal mythological motifs, primeval schemes of thought, fundamental and universal for all of humankind, lying at the roots of any artistic structure, among which mythological structures, without necessary connection to the teaching of Jung.]

10. From here we may draw a line to a specific feature of modern literature. As I see it, there exists a typological connection between what Toporov calls archaic conceptions, active forces of nature, and certain fantastic literary elements in modern literature that may have reached us via folklore.

11. Toporov himself was inspired by the ethnographer Leroi-Gourhan, cf. Mify 1982, II: 352-3.

12. With respect to certain writers, Toporov (1983: 251) speaks about a particular "spatial" talent. In the work of, e.g. Goethe, Hoffmann, Gogol', Dostoevskij, Kafka, Thomas Mann, Belyj and Platonov, space plays a role that could be called above average. According to Toporov, these authors possess a specific psychological predisposition which enables them to "listen" to space. Besides these specially "gifted" writers, there exists of course another group, more or less indifferent towards spatial language.

All this sounds rather "vague" from a strictly scientific point of view, one must admit however that in some works of literature space plays a more prominent role than in others. Sometimes, space may be even absent from descriptions and narration, but in the mind of the reader it is always present as the indispensable background for imagining and visualising the related events.

13. On the interrelation of the different narrative categories during Russian Realism and Romanticism respectively, cf. also John Mersereau Jr. 1971 and 1973.

Part II

CHAPTER I

The structure of space in Lermontov's "Mcyri"

1.0 introduction

In this chapter I will examine the peculiarities of the structure of space in a literary text of the period of Russian Romanticism. In Russian literary history, this movement is generally situated between 1815 and 1840, so that roughly speaking Romanticism occupies the first half of the nineteenth century, initially embracing Sentimentalism, from which it evolved, and coexisting for some time with Realism in the ultimate years.

A fundamental aspect of the romantic worldview, particularly with respect to the category of space in romantic works of art, is the orientation towards another world. The romantic code, as it were, prescribes the evocation of an alternative world, onto which all kinds of ideals can be projected. The attention of the Romanticists is attracted not by the *hic et nunc*, but by worlds of the past (or future), by irrational phantasmagories or the marvels of unknown and strange countries. This results in a basic bipartition of the world-picture, designated as *dvoemirie*, i.e. a system of two contrasting or even antipodal worlds. Furthermore, the conflicting worlds in secondary systems are believed to be incommensurable (Van Baak 1983: 33) or asymmetrical (Lotman 1979: 167) in principle, which means that they involve sets of non-interchangeable elements:

> Conflict space in such cases will be a compound of incommensurable spaces, emerging from the polarities between two distinct worlds with their own modalities, one of them being imaginary and infinite, unbound and not subject to the limitations, time and causation of 'primary style' worlds. (Van Baak 1983: 33)

The distinction of two worlds determines the structure of the text on different levels - spatially, it is expressed as an opposition between "here" and "there", "proximity" and "distance", "this side" and "the other side". Döring and Smirnov notice that in secondary style works words refering to the "other" world occur frequently:

> Высокий удельный вес слов "тот", "иной", "чужой", "дальний", "нездешний", в лексическом репертуаре "вторичных стилей".
> (1980: 33)
> [The high specific gravity of words like "that", "the other", "strange", "distant", "not here" in the lexicon of "secondary styles".]

Obviously the *dvoemirie* influences other modalities of the text as well. It is, for instance, expressed temporarily (opposition between "now - then", "present - past/future"), or causal/logical: "rational - irrational/fantastic".

In the spatial structure of texts in which orientation towards an alternative world is a distinctive feature of the world-picture, the border between the two worlds is of great modelling importance (cf. Lotman 1968, 1971). It is the romantic hero who emphasises the separating role of the border. His primary actions are aimed at crossing that border.

49

This pursuit causes the romantic conflict, in which there is always a clashing between the hero and his surroundings. Or, to put it in another way, a central aspect of Romanticism is the conflict between the hero and his environment. The romantic hero views himself as an outsider, "я - чужой" [I am the other][1]. He is either fleeing his own country in pursuit of happiness elsewhere, or he is an alien in a foreign land. In both cases the romantic hero embodies a confrontation between two worlds.

Typologically, the romantic bipartite model of the world could be summarised in the opposition "свой, родной vs. чужой" ["own, familiar (svoj) vs. alien (čužoj)"]. This opposition, however, appears to be of a highly ambiguous nature. It is for instance not always easy to ascertain which part of the *dvoemirie* corresponds with "svoj" and which one with "čužoj". The definition depends strongly on the point of view of narrator and/or characters. "Svoj" is not necessarily identical with the "here and now", in fact, it probably more often is not. For instance, in the very popular conflict situation in which the hero longs for a place where he is not - "dort wo du nicht bist ist das Glück", the romantic hero often feels a stranger among his fellow countrymen. In such case, the hero's point of view will define the place where he is as "čužoj" and the place where he is not as "svoj". From the point of view of society the definition is exactly the opposite. To make things even more complicated, the point of view of a focalisator may shift as the story progresses. What was experienced as "svoj" at first, may turn "čužoj" in the course of events, and vice versa.

The typological definition of Romanticism as a conflict between two worlds, opposed according to the principle of "svoj" vs. "čužoj", must therefore be handled with care. Points of view and nuances must be taken into account in order not to simplify the complex and often contradictory romantic worldview.

While the following enumeration renders only a very incomplete picture of the many-faced movement of Romanticism, the works of this period can be grouped thematically, according to the nature of this "other world". Typical for Russian as well as for European Romanticism are stories about a) the historical past, b) the world of the fantastic or supernatural, c) exotic cultures, and d) the contemporary high society. These themes were treated in the form of both prose - the short story in particular -, and poetry, especially the genre of the verse tale, the "poèma".

2.0 the genre of the Eastern Tale

In the present chapter, I have singled out the exotic category, because it is here that we encounter the romantic world-picture in its most typical Russian form. Northern and southern thematics both play a role in the Russian romantic need for the exotic and as a consequence the opposition north - south is of importance in the modelling of world-views[2]. In the case of such an opposition, Russia is conceived as a central chronotope, opposed to culturally and geographically peripheral locations such as Finland, the Baltic countries, Siberia, the Ukraine or the Caucasus.

The north or the south may also function as an autonomous, exotic conflict space. An example of this variant are stories situated in the northern city of St. Petersburg ("Mednyj vsadnik", Šinel'" ["The Bronze Horseman", "The Overcoat"]), which is seen as a demonic, artificial and anti-human world (the exotic and fantastic sometimes merge), where there is no explicit north - south orientation[3].

Though the north plays its part as an exotic location, the south seems to stand out. Therefore, my attention will be focused more specifically on this particular theme in Russian Romanticism. Although not distant, newly discovered or occupied territories overseas, the provinces in the south and south-east of the empire became the setting for Russian romantic conflicts[4]. The "other" world in the Russian romantic stories and poems about the exotic is part of the material, tangible, geographically defined and "known" world, but emphasis is placed on the different cultures, customs, spectacular landscapes. This notion of foreignness is accentuated in all sorts of ways[5]. Furthermore, the foreign country is often preferred above the "own", because it is supposedly more authentic and less affected by the decadence of civilisation[6]. The climatological contrast between the harsh north and the much more hospitable south evidently plays a role as well.

In contrast to Sentimentalism, the Romantic utopia is either never reached, or, after it has been reached, is disappointing. The paradoxical situation in Puškin's "Kavkazskij plennik" ["The Prisoner of the Caucasus"] is exemplary. In this poem the hero has left his homeland (Russia) in search of a life close to nature, among a free people, but once he reaches the place of his dreams, he is taken prisoner and held captive, unable to share the freedom of those around him. In consequence, he yearns for home more and more.

Probably the most important aspect of the exotic world in relation to the "own" culture, the culture of origin, is the association with liberty and freedom, notions for which the Russian knows no less than three words, each with its own specific nuance of meaning, "свобода" [political freedom], "воля" [spiritual freedom] and "простор" [experience of freedom in space]. If one takes the socio-political background of the romantic movement in Europe into account, it is not surprising that these words figure so frequently in the romantic lexicon. The case of Byron is exemplary. What began as an individual love of freedom was to develop into a general and social fight for freedom. In Russia, the victory over Napoleon (1812) and the abortive Decembrist uprising against autocracy (1825) to which Nicolas I answered with reactionary despotism, played their part in determining the ideology behind the Romantic movement.

2.1 the Caucasus in Russian Romanticism

In the case of Russian Romanticism, the Caucasus became the exotic topos par excellence. This territory neighbouring Russia to the south-east, which joined the empire partly in 1783, and entirely and definitely in 1801, was a source of inspiration for many Russian authors in the first half of the nineteenth century. Owing to its proximity and the specific socio-political circumstances that brought Russians to the south, the Caucasian region was known to these writers either from their travels or from their own military experience. However, Russian culture of that time shows a rather ambivalent attitude towards the Caucasus and its inhabitants. There appears to be a discrepancy between historical and literary reality. In real life, the Romantic authors (Bestužev, Lermontov) participated in the Russian hostilities, aimed at oppressing the Caucasian peoples. The behaviour of the Romantics seems to indicate that they were not in favour of this region's independence. In their literary works, however, the same authors depict these peoples with sympathy and understanding, even with admiration for their unconditional, zealous fight for freedom and liberty, cf. Lermontov's "Izmail-Bej" (1832).

This inconsistency, the contrast between life and literature, leaves a complex impression of the Romantic relation with the Caucasus. The mountain tribes' armed resistance was to continue well into the second half of the nineteenth century. Therefore, the region was a continuous source of conflict, and as such a historical and a simultaneuously literary space of conflicts. In both cases, the region was identified with danger and battle (heroism) on the one hand, and with the spirit of freedom on the other. These notions were rapidly accepted into literature and became an obligatory part of the romantic code. The second permanent component was description of the striking natural beauty of the mountains, that did not fail to become literary cliches and were mocked by later generations of writers, for instance Tolstoj in his story "Kazaki" ["The Cossacks"] (1852-1862), (cf. Van Baak 1984).

The Caucasus in Russian literature of the first half of the nineteenth century, therefore, represents all kinds of contrasting notions simultaneously, such as war and peace, freedom and captivity, love and animosity, life and death. This identification of one and the same location with such mutually contradictory concepts, accounts for a complex setting, which is filled with conflict and which is highly emotional. Van Baak speaks of the Caucasus as a cluster of chronotopes (1984: 368), using Bachtin's well-known term for the merging of place and time. In Russian Romanticism, the Caucasus became one of the most famous and popular chronotopes, owing to the characteristic identification of locations, actions, and emotions in stories and poems with a Caucasian setting.

An example of such a chronotope is the river Terek, which functions as a border in the structure of literary space and divides the literary universum into two "poles". This is especially the case in stories and poems in which a contrast between two hostile cultures, the world of Russia to the north and the world of the Caucasus to the south of the Terek, is established. In romantic literature, the crossing of the Terek creates suspense, entailing an incident, the clashing of north and south and a changing of the status quo.

3.0 Lermontov and "Mcyri"

The most prominent representatives of the romantic exotic Caucasus-theme in Russian literature are Aleksandr Bestužev-Marlinskij (1797-1837), Aleksandr Puškin (1799-1837) and Michail Lermontov (1814-1841). Puškin's "Kavkazskij plennik" (1820-21) opens a series of verse and prose tales, among which Marlinskij's - at that time extremely popular - "Ammalat- Bek" (1832) stands out, and of which Lermontov's "Mcyri" ("The Novice") (1839-40) forms the concluding piece. Lermontov can, perhaps, be regarded as the greatest and purest representative of Russian Romanticism. For one thing, this is due to the great passion with which he treats the traditional romantic topics of freedom and captivity, of melancholic yearning, of loneliness and of the majesty of nature[7], onto which he added a philosophical dimension. He deals with the problem of good and evil, fate and free will, heaven and earth, time and eternity recurrently.

Furthermore, life and art have hardly ever been more intertwined than in Lermontov's tragically short biography. For this reason, Lermontov can also be called the Russian Byron. It is not surprising that Lermontov's work has often been treated from an autobiographical point of view, an approach fostered by the enigmatic and contradictory nature of the poet's character and the sometimes nearly prophetic dimension of his work.

In the traditional allegorical reading of the poem "Mcyri", the mcyri is identified with the person of Lermontov himself (or with his entire, "lost" generation), the mcyri's loneliness with Lermontov's isolation in the oppressive czarist Russia of Nicolas I, and the mcyri's unsuccesful search for his native country with the poet's striving for a freer (and juster) society[8]. Without wanting to deny the existence of such a symbolical dimension, the present discussion of the poem will focus on the structure of space and the world-views connected with it.

3.1 the place of "Mcyri" in literary history

Although its date of appearance places "Mcyri" on the borderline of Romanticism and Realism, the tale is still completely faithful to the romantic code. The topics Lermontov treats in his last big lyrical work[9], captivity and escape, freedom and loneliness, longing and nostalgia for a lost homeland, fate and individuality, and last but not least, the majesty of nature, had all been dealt with exhaustively before. On the other hand, "Mcyri" lacks some of the other traditional romantic themes and motifs. The obligatory battle-scenes and love-story are reduced to an absolute minimum. Even the compulsory mysteriousness of the hero (in the Byronic sense of the word), associated with his enigmatic past or puzzling physiognomy, is modified. Notwithstanding these facts, "Mcyri" is still one the most complete and powerful creations of Russian Romanticism, and can therefore be regarded as one of the corner-stones of this movement[10].

4.0 the story

"Mcyri" - its title is a Georgian word designating a novice, but also a stranger or a lonely person without relatives (cf. Lermontov, 1989: 650) - belongs to the typical Romantic genre of the lyrical verse tale, a genre associated with the name of Byron in the first place, and in Russian literature with Puškin and Lermontov[11]. It is written in iambs and consists of 748 lines, divided into 26 stanzas of unequal length.

The poem relates the peregrinations of a young man, who flees the monastery where he grew up, in search for his lost motherland - his "rodina". The mcyri's story - the young man stays anonymous throughout - is told in first person as a long apologetic monologue before he dies. A brief auctorial introduction precedes this "confession" (stanzas I + II)[12]. Here the narrator/author outlines the historical and geographical setting globally. The monastery, though in ruins, is still existent (a reminiscence of the elegiac introduction to Karamzin's *Bednaja Liza* [*Poor Liza*]) at the confluence of the rivers Aragva and Kura. The narrator gives a short account of the mcyri's life, who was kidnapped from the mountains as a child by a Russian general, and abandoned at the monastery, mortally ill. Here a monk saved his life, and raised him according to the ways and customs of the monastery. He was already preparing to take the vow and stay for good, until, one night, he mysteriously disappeared. Three days later the monks found him barely alive in the steppe. His own account of his wanderings follows, a description of an extatic experience of freedom in open space, a world of storms and struggles, of beautiful girls and ferocious animals. The mcyri, however, fails to find the path to his homeland, and he involuntarily returns to the monastery where he realises that his fate is to stay in the monastery and to die and be buried there.

During his journey through free and open space, to which he consequently refers as "volja" - "на воле" [freedom], the mcyri has a number of very intense emotional experiences. These are above all the revelation of the magnificence of the universe (VI), the recollection of scenes from his childhood (VII) and the perception of his unity with nature (IX). In another deeply moving moment during free life outside the monastery, he experiences feelings of love for a Georgian girl whom he watches secretly while she fetches water from the river (XII,XIII). During his second night of wandering, the novice gets lost in a dark wood which bears resemblance to a mythological forest[13]:

Все лес был, вечный лес кругом,
Страшней и гуще каждый час;
И миллионом черных глаз
Смотрела ночи темнота
Сквозь ветви каждого куста...
(XV)
[The giant woods on every side
In dreary walls began to loom
Each hour. Deep night alone, in gloom,
In leaf and branch with sullen sighs
Stared at me with a thousand eyes.][14]

In this terrible and frightening place, another experience is in store for him, the encounter with a wild animal, which he kills heroically in a life-or-death struggle (XVI,XVII,XVIII). In a final effort, the mortally wounded young man manages to find his way out of the forest. Disillusioned, he recognises the site of the monastery and realises with despair the futility of his struggle for freedom. His last wish is for a view of his beloved Kavkaz, so that he may die at least in a spiritual reunion with his homeland.

5.0 on the structure of space in "Mcyri"

5.1 the setting

Apart from the brief description in the first stanza about the topographical and socio-historical circumstances of the events in "Mcyri", the setting of the story is extremely vague, and described only in very general terms. This lack of topographical detail seems to be a characteristic of the genre. The precision in the Caucasian prose stories of A.A. Bestužev-Marlinskij[15] is, for instance, striking in comparison to the nearly total lack of indications concerning time and place in the lyrical verse tale of Lermontov (or Puškin).

The description in stanza I about the location of the monastery at the confluence of the two rivers and a vague reference to the date of union between Georgia and Russia are the only concrete details about the setting of the "story". And even these details are conspicuously absent in the mcyri's own account of his three days of wandering. Whereas the auctorial introduction renders at least some information about time and place, the mcyri himself seems to be entirely ignorant of his whereabouts. This creates the impression that he is in a kind of trance during his wanderings, and that he therefore does not notice (and does not care) where he really is. This situation may be seen as a psychological explanation of the way in which the hero describes his surroundings. The mountains are designated only very generally as "зубцы далеких гор", "скалы", "горные хребты", "вершины цепи" [jagged peaks, crests of mountains], (only twice as

"Caucasus"); he mentions a river - "ручей", "поток", but no proper name; a hamlet with two humble huts - "сакли"; and a wood with archetypic features - "вечный лес", "темный лес".

This almost schematic abstraction in the outlining of the natural surroundings leads to a number of cliche formulations, which can be generally connected with secondary style literature. An example of this is the circumstance that the "rodina" or motherland, the place on which all the young man's striving and attention are focused, is situated in the east: "Смотрел вздыхая на восток"(II) [He gazed eastward to a land unknown], "К востоку направляло бег"(VI) [To wander toward the sacred East]. How does the novice know, whether it is to the East he must look for his native village? It could also very well be to the north, if one takes into account that the road the Russian general took to Tiflis probably runs north-south[16].

Another aspect of the romantic convention is an anthropomorphic description of nature (cf. also Van Baak, 1984: 370; 372). The following passage is but one out of the many examples of personified nature to be found in "Mcyri":

Внизу глубоко подо мной
Поток, усиленный грозой,
Шумел, и шум его глухой
Сердитых сотне голосов
Подобился. Хотя без слов,
Мне внятен был тот разговор,
Немолчный ропот, вечный спор
С упрямой грудою камней;
(X)
[A swollen flood in a deep ravine
Below me thundered far, unseen,
Resounding in a wild loud tongue
As if a thousand voices strong
In anger rose. I understood
The ever-roaring multitude,
The speech of waters striving long
In silence or in storm, but strong
In never-ending war, alone
Against the stubborn crags of stone.]

5.2 the two world-views

Two cultural systems are contrasted in "Mcyri", the world of the monks of the monastery, an enclosed and static community, and the free natural world outside, inhabited by the mountaineers, which is the young man's homeland and represents open and dynamic space. This contrast is brought about through the person of the romantic hero, the mcyri, whom we may call the dynamic element in a static world. It is part of the romantic code that he will remain an "outsider", notwithstanding all the efforts to make him part of the system. In the second stanza of the introduction, the narrator describes the hero in well-known, romantic terms, as a lonely, melancholy stranger:

Но, чужд ребяческих утех,
Сначала бегал он от всех,
Бродил безмолвен, одинок,
Смотрел вздыхая на восток,
Томим неясною тоской
По стороне своей родной.
Но после к плену он привык,
Стал понимать чужой язык.
(II)
[He shunned the games all children play;
He fled from strangers in dismay.
He wandered silent and alone,
Gazed eastward to a land unknown,
And wasted from some secret ills
And dreams of home beyond the hills.
By steady discipline erelong
He came to speak the foreign tongue.]

One may, therefore, conclude that from the point of view of the narrator, the mcyri is perceived as a Byronic hero, "on - čužoj" [he is a stranger]. The way the narrator refers to the hero emphasises this strangeness. The young man is not given a proper name, instead he is called "mcyri", a word with a strange, exotic connotation, which underscores the fact the hero is "different". The feeling of being a stranger is also expressed by the mcyri himself: "ja - čužoj" [I am a stranger].

It is important to understand that this alienation means an estrangement from his own world as well. The mcyri's tragedy lies in the fact that he is an outsider in relation to *both* worlds. This truth is revealed to him at the end of his journey, when he finds himself again in the proximity of the monastery walls, and realises that he has returned to his prison:

И смутно понял я тогда,
Что мне на родину следа
Не проложить уж никогда.
(XX)
Да, заслужил я жребий мой!
Могучий конь в степи чужой,
Плохого сбросив седока,
На родину издалека
Найдет прямой и краткий путь...
Что я пред ним?
(XXI)
[And I divined
In my despair I shall never find
My native home among my kind.
But I have well deserved my fate.
A horse will shrewdly use his gait
To bring a clumsy rider prone,
And find, by instinct, to his own
The shortest way, without a rein.
But I, not so!]

In spite of the mcyri's initial feeling of unity with nature (IX), he now comes to realise his inevitable human shortcomings. He lacks the intuition and keen sensory perception of animals (the horse) that would lead him home. Thus the images in this passage stress once again his isolation and exclusion from nature and the animal world, and from home.

5.3 the spatial contrasts

The confrontation between the two cultural systems in "Mcyri" is brought about by three important spatial oppositions: a) "inside vs. outside" or "closed vs. open" space, b) a vertical spatial orientation and c) "proximity vs. distance".

5.3.1 Confinement versus Freedom

Though in fact the young man is not kept as a prisoner, he views his life inside those monastery walls as captivity, and himself as a captive and slave - "жил в плену"(III) [I lived a slave]; "И я, как жил, в земле чужой/умру рабом и сиротой."(IV) [And, as I lived, I die-a slave/And orphan in an alien grave]. It is noteworthy that in the introduction, i.e. seen from the point of view of the narrator, this same monastery is not at all conceived negatively. On the contrary, the narrator speaks of the protective walls - "в стенах/Хранительных остался он/Искусством дружеским спасен"(II) [A friendly monk in pity gave/Him care and saved him from the grave;/And thus, among the meek and true,/Behind monastery walls he grew]. Whereas the mcyri calls these same walls gloomy and the atmosphere inside oppressive- "Я вырос в сумрачных стенах" [I lived in gloom, behind a gate].

The images of the monastery as a prison and the young man as a captive are favourite ones in Romanticism[17]. Lermontov himself, for instance, used them in his earlier verse-tale "Bojarin Orša" (1835). In this tale the novice Arsenij was indeed kept as a prisoner in a monastery, so that the place was correctly designated as a prison.

Prior to the novice's escape, the notion of confinement and threat is also attributed to the world outside the monastery walls: "Темный лес/Тянулся по горам кругом" (II) [the gloomy wood/And thickets where the cloister stood]. During his wanderings through free and open space, the mcyri remembers his imprisonment. He explains the reason for his escape in the following, famous words: "Узнать для воли иль тюрьмы/На этот свет родимся мы"(VIII) [to know/If man as freeman or as slave/Must live from birth unto his grave].

When the young man eventually breaks out of this enclosed, protecting, yet passionless and dull world, it is in search of his "rodina", a world of agitation and danger, in other words of "real life". The image of "rodina" is, however, a rather complex and complicated one. It appears to consist of two sub-images, in the first place the actual home, the house of his father ("отцовский дом"), the village where he was born and where his relatives and friends still live ("милых близких и родных") - the novice recollects blurred memories of this place in stanza VII - and in the second place the free world of fighting and trouble ("мир тревог и битв") governed by "воля дикая " (untamed freedom) and symbolised in the tempest - "гроза". These images merge in the mcyri's mind:

В тот чудный мир тревог и битв,
Где в тучах прячутся скалы,
Где люди вольны как орлы.
(III)
[To freedom, life, - to live and dare
Among the cliffs that pierce the sky,
Where men, like eagles, live on high.]

Сгонял виденья снов живых
Про милых близких и родных,
Про волю дикую степей,
Про легких, бешеных коней,
Про битвы чудные меж скал,
Где всех один я побеждал!
(XX)
[How oft it had destroyed my dear
Familiar dreams of home all near
To me, my dreams of open plains,
Of swift wild horses and campaigns,
Of wars among the cliffs on high
And victories beneath the sky!]

Throughout his account, he idealizes the world of his fathers, the free mountaineers, the fighting and bravery as favourable notions, and they are preferred to the calm and peaceful, but also apathetic world of the monks. The world outside is one of storms and struggles, affections and fears, elements alien to the inside world. As the mcyri relates his secret nightly escape, this contrast is presented in expressive terms:

И в час ночной, ужасный час,
Когда гроза пугала вас,
Когда, столпясь при алтаре,
Вы ниц лежали на земле,
Я убежал. О я как брат
Обняться с бурей был бы рад!
Глазами тучи я следил,
Рукою молнию ловил...
Скажи мне, что средь этих стен
Могли бы дать вы мне взамен
Той дружбы краткой, но живой,
Меж бурным сердцем и грозой?
(VIII)
[Then in the night, a night of dread,
When, fearful and uncomforted,
You lay in prayer upon the floor
Beside the altar, I fled before
The thunderstorm. Out, out in space,
The wind and thunder to embrace,
I fled. I hailed the clouds and lands!
I caught the lightning in my hands!...
What gift of life is yours to give
Within this prison where you live,
To gratify that friendship warm
Between my wild heart and the storm?]

At the end of his ramblings, the novice at last returns to the point of his departure, the wrong track has in fact led him round in a circle. At this point of the story the theme of captivity is reintroduced - the return to the prison - and the opposition of "interiority - exteriority", between open or outer space and closed or inside space regains importance. Thus, his words on returning to the monastery are:

И страшно было мне, понять
Не мог я долго, что опять
Вернулся я к тюрьме моей;
(XX).
[I gazed in terror either way!...
I saw my prison world again;
I knew my fleeing was in vain.
I found it hard to comprehend.]

In the last stanzas, the contrast between an inside and an outside world shifts from the direct, spatial level to the metaphorical level.

На мне печать свою тюрьма
Оставила...Таков цветок
Темничный: вырос одинок
И бледен он меж плит сырых,
И долго листьев молодых
Не распускал, все ждал лучей
Живительных. И много дней
Прошло, и добрая рука
Печалью тронулась цветка,
И был он в сад перенесен,
В соседство роз. Со всех сторон
Дышала сладость бытия...
Но что ж? Едва взошла заря,
Палящий луч ее обжег
В тюрьме воспитанный цветок.
(XXI)
[I seemed a weak slow-dying fire,
A dream, a sickness of the brain
Infirm, the seat of evil bane
And prisoned youth. Thus grows a flower
Immured, alone, and paler hour
By hour, in dampness pent about,
Too frail to put its young leaves out,
But waiting for the living rays
To quicken it to brightness; days
Pass by till some compassionate
Fair hand, in pity at its fate,
Removes it to the garden where
With neighbor roses it may share
The sun and air. On every side
Life blooms in sweetness and in pride.
But lo! beneath the blazing skies
The poor spent flower droops and dies.]

The simile of the fading flower is in a way the psychological explanation of the mcyri's failure in search of his "rodina" and his premature death. The monastery has left its mark on him, he says. It is therefore not an exterior obstacle but an interior barrier that prevents him from finding the right road. Thus, the inner and outer worlds are contrasted once more, this time on a mental level. The conflict of the mcyri with the surrounding world takes on the features of a problem of his inner self.

5.3.2 High versus Low

The spatial structure of the narrative poem "Mcyri" is to a considerable degree dominated by a vertical orientation. This is of course a result of the geological formation of the natural surroundings and therefore by its very nature a constant feature of the literary Caucasus. The notion of verticality permeates every description of surrounding space. The world seems to equilibrate between steep cliffs above and deep foaming rivers below.

Verticality is, however, also a feature of secondary styles in general. "Vertical modelling of the conflict space supports the previously mentioned incommensurability of the conflicting worlds in secondary systems" (Van Baak 1983: 35). [E.g. the vertical modelling of space in Gogol's "Nevskij prospekt", which is discussed in the next chapter.] In contrast to the horizontal modelling of conflict space, which would be typical of primary style periods such as Realism, and in which a neutralisation of the opposition between the juxtaposed models of the world can be attained (Döring & Smirnov 1980: 20 and Van Baak 1983: 34), vertically opposed cultural systems are in principle irreconcilable.

In "Mcyri" the two cultural systems are opposed along the axis of verticality, the world from which the boy originates, somewhere high up in the mountains as an idealized and never actually reached land, and the monastery down in the valley near the two rivers. The two worlds are contrasted as early as stanza II, when the narrator starts his account with the following words: "Однажды русский генерал/Из гор в Тифлису проезжал;" [A Russian general rode down/The hills one day to Tiflis town], thereby creating a contrast between height (mountains) and depth (Tiflis). Other contrasts in this clause would be those between north and south, or nature and civilisation.

The vertical spatial orientation also determines the typical behaviour of the novice during his three days outside the monastery walls, which are characterised by downward and upward movement. The novice's climbing of a tree in a fit of panic is a very significant moment:

Я стал влезать на дерева;
Но даже на краю небес
Все тот же был зубчатый лес.
Тогда на землю я упал;
(XV)
[I climbed the trees. I climbed to find
My way again. The woods rose high
Far to the edges of the sky.
I fell upon the ground in wild.]

This scene can be interpreted as a metaphor of the hero's struggle, the downfall as a symbol for the impossibility to reach the goal and to realise his dream. All the images of descent and depth are contrasted with the height of the mountains. Up to the very last moment, the young man keeps longing and trying to reach his homeland. Physically, he can not realise this wish, but his last desire before he dies is a view at mount Kavkaz:

Оттуда виден и Кавказ!
Быть может, он с своих высот
Привет прощальный мне пришлет.
(XXVI)
[There looms the Causasus in sight!
Perhaps its peaks of gleaming light
In cooling breeze and storm will blow
A farewell word to me below.]

5.3.3 Distant versus Near

The third important modelling parameter in "Mcyri" is the spatial opposition "proximity - distance". At certain points, this opposition is connected to the notion of verticality. The second member of the opposition, "distance", is especially accentuated and plays a decisive role in establishing the world picture. As a typical romantic hero, the novice longs for his far homeland, for freedom and a life full of passions and struggles. His only desire in life is to take a look at this remote land of his dreams:

Я знал одной лишь думы власть,
Одну - но пламенную страсть:
Она как червь, во мне жила,
Изгрызла душу и сожгла.
От келий душних и молитв
В тот чудный мир тревог и битв,
Где в тучах прячутся скалы,
Где люди вольны, как орлы.
(III).
[One dream to me in prison came;
One passion burning like a flame
I knew in my captivity.
A gnawing worm, it lived in me;
It roused my thought of liberty;
It called me from my cell and prayer
To freedom, life, - to live and dare
Among the cliffs that pierce the sky,
Where men, like eagles, live on high.]

The novice projects all his ideals onto someplace "distant" - "dal'nie polja", high up in the mountains, so high that you can almost touch the clouds.

В дали я видел сквозь туман,
В снегах, горящих как алмаз,
Седой, незыблемый Кавказ,
И было сердцу моему,
Легко, не знаю почему.
Мне тайный голос говорил,
Что некогда и я там жил.
(VI)

[Above the mists, in robes of snow,
Like diamonds in the sky aglow,
I saw the Caucasus. I know
Not why my heart felt sudden light,
Or what the cause of my delight.
Some inner voice said secretly
That once those peaks had nurtured me.]

However, the paradox and the tragedy of the mcyri lie in the fact that he fails to recognise the world outside the monastery as the land of freedom and struggles he was actually looking for. The world he is entitled to live in for three blissful days resembles the world of his dreams: "Ты хочешь знать что видел я/На воле? - Пышные поля"(VI) [You wish to know what I have seen/In freedom? - Meadows waving green]. He finds an earthly paradise: "Кругом меня цвел божий сад"(XI) [Around me a heavenly garden was blossoming]. And the encounter with the Georgian girl offers the possibility of a life of love and friendship, maybe even relatives and a family of his own. The romantic hero, however, does not grab this opportunity:

В знакомой сакле огонек
То трепетал, то снова гас:
На небесах в полночный час
Так гаснет яркая звезда!
Хотелось мне ... но я туда
Взойти не смел.
(XIV)
[In the familiar hut a light
First died, then flickered in the night:
Thus in the midnight sky a star
With trembling burns and dies afar!
I yearned for her but did not dare
To go.]

Once the "distant" ideals have come "nearby", the romantic heart begins to long for still farther places: "Я цель одну/Пройти в родимую страну/Имел в душе" (XIV) [One aim was mine, one care/To find my home!].

The motif of the road is associated with the motif of the search or quest. The path that could lead the young man home is a rather complicated one. At first he does not seem to know at all where he is going. After the episode with the Georgian girl the path appears clear and easy, but only for a short while.

Бежал я долго - где, куда,
Не знаю! ни одна звезда
Не озаряла трудный путь.
(IX)
[And so I ran, but where, how far,
I hardly knew. No kindly star
Came out to light my troubled way.]

И вот дорогою прямой
Пустился, робкий и немой.
Но скоро в глубине лесной
Из виду горы потерял
И тут с пути сбиваться стал.
(XIV)

[And then, in fear, I took my flight
In tangled woods and dark of night.
The mountains vanished from my sight;
And soon the forest gloom astray
I knew I'd lost in the night my way.]

The spatial opposition "far - near" is also important in the modelling of affections. Metaphors of nature represent the mcyri's loneliness, his remoteness from other humans. At other moments, the novice perceives nature around him as filled with images of friendship, fellowship and unity: "Недалеко, в прохладной мгле/Казалось, приросли к скале/Две сакли дружною четой" (XIII) [Two hovels like a friendly pair], images that constantly remind him of his own solitude.

Я видел груды темных скал
Когда поток их разделял,
И думы их я угадал:
Мне было свыше то дано!
Простерты в воздухе давно
Объятья каменные их
И жаждут встречи каждый миг;
Но дни бегут, бегут года -
Им не сойтися никогда!
(VI)
[I saw the massive cliffs cut through
By swollen torrents, and I knew
The doom that brooded in their heart,
For heaven gave to me the art
Of deeper sight. The cliffs, apart,
Reached far across dividing space,
Their stone arms yearning to embrace
Again; but days and ages fleet
Will pass, and ne'er the cliffs shall meet.]

5.4 the moral transgression

The problem of conflicting worldviews in "Mcyri" can also be linked to the poem's epigraph. Lermontov took a line from the first book of Samuel: "Вкушая, вкусих мало меда и се аз умираю" [I did but taste a little honey.../and, lo, I must die]. Since no real honey is found in the story, we must look for a symbolic meaning of this biblical verse. The quotation speaks of a transgression (of a prohibition of eating) for which the offender must pay with his life. With regard to the thematics of "Mcyri", the honey can be understood as a symbol of freedom (cf. also Maksimov, 1959: 267). The epigraph therefore refers to the mcyri's transgression, his crossing of the border when he leaves the monastery and tastes the smell of freedom. And for this breaking of the law he must die, a judgement he seems to accept without protest. Therefore, this epigraph seems to suggest the existence of yet another point of view, a moral and ethical standard that is superior to the worldviews in the story as such, to which ultimately everything and everybody must submit, even the romantic hero, the eternal outsider.

6.0 conclusion

In the light of a metaphorical reading of "Mcyri", the novice's quest for his lost homeland can be understood as a search for his self. The journey represents a growing self-knowledge which culminates in the understanding that he will never reach "utopia". In this respect, the seeds of later nineteenth century psychological Realism are already present in Lermontov's last verse tale.

Apart from this, the analysis of the structure of space in "Mcyri" and the world-views connected with it demonstrate some of the typical secondary style features of this poem. A particular dualism determines the "kartina mira", resulting i.a. in a bipartition of literary space. Contrasts play a crucial role in the modelling of the world and the establishment of meaning. Apart from the spatial contrasts discussed in this chapter, other oppositions such as those between day and night, heat and cold, sleep and wake, life and death are of great importance.

"Mcyri" is one of the many works of romantic literature in which the romantic hero - probably the strongest exponent of the romantic code - seeks to overcome this division of the world but comes to grief. The novice perishes in pursuit of his goal, in search of the "svoj" among the "čužoj". His failure proves the irreconcilability of "this" world and the "other" world, which lies at the basis of so many secondary style works of art.

1. «"Вторичные стили" мыслят свое как чужое» ["Secondary styles" regard as alien what is their own], leading to a fundamental "отчуждение" - alienation. Cf. Döring & Smirnov 1980:2.

2. An example of this North-South orientation is Lermontov's famous translation from Heine: "На севере диком стоит одиноко" ["Ein Fichtenbaum steht einsam"].

3. A survey of the northern theme in Russian literature is given by Van Baak 1988.

4. "Easy access to contiguous colonial possessions was to make of the Caucasus, the Crimea and Bessarabia, [...] exotic topoi unparalleled in any other European variant of Romanticism" (P.M. Austin, 1984: 233).

5. Foreign words from local languages in these romantic tales and stories emphasize the exotic on the lexical level.

6. These could be called "echoes from Rousseau": "Отдаленный край, населяющий его первобытный народ, являлись целью бегства и скитательства центрального персонажа. Именно там стремился он найти (и в той или другой мере находил) воплощение вытесняемых цивилизацией, незамутненных идеалов Природы" (Ju.Mann, 1976: 43). [A distant region, inhabited by an authentic people, was the goal of the flight and wanderings of the central character. It was there that he hoped to find (and to a certain extent he did find) the embodiment of the unclouded ideals of Nature, suppressed by civilisation.

7. It is of interest to note that by 1841 Lermontov began to distance himself from the romantic depiction of the Caucasus. In *Geroj našego vremeni*, that stands as a Janus face at the convergence of Romanticism and Realism, one may read:
Избавляю вас от описания гор, от возгласов, которые ничего не выражают, от картин, которые ничего не изображают, особенно для тех, которые там не были, и от статических замечаний, которых решительно никто читать не станет,[...].
[I will spare you the description of mountains, and shouting, that do not express anything, the pictures that do not depict anything, especially not for those, who have not been there, and the static remarks, that, frankly speaking, no one is likely to read.]
However, in the same book the reader may still encounter the kind of romantic descriptions, rejected so ironically in this passage.

8. Cf. on this subject D.Maksimov, 1959: 259ff. Nineteenth century critics like Belinskij, Herzen and Ogarev (ibid.: 273-4), of which especially the latter two were known for their social and political commitment, stressed the symbolic meaning of Lermontov's work. They regarded him as a realist writer, who portrayed his own generation and the political situation of Russia in the 1830s. They interpreted the mcyri mainly as a rebellious, protesting hero, and declared the themes of prison and freedom to be the central ideas of the poem.

9. According to Maksimov (1959: 237) it would be more appropriate to rank "Mcyri" (1839) after "Demon", which was almost entirely written 1838 (and only completed in 1841). Consequently "Mcyri" should be regarded as the last of the great romantic "poemas".

10. Cf. Boris Ejchenbaums words: «"Мцыри" не является новым жанром и не открывает собой нового пути. Наоборот - это последнее слово, итог развития русской лирической поэмы, поглощающий в себе опыты Жуковского, Козлова, Подолинского и др.», (1987:217).
["Mcyri" is not a new genre, nor the beginning of someting new. On the contrary, it is the last word, the summary of the development of the Russian lyrical versetale, and it combines the experiences of Žukovskij, Kozlov, Podolinskij e.a.]

11. Cf. B.M. Žirmunskij "Bajron i Puškin" 1970 (1924).

12. References will be made by indicating the stanza in question with Roman numerals.

13. Cf. on this wood: Maksimov 1959: 292-3.

14. English translations are derived from Lermontov, *The Demon and other Poems*, 1965.

15. The reader could very well, so to say, imitate the journeys of heroes like Ammalat-Bek or Mulla-Nur.

16. P.M. Austin 1984: 242 explains the occurence of the term "East" in Russian literature as an influence of western European romantic terminology.

17. Byron's "Prisoner of Chillon", Puškin's "Kavkazskij plennik" and "Uznik" are wellknown examples. P.M. Austin 1984 gives an interesting account of the source of this theme.

CHAPTER II

The structure of space in Gogol's "Nevskij prospekt"

1.0 Gogol and the Petersburg stories

It is generally agreed upon that the years 1833/4 were a period of transition in Gogol's development as a writer, marked by the appearance of *Arabesques* in 1835. From the romantic, bright and colourful rural setting in the Ukrainian stories, the author turns to the gloomy, bleak St. Petersburg. A change on the thematic level accompanied this shift in location. The exotic, often fantastic, sometimes sentimental world of *Dikan'ka* and later *Mirgorod* (though this second Ukrainian cycle appeared in the same period as *Arabesques*, it must be seen rather as the conclusion of a previous period), gives way to the world of bureaucracy, ranks and uniforms, glamour and pretence of the Northern capital. In his Petersburg stories, as they came to be called later, Gogol describes locations familiar to the contemporary reader, such as the Nevskij prospekt and adjoining streets like Morskaja, Meščanskaja, Gorochovaja and Litejnaja ulicy. Still, in this most realistic St. Petersburg, rather unusual, sometimes absolutely incredible events occur: noses walk around in uniforms, lapdogs keep up a correspondence, etc.

Van der Eng (1984) argues that literary works sometimes do make use of contrasting, even paradoxical and mutually exclusive ways of modelling existence (Modellierung des Daseins) in order to heighten the expressiveness of the text. "Die Intensivierung der dargestellten Welt geschieht durch Einbezug von Bereichen, die von der Ratio ausgeschlossen werden, die aber trotzdem, wie die Erfahrung lehrt, sehr wesentliche anthropologische Konstanten darstellen und anscheinend selbstverständlich an literarische Formen mit ihren sinnlich suggestiven Elementen der Dramatisierung, der Tragik, des Strebens nach Glück, der Katastrophe usw. anschlieszen können, (Van der Eng, 1984: 123-4).

1.1 Fantastic Realism

I take the view that this so called "fantastic realism" is brought about by means of a double construction. The world of the Petersburg stories actually consists of two worlds, one of them is physically tangible, with logical topographical indications of existing locations, the other is an imaginary world, actually "made out of air", a *phantasmagoria*. The curious thing about St. Petersburg in Gogol's stories is that it is both worlds, both types of space, at the same time. The city shows itself now in its true colours, now in its ghostly shape. Both hypostases, the realistic and the fantastic one, are contained in the total image of the city. It is the capability of transformation, of metamorphosis from one type of space to another, completely different type of space, with other rules of logic, that will be the object of investigation in this chapter[1].

Furthermore, the change of form results in two variants of the fantastic city, a harmless, comic one, and a fatal, tragic one. We deal either with the merry world of

"Nos" ["The Nose"], the carnivalesque travesty, where man in the end stays unharmed, or with the demonic, frightening world of "Šinel'" ["The Overcoat"], that destroys and kills. In this respect, "Nevskij prospekt" is an ambivalent story, because both the comic and the tragic version of the city's metamorphosis are represented. "Nevskij prospekt" is not by chance the opening story of the collection. Presumably, in it the author formulates his own ambivalent attitude to the city of Peter, his love, admiration and fascination, and his simultaneous feeling of repulsion and fear.

What I have called the *metamorphosis* of the city can be expressed by the following general transformation-formula: the surrounding world changes from a place where man rules over space into a place where man is himself dominated. Or, as it was put by Walter Koschmal: "Der Raum wird zum Agens, die ursprünglichen Aktanten zu Objekten, zum Patiens" (Koschmal, 1987: 198).

In the story at hand the street and some of its attributes such as houses and streetlamps, take over in leading the action. The characters are reduced to objects that undergo the action, to passive paticipants, whose actions are ruled and controled by the space they inhabit. Gippius has already drawn attention to the similarity between the characters in "Nevskij prospekt" and puppets or marionettes: "Все происходящее на Невском проспекте нарисовано в тонах кукольного театра" (1924: 53) [Everything that happens on the Nevskij prospekt is depicted in puppet theatre colours][2].

2.0 composition and story

As far as the composition of "Nevskij prospekt" is concerned, it is that of a typical frame-story with a clear and symmetrical construction. "Nevskij prospekt" starts with an exceptionally long exposition, a lyrical description of the empire's most famous boulevard. But the picture of delight and beauty created at the beginning of the story will be unmasked at the end. In the concluding passage, the narrator formulates the famous sentences of "Nevskij prospekt": "Все происходит наоборот" [Everything goes contrary to what we expect], "Все обман, все мечта, все не то, чем кажется" [Everything is a cheat, everything is a dream, everything is other than it seems], and: "Он лжет во всякое время, этот Невский проспект" [It deceives at all hours, the Nevsky prospekt does], (III: 37 - 38)[3].

The general deceitfulness of this street is actually the main theme of the story. Considering metonymy to be the most important poetical device in "Nevskij prospekt" [4] , these sayings might as well concern the city as a whole and may even bear on the entire world. The story then actually relates how man is blinded by appearance, it unveils the treacherous nature of beauty and shows the world in its true colours.

The inner story consists actually of two separate, independent tales, with the Nevskij prospekt as connecting link. Here the vicissitudes of the two heroes take a beginning. The painter Piskarev and the lieutenant Pirogov are startled by two girls, a blond and a brunette one, who appear on the street where no events had occured until then. The two friends are very different in character, Piskarev is struck by the beauty of the brunette, whom he compares to an Italian Renaissance painting, whereas Pirogov prefers the blond one. They part so that each of them can follow "his" girl, forgetting the general deceitfulness of the Nevskij. Subsequent events show that they are each following the "wrong" girl.

68

Piskarev is an artist, a painter with a sensitive character who believes in divine beauty. He is misled by the outward appearance of the girl, and only when he enters the brothel, does he realise that the brunette is not a Bianca by Perugino but a girl of easy virtue. Piskarev is not able to cope with the vileness of life in the capital. The confrontation with reality, the unveiling of the true nature of beauty shatters his ideals. He flees into opium induced hallucinations, by which he hopes to restore the former image. But after a desperate proposal of marriage to the girl, that she rejects crudely, his life ends meaninglessly. Piskarev commits suicide.

Lieutenant Pirogov, on the other hand, is not an extremely conscientious man. Being a military officer, he, in fact, personifies the life of outward appearances that is so typical for St. Petersburg. All he seeks is to have a good time. He is depicted as a superficial, empty-headed person, without any true ideals. His confrontation with reality, therefore, does not lead to his destruction, for there is nothing to be destroyed. Unlike the innocent artist, his expectations of life are banal, and he is merely interested in superficial pleasure with women. He has also followed the wrong girl, and ends up with a chaste, German housewife. Not in the least embarrassed by these circumstances, he makes a futile attempt to seduce her. His reward is an appropriate thrashing by the woman's husband, the tinsmith Schiller, and his friend, the cobbler Hoffmann. The lieutenant leaves humiliated, but he treats himself to a couple of pastries, and that very evening shakes off his misfortunes at a dancing party at a colleague's home.

Like Piskarev in the first story, Pirogov does not reach his goal. He too is deceived by reality. But while the former is destroyed by delusion, killed by a treacherous world, the latter is merely made ridiculous and comes through unscathed.

3.0 unclean space

In my opinion, in order to understand the nature of the fantastic image of the city in "Nevskij prospekt", the roots of this image have to be sought in folklore and mythology. Meletinskij (1976: 285) points out the impact of mythology on literature during the period of Romanticism, especially when the evocation of a mysterious and transcendental atmosphere is intended. In connection to the present subject, I have in mind concepts of unclean space, "нечистое пространсвто", locations ruled by the powers of darkness, which play an important role in archaic concepts of the world[5]. The peculiar, fantastic features of space in the Petersburg stories generally stem from the northern setting of these stories. Various scholars have pointed out the demonic interpretation of the North in works of literature, (i.a. Meletinskij 1976, Van Baak 1988). Such a negative interpretation derives from an identification of the North with the land of the dead, a land inhabited by evil spirits, hostile to human beings (cf. Meletinskij, 1976: 284). Hence I am of the opinion that the North can be regarded as an unclean and unholy territory.

Another important concept, derived from archaic thinking and related to the idea of the demonic North, is the division of space into "svoj" and "čužoj", "this land" being associated with "holiness", "order", "safety", to name but a few connotations, while the "alien" space is conceived of as "satanic", "chaotic", "illogical", "hostile" and "frightening".[6]

According to popular belief, the working of evil forces is related to certain strange, unknown, dangerous places, such as the forest or the water (rivers, swamps). Russian folkore includes incarnations of these taboo locations in the form of demons, such as the "леший", "водяной", "русалка", "полевой" (wood-, water-, river-, and field demons respectively), which personify the hostile forces of nature[7].

Apart from "unclean" places, popular belief also knew of certain dangerous moments at specific times, such as the unstabile period between day and night during sunset, the midnight hour, and also the transitional periods between the seasons. (This temporal circumstance will be discussed later). The archaic schemes of spatial bipartition may, in a more or less transformed way, be reactivated in modern literature.

3.1 carnivalism

The other aspect of "Nevskij prospekt" which derives from folkore is the fact that the image of the Nevskij prospekt as created in the exposition of the story evokes a *carnivalesque world*. On several occasions, the narrator stresses the difference between this part of town and other streets. He emphasizes its uniqueness, its festive spirit and gaiety. As soon as people set out on the Nevskij, their behaviour, even their very nature, changes.

> Единственное место, где показываются люди не по необходимости, куда не загнала их надобность и меркантильный интерес, объемлющий весь Петербург.
> (6)
> [This is the one place where people put in an appearance without being forced to, without being driven there by the needs and commercial interests that swallow up all Petersburg.]

The caleidoscopic description of the passers-by on Nevskij prospekt on the pages which follow, reminds very much of a carnival procession, especially during those moments when grotesque details replace the actual walking person. During this introduction, amusement and laughter dominate the world of "Nevskij prospekt".

At this point it is necessary to elucidate the concept "carnivalesque" in relation to Gogol. It is the merit of the great Russian scholar Michail Bachtin that he has again paid attention to the correlation between the work of Gogol and folk culture. In his search for the origins of this writer's humour: "творчество Гоголя - самое значительное явление смеховой литературы нового времени" [the oeuvre of Gogol is the most outstanding example of the modern literature of laughter], Bachtin pointed at the fact that Gogol stayed faithful to popular laughter throughout his whole literary career.

> Народная основа гоголевского смеха, несмотря на его существенную последующую эволюцию, сохраняется в нем до конца.
> (both quotations: Bachtin, 1975a: 486)
> [The folklore roots of Gogol's laughter was preserved until the very end, not regarding its fundamental subsequent evolution.]

Lotman extends these thoughts in the following statement: "Gogol is the writer who synthesized the most diverse elements of national life. The accute contemporaneity of his works was combined with a capacity to penetrate into deep strata of the archaic folk consciousness" (Lotman, 1976: 298). He warns, however, not to misinterpret Gogol's humour in the light of Western-European carnival tradition (as it was described by Bachtin in his book on Rabelais, 1965). For a correct understanding of the nature of Gogol's laughter, one must bear in mind the essential difference between Western-European and Russian-Orthodox "laughter culture". Whereas in the former, laughter is meant to abolish fear, in the latter laughter implies fear. Unlike in the West, the Eastern-European attitude toward carnival, and laughter more generally, was unambigous: "Permission for carnival behaviour at certain times was linked with the belief that at that time God permitted the Devil to rule the world" (Lotman, 1976: 298).

One cardinal feature of the system of carnival is of special interest in relation to the present subject, namely the theory of carnival as an inversion of norms and values, a world inside-out. In carnival, these inversions primarily affect the social position of members of society, the lower classes become highest during carnival, the fool is made king. But the principle of inversion actually influences any kind of binary opposition - male and female, heaven and hell may change places - because the world of carnival is reigned by a *logic of opposites*, in which every aspect from official life is turned inside-out, vice versa or upside down.

This is where the two concepts, "unclean space" and "carnival behaviour", meet. In my opinion, the category of space in "Nevskij prospekt" can be understood in the light of a demonic interpretation of the world. During certain hours of the day, namely during dusk, the world undergoes a radical change. The Nevskij prospekt and the other, derived, locations in which the action takes place, turn into a place with a different, unfamiliar order, where man is at a loss and an easy prey to the demons that come to rule the world during that period of time. Man's mind is clouded through the working of these magic forces, which take advantage of the fact that man's faculty of sight fails him during dusk.

In the new, chimerical world, established at nightfall, the normal rules of logic are violated, the transformation of the surrounding world leads to instability and induces uncertainty that may, but not necessarily does, lead to terror and fear. Most important is the fact that in this world, laughter and horror reign simultaneously. The world of "Nevskij prospekt" is funny and frightening at the same time. The parallel stories of Piskarev and Pirogov exemplify this ambiguity.

4.0 the Nevskij prospekt

One of the characteristics of the fantastic world in Gogol's stories, is the possibility of a well-known, familiar place to change into someplace foreign and unreal, either frightening or simply absurd. The usual spatial distinction into "svoj" and "čužoj" breaks apart in "Nevskij prospekt", since both types occupy the same territory simulaneously. This is the cardinal difference between the archaic worldpicture and its subsequent transformation in Gogol's stories, in which a deformation of space is brought about.

In "Nevskij prospekt", the initial six page description of St. Petersburg's main street is built up on the theme of transformation. This typical phenomenon is illustrated by descriptions of the prospekt's appearance during different hours of the day:

Какая быстрая совершается в нем фантасмагория в течение одного только дня! Сколько вытерпит он перемен в течение одних суток!
(7)
[What changes pass over it in a single day! What transformations it goes through between one dawn and the next!]

В три часа - новая перемена. На Невском проспекте вдруг настанет весна.
(10)
[At three o'clock there is fresh change. Suddenly it is like spring on Nevsky prospekt.]

The enumeration of the merry and funny changes of the street seems rather harmless at first sight. But things are never quite what they seem in this world of outward appearances. Very soon after Piskarev's unexpected meeting with the lovely girl, his surroundings take on rather strange features, surrounding objects begin to move, and what was moving at first comes to a standstill. The opposition "mobile - immobile" is reversed, space and the objects in it are set in action.

Он весь задрожал и не верил своим глазам. Нет, это фонарь обманчивым светом своим выразил на лице ее подобие улыбки; нет, это собственные мечты смеются над ним. Но дыхание занялось в его груди, все в нем обратилось в неопределенный трепет, все чувства его горали, и все перед ним окинулось каким-то туманом. Тротуар несся под ним, кареты со скачущими лошадьми казались недвижимы, мост растягивался и ломался на своей арке, дом стоял крышею вниз, будка валилась к нему навстречу, и алебарда часового вместе с золотыми словами вывески и нарисованными ножницами блестела, на самой реснице его глаз.
(14).
[He trembled all over and could not believe his eyes. No, it was the deceptive light of the street lamp which had thrown that trace of smile upon her lips; no, his own imagination was mocking him. But he held his breath and everything in him quivered, all his feelings were ablaze and everything before him was lost in a sort of mist; the pavement seemed to be moving under his feet, carriages drawn by trotting horses seemed to stand still, the bridge stretched out and seemed broken in the center, the houses were upside down, a sentry box seemed to be reeling toward him, and the sentry's halberd, and the gilt letters of the signboard and the scissors painted on it, all seemed to be flashing across his very eyelash.]

Space in its transformed, topsy-turvy appearance is not only funny, it is also alarming ("он задрожал") and threatening. The behaviour of objects can be seen as the harbinger of danger. This manifests itself in the following encounter between Piskarev and the four-storied house the girl lives in:

Он даже не заметил, как вдруг возвысился перед ним четырехэтажный дом, все четыре ряда окон, светившиеся огнем, глянули на него разом, и перилы у подъезда противостояли ему железный толчок свой.
(15)
[He did not even notice a four-storied house that loomed before him; four rows of windows, all lighted up, burst upon him all at once, and he was brought to a sudden stop by striking against the iron railing of the entrance.]

Staring windows and the hostile resistance of iron bannisters are more than mere metaphors. In the light of a demonic interpretation of space in the tragic story of Piskarev, these are examples of animated space, objects come to life - the many-eyed house reminding of a mythological monster, start an autonomous life and make human beings their "victims".

In the humorous story of Pirogov, the hero is confronted with another type of transformed space. The scenes situated at the house of the German beauty are burlesque and comical: during his first visit to the German apartment, Pirogov witnesses a grotesque and absurd spectacle, in which drunken Schiller asks Hoffmann to cut off his nose, since he is spending far too much money on snuff. During his last visit, Pirogov's own behaviour becomes absurd when he starts to dance the gavotte, and the burlesque reaches its climax in the subsequent flogging-scene[8]. All actions in this second tale are senseless and illogical and we can not by any means take them serious. The house of the German craftsman can be seen as an inside-out, carnivalesque world. What was supposed to be a girl of easy virtue appears to be a chaste, dull housewife. Pirogov's expectations, that he would enjoy himself and have a good time with her, are rewarded with a spanking. The Russian officer, who should be respected for his rank and uniform, is debased, even by foreigners of much lower standing. Pirogov - nomen est omen - ends his misfortunes with the eating of pastry ("съел два слоеных пирожка" (37) [ate two cream puffs]) and instead of reporting the Germans' "crime" to the police, enjoys himself dancing the mazurka, an absurd and senseless ending to a likewise absurd and banal story.

4.1 enchanted space

Spatial metamorphosis was already typical for many settings in Gogol's Ukrainian stories. He uses it, for example, in the tragic story "Vij", in which the church is no longer a refuge from the forces of the evil, but in fact the place where the hero of the story is killed. Man is deceived by space, and the "holy" reveals itself as "demonic", or even "satanic". Another, more harmless, transformation of the surroundings occurs in the story "Zakoldovannoe mesto" [A Place Bewitched], in which man is betrayed and laughed at by the "unclean", the devil, but not destroyed. Jurij Mann connects instances of "zakoldovannoe" - bewitched, enchanted or magic - space in the work of Gogol, to an intriguing folklore motif called *obmoročnoe mesto* (1978: 20). He quotes an article by N.I. Petrov from 1902:

> Обморочные места, по народным понятиям, обладают особой силой потемнять сознание
> случайно зашедшего на них человека до невозможности найти выход. На такие места
> чаще наводят особые полночные духи - полуничка, мара или черти в различных образах.
> (Ju. Mann 1978: 20).
> [In popular belief, so-called places of impotence have the power to obscure the mind of a person
> that has entered it by accident, untill a point of no return. Special midnight spirits, devils and
> demons lead man to such places.]

The Nevskij prospekt-location, as I understand it, resembles this folkore motif. At certain moments, the surrounding world changes into an instable, indeterminate place in which man falls victim to uncertainty, blindness or madness. A prey to delusions, he is either laughed at and humiliated or tragically ruined.

4.2 the structure of space

In "Nevskij prospekt", the ideological, psychological as well as ethical modelling of the world are structured according to the axis of verticality. This model manifests itself by means of the following spatial parameters: "high - low", "up - down", "top - bottom", "heaven - earth". Primarily, these parameters determine the structure of literary space of the story, that is, the space in which the action takes place, the space in which the heroes live. At the same time, part of the poetical language is governed by spatial orientation. The notion of verticality is expressed through metaphors as well.

Здесь вы встретите улыбку единственную, улыбку верх искусства, иногда такую, что можно растаять от удовольствия, иногда такую, что увидите себя вдруг ниже травы и потупите голову, иногда такую, что почувствуете себя выше адмиралтейского шпица и поднимете ее вверх.
(9)
[Here you meet whith a unique smile, a smile that is the acme of art, that will sometimes make you bow your head and feel lower than the grass, sometimes make you hold it high and feel loftier than the Admiralty spire.]

The exaggerated upper part of the opposition "high -low" - the image of the elevated spire - must be understood as a first indication of the stressed importance of the "height" and "top". In the official world of bureaucratic St. Petersburg the one and only thing that really counted were the civil and military ranks. The single serious fact in life was the hierarchy in the table of ranks, from which all other items derived their meaning. Moving up along the scale of ranks was the sole purpose of life in the capital, and this is why the top, towards which everyone strives, is of such crucial importance.

Apart from this social interpretation, the opposition "high - low" may acquire other meanings as well. With the launching of the plot at the appearance of the two girls, this opposition is connected to the theme of femininity. Gogol's attitude toward woman is a very complicated and ambiguous one[9], a conflict that permeates a great part of his literary work. In "Nevskij prospekt", it even becomes one of the main themes.

Basically, there are two images of woman in Gogol's work. One is the incarnation of divine beauty, harmony, purity and virtue. She is the spiritual ideal, a Madonna, who helps man in his mystical striving for perfection. Naturally, this type of woman is associated with an angel from heaven, and the longing for her is expressed in an upward movement - "стремление ввысь" . The other image of the female may be called the manifestation of the destructive and demonic forces (think of the witch in "Vij"). This type of woman will mislead man with her beauty, trap him in her nets and tear him down into the lowest regions of the universe.

I will now show how these ideas are expressed in the spatial structure of the story under discussion. Struck dumb by the beautiful young brunette, Piskarev rushes after his "Perudžinova Bianka".

Ему хотелось только видеть дом, заметить, где имеет жилище это прелестное существо, которое, казалось, слетело с неба, прямо на Невский проспект, и, верно, улетит неизвестно куда.
(12)
[All he wanted was to see the house, to discover where this exquisite creature lived who seemed to have flown straight down from heaven onto the Nevsky prospekt, and who would probably fly away, no one could tell where.]

Piskarev almost panics at the thought to lose track of her. When she notices his pursuit, she stops to throw a glance at him. He lowers his eyes with the following thoughts:

Но как утерять это божество и не узнать даже той святины, где оно опустилось гостить.
(14)
[But how could he lose this divine being without discovering the sanctuary in which she was enshrined?]

The girl's celestial appearance evokes associations with heaven, "flying" and "descent" emphasize a vertical spatial orrientation. Furthermore, the godlike creature is associated

74

with holiness, her dwellings with a sanctuary. Oppositions "high - low" and "holy - unholy" are activated through these metaphors. The poetical use of spatial language is subsequently transposed into the description of the setting. Piskarev suddenly finds himself in front of the four-storied house, and sees "как незнакомка летела по лестнице" (15) [how the unknown woman flew up the stairs.] The stairs, first introduced at this point, will play an extremely important role in the structure of literary space and consequently in the modelling of a world-picture in "Nevskij prospekt", mainly in Piskarev's story[10].

Traditionally, the staircase or a ladder symbolizes the connection between earth and heaven, like the ladder in Jacob's dream. It enables the contact and communication between the upper and lower part of the universe, and represents the possibility to improve, upgrade and rise, or, on the contrary, to be degraded and fall down. This is why the image of the stairs has become one of the symbols of a happy fate, of holiness and richness or, on the other hand, the symbol of danger, misfortune, even death (Mify 1982, t.II: 50-51).

As a consequence, in literature the stairs have obtained chronotopical function, i.e. a place of crucial importance in the fate of a hero which represents a state of expectation and a decisive moment in a person's life. When Piskarev starts climbing the stairs, he leaves the materiality of everyday life, the dullness of his poor existence as an artist in a land of snows behind him. He climbs the staircase expecting to find a new and different life at the top.

Он взлетел на лестницу.
(15)
[He flew up the stairs.]

Лестница вилась, и вместе с нею вились его быстрые мечты.
(15)
[The staircase went around and around, and his thoughts whirled around and around with it.]

When he enters the girl's appartment, her true nature is revealed to him. Actually, it is the room itself and the objects in it that unmask her (16) and show who she really is. In a flash - "Боже, куда зашел он!" (16) [Good God, where had he come!] -, the world regains its true colours. At this moment of disillusion the erroneous world is turned upside down; what was supposed to be virtuous and superior is really a cesspool of vice, the lowest of all places. "Он зашел в тот отвратительный приют, где основал свое жилище жалкий разврат" (ibid.) [he had come into one of those revolting places in which the pitiful vice [...] finds shelter]. The room that was supposed to be a sanctuary is unmasked as a brothel, "holy" changes into "sinful", the house into an anti-house, "heaven" becomes "hell". An inversion of oppositions takes place on several levels. Piskarev's way up, his upward movement along the stairs actually becomes his downfall and destruction.

The vertical modelling of space is, it seems to me, less important in the second story. Since no ideals are shattered during Pirogov's adventures, the opposition "high - low", which structures the axiological and ethical model of the world, and in which verticality obviously plays an important role in modelling the hierarchy of values, is not as strong. The stairs occur only once (30). But the order of the world is also turned upside down in Pirogov's tale, where the inversion concerns oppositions such as "vice - virtue", "honour - dishonour", "respect - disrespect".

Finally, I will deal with the question of what causes and who is responsible for the inverted world in "Nevskij prospekt". Twilight, the time between day and night, is of particular importance for the activity of hostile "creatures" as defined in Russian folkore[11]. In the mythopoetical tradition, the setting of the sun, the borderline moment when day and night meet, is pre-eminently the period for the powers of chaos to infringe upon the world and man. This is why sunset was conceived of as a particularly dangerous time (cf. Toporov, 1973: 238).

Но как только сумерки упадут на домы и улицы и будочник, накрывшись рогожею, вскарабкается на лестницу зажигать фонарь, а из низеньких окошек магазинов выглянут те эстампы, которые не смеют показаться среди дня, тогда Невский проспект опять оживает и начинается шевелиться. Тогда настанет то таинственное время, когда лампы дают всему какой-то заманчивый, чудесный свет. [...] В это время чувствуется какая-то цель, или, лучше, что-то похоже на цель, что-то чрезвычайно безотчетное; шаги всех ускоряются и становятся вообще очень неровны. Длинные тени мелькают по стенам и мостовой и чуть не достигают головами Полицейского моста.
(11)
[But as soon as dusk descends upon the houses and streets and the policeman covered with a piece of coarse material climbs up his ladder to light the lamp, and engravings which do not venture to show themselves by day peep out of the lower windows of the shops, Nevsky prospekt revives again and begins to stir. Then comes that mysterious time when the street lamps throw a marvelous alluring light upon everything. You meet a great number of young men, for the most part bachelors, in warm frock coats and overcoats. There is a suggestion at this time of some aim, or rather something like an aim, something extremely unaccountable; the steps of all are more rapid and altogether more uneven; long shadows flit over the walls and pavement and their heads almost reach the Police Bridge.]

Space is brought to life by the light of a streetlamp, but like this kind of light, nightlife is artificial and false. At nightfall, the world is transformed into something uncontrollable (что-то чрезвычайно безотчетное [something extremely unaccountable]) by reason or willpower (шаги неровные [uneven steps]). Chaos encroaches into the worldorder, and shapes are distorted owing to the curious and tempting light of the streetlamps. Under the light of the streetlamp, Piskarev the painter is enchanted by the girl (12; 14). However, only towards the end of the story, will the narrator disclose the secret of the streetlamp's spell. His warnings against the mendacity of the Nevskij prospekt are accompanied by warnings against the streetlamp.

Далее, ради бога, далее от фонаря! и скорее, сколько можно скорее, проходите мимо. Это счастие еще, если отделаетесь тем, что он зальет щегольской сюртук ваш с вонючим своим маслом. Но и кроме фонаря, все дышит обманом. Он лжет во всякое время, этот Невский проспект, но более всего тогда, когда ночь сгущенною массою наляжет на него и отделит белые и палевые стены домов, когда весь город превратится в гром и блеск, мириады карет валятся с мостов, форейторы кричат и прыгают на лошадях и когда сам демон зажигает лампы для того только, чтобы показать все не в настоящем виде.
(38)
[Keep your distance, for God's sake, keep your distance from the street lamp! and pass by it quickly, as quickly as you can! It is a happy escape if you get off with nothing worse than some of its stinking oil on your foppish coat. But even apart from the street lamp, everything breathes deception. It deceives at all hours, the Nevsky prospekt does, but most of all when night falls in masses of shadow on it, throwing into relief the white and duncolored walls of the houses, when all

the town is transformed into noise and brilliance, when myriads of carriages roll over bridges, postilions shout and jolt up and down on their horses, and when the devil himself lights the street lamps to show everything in false colors.]

This final revelation is in support of my demonic interpretation of the world of "Nevskij prospekt". In my opinion, it even refutes a purely psychological interpretation which would restrict itself to a one-sided understanding of the fantastic, and attribute the occurences in space only to the perception of the characters. The curious spatial transformations and the sudden encounter with the girls must be blamed on the interference of supernatural powers. To a certain extent the two girls that enchant the men with their beauty can be seen as witches, incarnations of the evil.

To indicate the powers of darkness, responsible for the negative structure of the world, the narrator uses the general and rather indefinite term *demon* instead of the personal and individualistic Devil - that would be "черт" or "дьявол" in Russian. It therefore remains a formless, unstabile and elusive force, with mythological rather than Christian connotations.

Какой-то демон искрошил весь мир на множество разных кусков и все эти куски без смысла, без толку смешал вместе.
(19)
[It seemed as though some demon had crumbled the whole world into bits and mixed all these bits indiscriminately together.]

At nightfall, a demon rules the world. He uses the misleading lamplight as a tool to derange the natural order of things, and man is deceived by false appearance.

6.0 conclusions

In sum, in "Nevskij prospekt' a confrontation takes place between a rational and a fantastic concept of the world. Semantic contrasts play an important role in establishing the meaning of the story, by means of a contrast that can be traced back to an archaic dualistic worldpicture in which binary oppositions are very strong.

The effect of confusion in "Nevskij prospekt" results from the inversion of the members of these oppositions. What seemed to be a familiar street all of a sudden manifests itself as a strange location with magically moving objects. The familiar order of the world is deranged, space is disorganised and man desoriented. The positive, intelligible structure of reality is destroyed when the evil makes its appearance. This is why the meaning of "Nevskij prospekt" surpasses the level of the psychological, and of social criticism. In this demonic interpretation, the story acquires features of cosmic dimension.

The scheme of spatial bipartition, applied in this story to one and the same location, results in what I have called spatial metamorphosis. Contrast is established between the "real", the "familiar" and therefore "human" space and the "apparent", the "strange" and eventually "anti-human" space.

The romantic hero, the eternal outsider, who was, for instance, the central focus of attention in "Mcyri", plays a less outspoken role in Gogol's story. The behaviour and fate of Gogol's heroes can be explained realistically, i.e., in psychological and sociological terms. To a certain extent, Gogol's Petersburg stories, therefore, occupy a transitional position between Romanticism and Realism. This is also the result of the much more prosaic setting with its tangible, topographical indications, the mentioning of streetnames familiar to the contemporary reader.

It is remarkable that in "Nevskij prospekt" the function of the category of space, the setting, is conspicuously dominant, structurally as well as thematically. Descriptions of the famous *Nevskij* constitute the frame of the narration. Its exotic appearance at different hours of the day is extensively described in the exposition, and on the last pages the street again becomes the primary subject of the narration. Within this everyday setting, another world of fantastic dimensions and rules of magic, is created. The evocation of an alternative world, which is needed to replace the reality of everyday-life, is, as such, part of the romantic code, and it is the unusual and abnormal, not the ordinary and prosaic aspects of the Nevskij, that are stressed.

The central idea of the story, the falseness and treachery of apparent reality is primarily expressed in spatial language. This was to become an important issue in symbolist literature. From the point of view of literary evolution, the importance of Gogol's story may be, in part, that of a forerunner to the subsequent period of Symbolism and Modernism, when the destructive character of the city became a central issue. It was Gogol who first applied archaic motifs derived from folklore in order to model this specific worldview[12].

1. In connection with the same problem, i.e. the structure of space in Gogol's Petersburg stories, Lotman 1968 also speaks of "two types of space"; he calls the first one "bytovoe prostranstvo" - day-to-day space, and the second "mnimoe" or "fiktivnoe prostanstvo" - false, imaginary space.

2. Cf. also Lotman, 1968: 41-2.

3. All quotations are from N.V. Gogol', *Sobranie sočinenij v semi tomach*, 1976-1979. Translations are from Gogol, *The Collected Tales and Plays of Nikolaj Gogol*, 1964.

4. On the synecdochical construction of this story, cf. Gukovskij 1959:291 and Peace 1981:95.

5. This was, a.o., described by M. Eliade in his book "Das Heilige und das Profane", 1985 (orig. French 1965).

6. Such a dualistic worldpicture dominates, a.o., the medieval culture of Old Russia, as described by Lotman & Uspenskij 1977.

7. Note the recurrent mention of the fact that St. Petersburg was actually built on a swamp, "na finskom bolote", in literature with this place as a setting.

8. The function of dancing and thrashing in carnival behaviour was described by Bachtin 1965.

9. On this subject see Byrns 1975/6 and Zolotusskij 1979: 134-141.

10. Also Zolotusskij 1979: 98 draws attention to this image.

11. Toporov 1973 discusses the importance of this so-called spatio-temporal element in the work of Dostoevskij.

12. Flaker also mentions "Nevskij prospekt" as the first case of mythologisation of the city in modern literature, cf. Flaker 1987.

CHAPTER III

The structure of space in Gončarov's "Oblomov"

1.0 introduction

It is generally agreed that I.A. Gončarov's novel *Oblomov* (1857-8) deals with two conflicting pictures of the world. These worldviews have always been closely identified with the two heroes of the story and their opposite attitudes to life. Oblomov and Štol'c could be called the embodiment of the eternal dilemma: action or reflection - "whether 't is nobler in the mind to suffer, or to take arms against a sea of trouble". In the case of Gončarov's novel, this conflict can be described on different levels, such as the psychological, sociological or historical level, or from the viewpoint of literary evolution.

In this chapter, I will examine the conflicting worldviews in *Oblomov* in relation to the category of space. In addition, I will determine the novel's place in Russian literary history. This is a challenging task, because as a Realistic novel *Oblomov* obviously takes on a polemic attitude towards the preceding period of Romanticism, yet on other occasions it still makes use of the Romantic code.

In this analysis, the category of space will predominantly be connected to the block of characters. Van Baak has introduced the very appropriate term of *semiotic centre* to designate the literary character in its function of connecting the category of space to the other textual blocks (Van Baak, 1983: 80). He takes the view that the fictional world functions analogously to anthropological space, the world men act and live in. It seems to me that the semiotic centre may also designate the character's crucial function in the process of perceiving and interpreting literary space. On another level, that of literary communication, the narrator holds a similar position in relation to literary space, especially in passages where no characters are involved, e.g. description of landscapes or settings. Therefore, the term "semiotic centre" can in certain situations be extended to the category of the narrator as well.

Closely related to this problem is the issue of the point of view, or focalisation. In *Oblomov* this functions basically on two levels, that of the narrator and that of the characters. These levels can be divided into a number of groups - the so called Oblomov-group, which holds Zachar and Agaf'ja Matveevna among others, - the Štol'c-group which comprises Ol'ga and Tarant'ev among others, and eventually a third group, namely the visitors in part I, chapter 2. Besides focalisation by these groups, there is focalisation by the narrator, who navigates between the "parties", identifying himself with one of them at certain moments, or taking on a "neutral" position at others.

In each new situation it will be necessary to pay attention to the question "who" is looking at space. It will prove to be of crucial importance that in *Oblomov* the same location holds a different significance for different heroes.

The above mentioned classification of the characters into two groups can be related to one of the important oppositions in the novel, that of a *static* and a *dynamic* concept of space. Each group of characters will be identified with one of the members of this

81

opposition. On another level, these spatial parameters are related to the worldviews in the novel. They happen to play a decisive role in "distinguishing between the two most fundamental ways of culturally perceiving space" (Van Baak, 1983a: 29). Two conceptions of the world are presented: a static one, in which notions of inactivity, stability and permanence dominate; and a dynamic one, focussed on change and activity.

As far as the plot is concerned, the static obviously dominates the dynamic, hardly anything happens, and in this respect it is more appropriate to speak of *behaviour* rather than of action in space (cf. Van Baak, 1983: 12). This peculiarity of Gončarov's novel stems mainly from the fact that the author was concerned with portraying a certain *type* of man, a character that was the result of a process (psychological, socio-historical), rather than with depicting those processes themselves. Lichačev connects this tendency of the novel to the aesthetics of the "натуральная школа" - the naturalistic school, where "приемы обобщения и типизации" - the devices of generalization and typisation were used (Lichačev, 1967: 313)[1].

A final assumption is the following: in *Oblomov* certain archaic, mythological structures are activated. These manifest themselves in certain aspects of the structure of literary space, namely the meaning that is attributed to certain topological oppositions and to certain "archetypal" locations such as, for instance, the river and the abyss.

2.0 the story

The reader encounters Oblomov together with his servant Zachar on a springday in one of the rooms of his St. Petersburg apartment, which he will not leave until well into the second part of the novel. During this exceptionally long exposition, the reader is introduced to the hero's peculiarities and oddities: he is lying in bed and grumbling at his servant. His problems with his accommodation, with his health and with his financial affairs are extensively described. Notwithstanding his proverbial laziness, Oblomov seems to be extremely busy this one day, receiving visitors and making a "spiritual journey" to the land of his childhood, Oblomovka, during the dream-chapter (ch. 9 of part 1).

The end of part one is marked by the long-awaited appearance of his friend Andrej Štol'c. He is the one who finally sets Oblomov in motion and introduces him to Ol'ga Il'inskaja. This acquaintance soon develops into a love affair, which is the subject of the second and third parts of the novel. Their mutual love grows and blossoms during one summer season at a St. Petersburg dača and culminates in a secret engagement. The end of part 2 and beginning of part 3 mark the turning point, Ol'ga and her aunt move back to their apartment on Morskaja Street in the centre of the town, whereas Oblomov now finds himself "banned" to the northern outskirts of the capital.

As autumn progresses, Ol'ga and Oblomov's relationship becomes more and more problematic, and eventually ends in a failure, a definitive breach at the end of part 3. Clouds gather over Oblomov's head and, as a result of his own incapability to restore order in his affairs, he is constantly short of money. The first chapters of part 4 describe his deplorable situation in the house of the widow. Due to his financial woes, his meals are no longer abundant like before, but increasingly sober. His clothes, his famous chalat and all of the things in his room make a threadbare impression. And finally, one day when he is drunk, Oblomov is forced to sign a most unfavourable IOU by dishonest "friends".

Juxtaposed with the main hero's decline Štol'c rises to happiness and prosperity (chapter 4, part 4). He meets Ol'ga on the streets of Paris by chance and accompanies her to Switzerland, where they fall in love and eventually get married. On his return to St. Petersburg, Štol'c finds Oblomov down and out in the Vyborg-district ("Vyborgskaja storona"). He arranges Oblomov's affairs energetically, annuls the IOU and henceforth guarantees for him a life without material troubles.

After several years, Andrej and Ol'ga start a family in their home on the Crimea, Oblomov finds peace, a wife and family in the house on the Vyborg-side, where he enjoys some years of harmony and happiness before he dies of a stroke in his sleep. The last two chapters, as a kind of epilogue, relate of Oblomov's son Andrej and the changes at Oblomovka.

3.0 the structure of space

3.1 Oblomov's room

The story of Oblomov starts with a description of the setting[2]. A single sentence suffices to outline the situation of the hero in space:

> В Гороховой улице, в одном из больших домов, [...] лежал утром в постели, на своей квартире, Илья Ильич Обломов.
> (7)[3]
> [One morning, in his flat in one of the big houses on Gorokhovaya Street, Ilya Ilyich Oblomov was lying in bed.][4]

The narrator gradually draws closer to the principal object of attention. He moves from a large space to an increasingly smaller space, and from open towards enclosed space. Thus, the author gradually allows the reader to enter the slumbering world of Oblomov's room in his St. Petersburg flat.

From the very start, the hero is located at the center of several *concentrically* wrapped protecting layers. He is encircled first by his bed, then by the walls of his room, next by his flat, subsequently by the big house and finally by the street, which immediately, although implicitly, makes clear that the setting is St. Petersburg around the middle of the 19th century[5].

This description clarifies the hero's position in space. First, a neutral description of the circumstances is presented. Focalisation will take place only subsequently, when the characters with their meanings and evaluations are introduced. Depending on the point of view, the situation of inclusion can have either a favourable meaning, like protection from a hostile, outside world, or an unfavourable meaning, such as confinement or imprisonment. The reader, therefore, is confronted with two views on space, a fact that influences his own interpretation of the text.

Different characters will give different interpretations of the opposition "inside - outside". Oblomov and his servant Zachar belong to the inside world, while the visitors of his room, Tarant'ev and Štol'c all belong to the exterior. Depending on the point of view, and, ultimately, depending on the worldviews that govern those points of view, the room and the world beyond the walls of that room have opposite meanings.

The first three pages provide an extensive description of the looks and features of Oblomov, as well as a detailed account of the room he inhabits. The descriptions of Oblomov and the space that surrounds him are intermingled. The room and its furniture are not only described for the sake of atmosphere, but they also carry additional information on the man who lives in that room. There is a semiotic (metonymic) relation between the character and his surroundings, the state of the objects being symbolic for the state of their owner. Oblomov, we are told, is fat and lies in bed for most of the time: "Лежанье [..] было его нормальным состоянием" (8) [lying was his normal condition]. The things in his room are heavy and dusty, and have not been moved for a long time so that you "could get the impression that no one is living here" (9). So *immobility* is introduced from the very start as an important characteristic both of Oblomov and of the things in his room.

Inclusion and immobility are subsequently contrasted with the exterior world and its dynamism. The initial harmony that reigns in Oblomov's room (focalisation by Oblomov) threatens to be disturbed by intrusions from the outside. First we are told about the letter from his bookkeeper and agent, "письмо из деревни" (10), which brings bad news and urges him to come to his estate to put things in order. Secondly, his landlord forces him to move out of the flat on Gorochovaja street (17). Elements of exterior space, which I propose to call *spatial intrusions*, thus penetrate into the interior world[6]. As a result, the outside world turns into a trouble-making, hostile entity in the eyes of Oblomov. It comes to him without being asked for.

"Он терялся в приливе житейских забот" (18) [He was lost in a flood of worldly cares]. Danger presents itself to Oblomov in the form of almighty forces of nature ("priliv" - the tide coming in) against which man is impotent.

In the second chapter, the exterior world is impersonated by several visitors, literary masks that stand for different aspects of life in Petersburg society. On this occasion a clear-cut boundary between interior and exterior space is mentioned for the first time. It is the door to his room that marks the line between "his", Oblomov's world and the world of "the others"[7].

The outside world which penetrates into his territory is divisible into a number of sub-categories. Volkov, the first visitor, stands for life in high society with its parties, shortlasting love-affairs, and boring evenings at the theatre (19-23). The second, Sud'binskij, embodies working life in bureaucratic society with its idle careerism (23-27). Thirdly, Penkin the journalist represents cultural life and bad taste (27-31). The fourth visitor is the faceless and nameless (32) Alekseev, a parasite[8].

Again I must stress that their negative image comes from Oblomov's perception. Each visitor stands for a certain part of the outside world, and together they make up the whole of the exterior world that is being qualified so negatively by Oblomov, he himself being the embodiment of interior space. Public life is contrasted with private life.

"Не подходите, не подходите, вы с холода" [Don't come near me, don't come near me; you're straight from the cold street], he repeats three times, (19,23,27). The cold weather can be seen as a symbol for the chilliness of the life and human relations in the world beyond the walls of Oblomov's flat. First of all, Oblomov mentions himself the cold weather. And secondly, we should note that it is the first of May, that cannot be an extremely cold day in St. Petersburg. Oblomov pities the people living in that world, "несчастный" [the poor wretch] he exclaims, and he calls that world inhuman: "Где же тут человек?" [What's there left of the man?]. On the other hand, the representatives of the exterior space look at their world as exciting and want him, Oblomov, to partake of it. One of the functions of these visiting scenes is, as it seems to me, a more precise definition of Oblomov's relation to the outside world from which he himself has retreated[9]. In Oblomov's mind, values like generosity, benevolence and kindness reign, whereas the St. Petersburg society, the world of the gentry and bureaucracy, is governed by egoist emotions, jealousy, malice and slander.

At this point the conclusion may be reached that until now, the opposition of the inside to the outside world was focalised only by Oblomov. A different, new qualification both of the interior and of the exterior is introduced with the arrival of the fifth visitor, Tarant'ev. He is one of the incorporations of yet another worldview, of which Andrej Štol'c is the primary representative. For the first time, an explicit statement is made about the opposition between Oblomov's room and St. Petersburg society.

В комнату, где царствовал сон и покой, Тарантьев приносил жизнь, движение, а иногда и вести извне.
(59)
[Into the room where sleep and peace reigned, Tarantyev brought life and movement and sometimes news from the outside world.]

This observation by the narrator announces a shift in the values connected to the oppositional pair "inside - outside". The sentence introduces a new view about the location of Oblomov's room. Seen through the main hero's eyes, the world of his room, his domain or territory, is a place of rest, an island of peace and safety amidst a sea of trouble and danger. He calls himself a lucky man, one who can stay at home and lie on his couch all day, keeping his human dignity - "человеческое достоинство" (41).

Visitors like Tarant'ev, and later on Štol'c and Ol'ga, view space in exactly the opposite fashion, to them exterior space means motion, progress and growth. Interior space is, on the contrary, motionless, filled with boredom and sleep, signifying degeneration, failure and loss.

Thus two different axiological qualifications of the same space emerge in this first part of the novel. This remains symptomatic for the whole book. As a consequence, a kind of dialectics or polyphony of spaces is established, perception of space from antipodal views.

In his stimulating article on space in Gogol's prose, Lotman introduced the term *bytovoe prostranstvo* - day-to-day space. Characteristics of that type of space are eventlessness, timelessness, immobility, fullness (objects), but also a sense of security, cosiness (Lotman, 1968: 18, 24-26). These characteristics of space of the *byt*, diagnosed by Lotman in "Večera na chutore bliz Dikan'ki" ["Evenings in a Village near Dikan'ka"] and "Starosvetskie pomeščiki" [Old-world Land-owners"] can all be ascribed to Oblomov's room as well. In another article, Lotman distinguishes plot-texts from mythological texts. The former describe a single event with marked categories of beginning and end, whereas mythological texts or myth is thought of as a mechanism which constantly repeats itself, dealing with events "which were timeless, endlessly reproduced and, in that sense, motionless" (Lotman, 1979: 163). In the light of this last remark, the spatial characteristics typical for the *byt* could be traced back to their roots in mythological times. A kinship between *byt* and myth may exist, but this question would need separate investigation. In the Oblomovka-locus, mythological world-views prevail, as will be shown below.

Oblomovka is not only a dream and an actual location "almost on the borders of Asia". Its relation to the rest of the novel makes it take on features of mythological dimensions. It is very well possible to speak about the Oblomovka-myth that governs one of the world-views in this book. This can be deduced from the fact that structures characteristic of the space in Oblomovka recur in other settings involving Oblomov, for example in the room of the big house on Gorochovaja street or at the widow's house. Before the chapter "Oblomov's dream" actually starts, some preliminary allusions are made to this piece of heaven on earth.

> Воспитанный в недрах провинции [...] среди кротких и теплых нравов и обычаев родины, переходя в течение двадцати лет из объятий в объятия родных, друзей, и знакомых, он до того был проникнут семейным началом...
> (58)
> [Brought up in the wilds of the country [...] amid the gentle and kindly manners and customs of his native province, and passing for twenty years from the embraces of his parents to those of his friends and relations, he had become so imbued with the ideas of family life...]

The Russian "v nedrach" ("the wilds" in this translation) designates the depth of the earth, the innermost - a similar form of enveloping as at the beginning of the novel, only this time by ancestral earth, parents and friends. The child is at the centre of the family, which is the centre of the estate, which is the centre of the province etc. Again the author sets up a concentrical structure of space, which gently protects our hero. This structure parallels the previous enveloped position in the Gorochovaja-apartment.

Another similarity arising from this enclosed position between Oblomovka and Oblomov's room is the opposition "inside - outside". Like before this spatial opposition is connected with notions like "safe - hostile" and "known/familiar - unknown/foreign". Space is structured concentrically around little Il'ja Il'ič, and this closed territory is surrounded by an unknown, maybe even hostile world (cf. the utter darkness mentioned on p. 108). "Весь уголок верст на пятнадцать или двадцать вокруг..." (115) [The whole place for ten or fifteen miles around], is another example of this enveloped situation.

The interior world of Oblomov's childhood acquires positive values - a feeling of intense security is the strongest association in this case - and a positive assessment of an idyllic world, which are transmitted to the opposition "town - countryside".

> Oblomovka resembles the "middle landscape" of a long tradition of pastoral Arcadias - those ideal terrains lying halfway between the forbidding and impersonal realm of raw nature (the sea and mountains) and the overcivilized city, idyllic places that in Russian novels (Sergey Aksakov, Turgenev, Tolstoy) are so often identified with the estates of the gentry.
> (M.Ehre, 1973: 176)

In other words, Oblomovka is also feudal space, the type of space that is marked by a strong relation between man and the land. The fact that the land carries the name of its owners is typical of this sort of space. Zachar represents the other aspect of the feudal system, the subordination of man to the land. The following explanation of his clumsiness is a good example:

Все это происходило, конечно, оттого, что он получил воспитание и приобретал манеры не в тесноте и полумраке роскошных, прихотливо убранных кабинетов и будуаров, где черт знает чего ни наставлено, а в деревне, на покое, просторе и вольном воздухе.
(73)
[All that, of course, happened because Zakhar had been brought up and acquired his manners not in the dark and narrow, but fastidiously furnished, drawing-rooms and studies, cluttered up with all sorts of fancy articles, but in the country, where there was plenty of room to move about.]

In spite of the narrator's obvious irony, this statement also contributes to the definition of the opposition "town - countryside". According to the vision formulated here, rural space is preferable to urban space. Life in the city is not real life, whereas life at Oblomovka - the real home - resembles heaven.

Ах! - горестно вслух вздохнул Илья Ильич. - Что за жизнь! Какое безобразие этот столичный шум! Когда же настанет райское, желанное житье? Когда в поля, в родные рощи? - думал он.
(80)
["Oh dear!" Oblomov sighed mournfully aloud. "What a life! How horrible these town noises are! When will the heavenly life come? When shall I return to my native woods and fields?" he thought.]

The major problem with the "dream-chapter" is the question *who is seeing the dream?* This is important for a correct understanding of the ambivalent attitude, as it seems to me, not only of the narrator, but also of the adult Oblomov, towards the Oblomovka-location. It appears that besides the dreaming hero, who sees himself as a child back at the Oblomovka of his youth, there is also a narrator commenting on the world of the dream. This narrator furnishes information the child would not be able to give.

Сон [...] перенес его в другую эпоху, к другим людям, в другое место, куда перенесемся и мы с читателем в следующей главе.
(102)
[Sleep [...] transferred him to another age and other people, to another place, where we, too, gentle reader, will follow him in the next chapter.]

What does this ethereal world look like? Oblomovka, at first sight, shares many features with the idyllic landscape as Michail Bachtin described it in his study on the chronotope[10]. However, upon a closer reading of the description of Oblomovka, it becomes clear that in the eyes of the narrator and in the eyes of Oblomov, this location is far from perfect. It is true, the chapter starts with a lyrical description of the landscape, but as soon as the inhabitants of Oblomovka are drawn into the picture, other, more critical sounds can be heard. The laziness, simplicity and backwardness of this archaic world are depicted together with its paralysing influence on the people who live in it. Therefore, the dream is all but a simply pleasant recollection - the dream recounts his repeated clashes (as a child) with the system of Oblomovka. What is more, the child plays the part of an outsider. He looks at the world with the amazement of a newcomer and behaves differently from all the other inhabitants (the adults), who want to subjugate him to the laws and regulations of Oblomovka. Time and again, the child tries to break out of this suffocating atmosphere, but eventually loses the battle. Toward the end of the dream chapter, the tone becomes increasingly negative about this apparent paradise, which has turned out to be a mere mock-idyll resembling an anti-paradise.

ie following details are especially striking about the place: nature always meets the expectations of the inhabitants, and never surprises them by excessive heat or cold (104-5), people seldom die (108), and when somebody passes from life to death, it is experienced as an amazing occurrence. As a matter of fact, nothing happens there (107-9) - no robbery, murder or other dreadful accidents. This dream-land resembles a fairy-tale country, it has the features of a world where mythological thinking is still very strong. Time, for instance, is experienced as cyclical instead of linear, one of the primary differences between myth and non-myth.

As far as the structure of space in mythology is concerned lines and boundaries - cf. the encircling rings already mentioned - are of special importance. The world of Oblomovka is literally filled with them. For the child, boundaries are obstacles, and they occur in the form of a window (111) marking the line between the closed, inside space of the house and the open, outside world, or in the form of the gates (113, 118) which separate the enclosed yard around the house from the rest of the property, or in the form of a treshold (122). The child longs to cross these forbidden lines and to go beyond these boundaries, yet this is prevented by the adults.

Certain locations in Oblomovka which are prohibited and dangerous to enter, such as the ravine and the forest are of equal importance. M. Ehre is very much on the mark when he compares these locations to *taboos* (1973: 177). The forest localises danger, and the ravine is identified with death. Danger and fear are very important factors in the main hero's definition of his position in the world. They explain his behaviour, the retreat into the safety of his room - his fear for cold is an indication - and will recur in subsequent chapters as a driving force. Therefore attributes of the mythological Oblomovka-worldpicture have power over the hero, even outside Oblomovka. The taboos, the identification of danger and death with a certain location, govern Oblomov's behaviour wherever he goes, and this eventually leads to "wrong" behaviour in the "wrong" place.

Other allusions to fairytales (107, 121, 123) and mythological thinking can be found in the ninth chapter. The worldview of the inhabitants of Oblomovka is described not without irony. They think of themselves as the centre of the world, the Volga-river being the frontier between them and "the others". It is the first instance in which the river fulfils its border-function in a typical archaic way. The river marks the line between two lands, "our" land and the land on the "other side", that is very often identified with the world of the dead (Nekljudov, 1972: 36): "к Волге, которая была их Колхидой и Геркулесовыми столпами" (108) [the Volga, which was their Colchis or Pillars of Hercules]. I will discuss this mythological border function of rivers below. As far as the role of space in this curious picture of the world is concerned, the following quotation is particularly expressive:

Они знали, что в восьмидесяти верстах от них была "губерния", то есть губернский город, но редкие езжали туда; потом знали, что подальше там, Саратов или Нижний; слыхали, что есть Москва и Питер, что за Питером живут французы или немцы, а далее уже начинался для них, как для древних, темный мир, неизвестные страны, населенные чудовищами, людьми о двух головах, великанами; там следовал мрак - и, наконец, все оканчивалось той рыбой, которая держит на себе землю.
(108)

[They knew that the administrative city of the province was sixty miles away, but very few of them ever went there; they also knew that farther away in the same direction was Saratov or Nizhny-Novgorod; they had heard of Petersburg and Moscow, and that the French and Germans lived beyond Petersburg, and the world farther away was for them as mysterious as it was for the ancients - unknown countries, inhabited by monsters, people with two heads, giants; farther away still there was darkness, and at the end of it all was the fish which held the world on its back.]

This picture is primarily ruled by the spatial opposition "near - distant", which is associated with notions of familiarity and safety and a feeling of growing threat and danger as the distance from home increases. The dream-chapter opens with an unusual description of the landscape (102-4). The narrator is obviously focalizing from an all-seeing, elevated position, comparable to B.A. Uspenskij's "Точка зрения птичьего полета" ["bird's eye view"] (Uspenskij, 1970: 86). Ostentatiously he replaces the *dynamic* Romantic landscape, traditionally full of action and passion, obstacles that have to be overcome and at the same time infinite and boundless, by a *static* one. In Oblomovka, nothing happens at all, even nature is permeated by a kind of motionless apathy.

An important function of the whole Oblomovka-episode is an attempt to explain adult Oblomov's behaviour and attitude to life through his childhood and therefore through the character of his homeland. The land is quiet and peaceful:

Как все тихо, все сонно.
Тихо и сонно все в деревне [...] Та же глубокая тишина и мир лежат и на полях.
(107)
[How quiet and sleepy everything is.
Everything in the village is quiet and sleepy [...] In the fields, too, peace and profound silence reign.]

Then the narrator turns his attention from nature to man, establishing metonymical relationship between them. More connections of the same kind are made, for instance the one between life at Oblomovka and the psychology of the grown-up Oblomov:

Тишина и невозмутимое спокойствие царствуют и в нравах людей.
(107)
[The same imperturbable peace and quiet prevail among the people of that locality.]

[...] у него навсегда остается расположение полежать на печи, походить в готовом, незаработанном платье и поесть на счет доброй волшебницы.
(121)
[He preserved for the rest of his life a predisposition for doing no work, walking about in clothes that had been provided for him, and eating at the fairy godmother's expense.]

In sum it must be stressed that the dream-picture of Oblomovka - as this place is seen by narrator and the main hero himself - is open to various, controversial interpretations. Oblomovka carries features of an archaic world-picture, its inhabitants still show a tendency toward magic or mythological thinking, and this affects their attitude towards the surrounding world. Life at Oblomovka is idealized, country life being preferable to city life. Yet, life at Oblomovka is criticised at the same time through the notion of captivity which strangles the child:

И Илюша с печалью оставался дома, лелеемый как экзотический цветок в теплице, и так же, как последний под стеклом, он рос медленно и вяло. Ищущие проявления силы обращались внутрь и никли, увядая.
(146).
[And sadly Oblomov remained indoors, cherished like an exotic flower in a hot-house, and like it he grew slowly and languidly. His energies, finding no oulet, turned inwards and withered, drooping.]

The following observations, while not related to the dream-chapter, are related to the Oblomovka-location as such. It is of interest that the other hero of the novel, Štol'c, demonstrates a very different view of this type of space. As demonstrated in the previous section, Andrej Štol'c is the representative of a different world-view, one which conflicts with Oblomov's. His behaviour in space, for instance, is diametrically opposed to Oblomov's: "Он беспрестанно в движении" (167) [He was continually on the move]. Here we recognize the introductory description of Oblomov's immobility. Oblomov is identified with the East, with Asia, where his estate is situated ("наследство чуть не в Азии"), whereas Štol'c, a descendant of German Saxony is a representative of the West. And it is during at trip abroad, to Western Europe (409-436), that Štol'c and Ol'ga fall in love.

However, Oblomov's friend and opponent (I cannot call him a real antagonist, for as far as the development of the plot is concerned, the only real antagonists are Tarant'ev and Ivan Matveevič, whereas in this respect Štol'c carries the function of helper) was in fact born in the same world, and Štol'c and Oblomov have even common roots in Oblomovka[11].

As far as the parameters "inside - outside" are concerned, in Štol'c case they are connected with very different values: the closed, inside world is equated to stagnation and death, while openness means life and progress. As for his attitude to Oblomovka, the fact that Štol'c wants to build roads and railways to pull this world out of its apathy and isolation is very significant. On the last pages of the novel this dream finally becomes reality.

[Штольц:] - твоя Обломовка не в глуши больше, до нее дошла очередь [...] она будет станцией дороги [...]. Прощай, старая Обломовка! [...] ты отжила свой век!
(498)
[Stolz: "It is useless to tell you that your Oblomovka is no longer in the wilds, that its turn has come [...] there will be a railway station there [...]. Goodbye, old Oblomovka! [...] You've had your day!"]

3.3. Oblomov at the dača

The dača-location seems to be the only one that is not debated by the characters. There are no instances of opposing points of view on this part of the literary space. This could be explained by the fact that Oblomov behaves in the normal, accepted way for the first (and only) time at the dača. For once, he is presented as a dynamic character, attempting to model his life according to his former plans, those of before his retirement, when he broke with the bureaucratic and, to him, banal Petersburg milieu. The episode is also a typical example of a change in the environment evoking a change of mood[12]. All of a sudden, Oblomov's behaviour changes radically, he rises early, reads books, goes out for walks, dresses correctly. How did this happen?

Вот он сидит у окна своей дачи (он живет на даче, в нескольких верстах от города). (195)
[Now he was sitting at the window of his country villa (he was staying at a villa in the country a few miles from the town).]

Oblomov's revival is narrated so that we first learn about his changed behaviour, and only after this we find out where he is. There is, of course, another very important explanation for his changed behaviour, namely his love for Ol'ga, who pulls him out of his isolation and apathy.

The dača-episode is the only instance in which Oblomov is portrayed in *open* space. It can be seen as an attempt to break out of his enclosed dream world, trying to start a new life. The structure of the dača-location differs from the previous one by a seeming absence of boundaries. The notions of inclusion and immobility have disappeared. Most scenes during the dača-episode take place in the open. In this respect the park has an important chronotopical function. Three important confrontations between Oblomov and Ol'ga take place there. This park is hardly described. Only a bench and a grove are mentioned. Apparently, the only element of importance is the fact that the love-scenes take place there. More significant, however, is the spatial structure of parks in general. They are cultivated pieces of land, which are as a rule fenced in, and have gates, or in other words are bounded space. Thus the term a "seeming" boundlessness, and therefore "seeming" dynamism seems more appropriate.

In the beginning, however, Oblomov is strolling through free nature and over hills:

[...] он читает с ней, посылает цветы, гуляет по озеру, по горам [...] он Обломов. (200)
На пять верст кругом дачи не было пригорка, на который он не влезал по несколько раз. (246)
[He read to her, sent flowers, went with her on the lake, on the hills - he Oblomov!
There was not a hill within a radius of five miles from his summer cottage that he had not climbed several times.]

This suggests that Oblomov regained natural vitality: he walks, acts, starts living again. This dynamism and activity are reflected by nature:

Природа жила деятельной жизнью; вокруг кипела невидимая, мелкая работа, [...] в траве все двигалось, ползало, суетилось. Вон муравьи бегут в разные стороны так хлопотливо и суетливо, сталкиваются, разбегаются, торопятся. (263)
[Nature carried on with her neverceasing work: all around him unseen, tiny creatures were busy [...] In the grass everything was moving, creeping, busling. Ants were running in different directions, looking very busy and engrossed in their work, running into one another, scampering about, hurrying.]

So, like the furniture in Oblomov's room, like the landscape in Oblomov's dream, the insect-world is a metonymical image of the hero's inner state.

At the end of the summer, however, the changes in Oblomov's behaviour turn out to have been merely apparent changes. The "seeming" dynamism belies any true changes in

Oblomov's behaviour and character. The trip to the dača was only an attempt to run away from real responsibilities that demand a real shift in space, such as a trip abroad (to improve his health) or, even more important, a trip to Oblomovka (to improve his financial position).

3.4 the house in the Vyborg-district

Before Oblomov actually moves to the house of the widow Pšenicyna, the place has already been mentioned several times. At first, he categorically rejects the whole idea of moving at all, and of moving to the outskirts in particular. In the Vyborg-episode, literary space is structured according to the topological opposition "central - peripheral". This is a typical opposition for literature set in St. Petersburg[13].

- Это что за новости? На Выборгскую сторону! Да туда, говорят, зимой волки забегают.
- Там скука, пустота, никого нет.
- Я туда не перееду.
- [здесь] от всего близко, тут и магазины, и театр, и знакомые [...] центр города, все ...
(48)
["What nonsense is that! Vyborg! Why, they say wolves roam the streets there in winter!".
"But it's such a dull place - a wilderness, no one lives.there".
"I'm not going there".
"[..here] its so near to everything, [...]. To the shops, the theatre, my friends - it's the centre of the city, everything..".]

First, it should be noted that these explicit statements, in direct speech, represent Oblomov's point of view on both types of space. He arranges the world according to the notions "tam" [there] and "zdes'" [here], which can be read as an opposition between "čužoj" and "svoj". The periphery or what is actually beyond it - the Vyborg-district is located on the *other side of the river* - is rejected. Bearing in mind mythological thinking, we could even say that the land on the other side is equated to the land of the dead. In the Oblomovka-section, I demonstrated that an attitude based on an archaic model of the world plays a part in Oblomov's world-view. The inhabitants of Oblomovka experience the Volga-river as the border between their world and the world of the others that is thought of as foreign and therefore dangerous. This same mechanism recurs in Oblomov's initial attitude towards the Vyborg district. I use the term "initial" deliberately, for we will see that the hero's attitude to, and interpretation of, the opposition "central - peripheral" will shift considerably.

The sly Tarant'ev, knowing exactly what Oblomov wants and needs, promotes all the advantages of the remote district on the other side of the Neva-river:

А там, подумай: ты будешь жить у кумы моей, благородной женщины, в покое, тихо; никто тебя не тронет; ни шуму, ни гаму, чисто, опрятно.
(49)
["You'll live in the house of a gentlewoman, a good friend of mine, in peace and quiet. No one to disturb you - no noise, clean and tidy".]

Oblomov refuses to leave the safety of the centre of town for an unsafe place. He says he is afraid of wolves. Again, anxiety is one of the main psychological motivations for Oblomov's withdrawal from the outside world. But before long, this location, qualified so negatively in the beginning, subtly changes into its opposite. The shift takes place slowly, at first on the level of the subconscious. When Oblomov sees himself confronted with the unavoidable questions and decisions of life, the Vyborg-side turns into a refuge.

Нет это тяжело, скучно! [...] Перееду на Выборгскую сторону, буду заниматься, читать, уеду в Обломовку [...] один!
(235)
[No, this is awfully boring! I'll move to Vyborg, I'll work, read, then go to Oblomovka - alone!]

Oblomov intuitively considers the Vyborg-locus as similar to the Oblomovka-locus. Understandably, Ol'ga interprets the Vyborg-side from her own point of view, as a threat to their relationship. After one of their reconciliation scenes, she asks him not to move to the Vyborg-district: "Вы не переедете на Выборгскую сторону?" (243) - [You won't be moving to Vyborg, will you?].

One summer-day, Oblomov undertakes his first trip to the Vyborg-district, to take a look at the place. The description of that journey, one of the few journeys Oblomov ever undertakes, and one of the very few that are described at all to the reader (for instance we learn nothing of his trip to the dača, all of a sudden he just happens to be there), augurs ill for the future.

The description of the journey can be linked to the hero's shifting attitude (cf. Van Baak 1983: 72). Some of the details the traveller notices along the way are signs of his inner state. By frequently mentioning of fences, Oblomov calls attention to the notion of inclusion. As must be obvious by now, this is one of the dominant features of Oblomovian space in general.

The cages of canaries and siskins in Oblomov's new apartment as well as the many fences in the Vyborg district and around the Pshenitsyn house, reinforce the sense of confinement. Oblomov becomes a captive of his atavistic yearning for Oblomovka.
(Lyngstad, 1971: 89)

Обломов отправился на Выборгскую сторону, на новую свою квартиру. Долго он ездил между длинными заборами по переулкам. Наконец отыскали будочника; тот сказал, что это в другом квартале, рядом, вот по этой улице - и он показал еще улицу без домов, с заборами, с травой и с засохшими колеями из грязи.
Опять поехал Обломов, любуясь на крапиву у заборов и на выглядывавшую из-за заборов рябину. Наконец будочник указал на старый домик на дворе [...].
Двор величиной был с комнату, так что коляска стукнула дышлом в угол и распугала кучу кур, [...] да большая, черная собака начала рватся на цепи [...] с отчаянным лаем.
(304)
[Oblomov went to his new flat in Vyborg. He spent a long time driving along narrow lanes with long wooden fences on either side. At last he found a policeman who told him that the house was in a different part of the suburb, and he pointed to a street where there were only fences and no houses, with grass growing in the road, which was full of ruts made of dried mud. Oblomov drove on, admiring the nettles by the fences and the rowan-berries peeping out from behind them. At last the policeman pointed at a house standing in a yard, [...].
The yard was the size of a room, so that the shaft of the carriage struck a corner and frightened a number of hens [...] a big black dog on a chain began to bark furiously.]

The resemblance between this isolated and provincial suburb of the capital and Oblomovka are implicitly given in this humorous, yet sad, description. Increasingly, the Vyborg-side turns into a "substitute-Oblomovka". Oblomov gradually abandons the idea of moving back to the centre, and gradually he regains his "normal" way of life, he sinks back into apathy.

> Однажды тишина в природе и в доме была идеальная [...] Илья Ильич лежал небрежно на диване...
> (328)
> [One day there was a perfect silence both at home and in nature: [...] Oblomov lay carelessly on the sofa...]

Again and again, Oblomov and his servant notice the resemblance between life at the widow's house and life in Oblomovka, thus equating the two locations.

> - Пирог не хуже наших обломовских,- заметил Захар.
> (314)
> - Деревню напоминают, Обломовку, сказал он [Обломов].
> (323)
> Тишина идеальная.
> (323)
> - Тихо, хорошо в этой стороне, только скучно! - говорил Обломов.
> (326)
> ["No sir," Zakhar said, "it's not worse than ours at Oblomovka...
> "They remind me of the country, of Oblomovka".
> There was a perfect silence all around.
> "It's nice and quiet here," Oblomov said [...] "but rather dull".]

The more he and Ol'ga drift apart, the more the Vyborg-house acquires the features of the "bytovoe prostranstvo", so typical of Oblomov's world - special attention for food, eventlessness, absence of movement, and what is new, but very typical of this kind of space, sexual drive. Bachtin, commenting on Gončarov's novel, calls the following features typically idyllic:

> В самой идилии (особенно на Выборгской стороне) раскрываются все основные соседства - культ еды и питья, дети, половой акт, смерть.
> (Bachtin, 1986: 267)
> [The idyll itself (especially in the Vyborg district) shows all the basic notions, such as the cult of food and drink, children, the sexual act, death.]

The growing distance between Ol'ga and Oblomov is symbolically reflected by the geographical distance between the centre and the outskirts. This distance is stressed increasingly. Along with this psychological drifting apart, in Oblomov's eyes the physical distance grows as well:

> А ездить ему какая даль! Едешь, едешь с Выборгской стороны да вечером назад - три часа!
> (312)
> Вечером, по грязи, этакую даль!
> (321)
> [And what a long journey it was! Driving from Vyborg and back again in the evening took him three hours.
> In the evening, through the mud, and all that way!]

94

What is more, the geographical barrier between the two lovers eventually becomes insurmountable because the river starts to freeze over (349-50). Again, the river functions as border between two worlds, but this time a border that is unbridgeable. A shift in Oblomov's orientation is indicated by the words "*ta* storona" [the *other* side]. What Oblomov once viewed as the periphery has slowly turned into the new centre of his world.

The fourth and last part of the novel presents contrasting points of view on the Vyborg-locus in particular and on Oblomov's space in general. It is precisely this contrast, or rather conflict between Oblomov's way of looking at his world and the way Štol'c and Ol'ga look at it, that brings the story to its climax.

The ninth chapter of the last part of the book is in several ways the culminating point of the story. In it the resemblance between the Vyborg-district and Oblomovka reaches its highest degree of similarity. The house is filled with objects, especially with food. The place is no longer dusty - "везде было светло, чисто и свежо" (484) [All the other rooms were bright, clean and airy]. Oblomov's harmony is finally complete: all threats to his ideal, his dream, have been overcome. And since Vyborg-district has turned into Oblomovka (heaven on earth), there is no longer any need to undertake the journey to the real Oblomovka. Oblomov decides that he has reached his goal - "жизнь его сложилась" (487) [he had attained the ideal of his life]. His daydreams are filled with Oblomovka, and there is no longer even a clear difference between dream and reality, for they have become so similar, a kind of diffusion of spaces (493).

Nevertheless the question why Oblomov does not return to Oblomovka (to return to one's estate after some years of civil or military service was a common phenomenon among the Russian gentry in the 19th century) must be approached from another angle as well. In the light of what has been said about the ambivalent attitude towards Oblomovka, it is possible to explain Oblomov's resistance to returning because he is conscious of the fact that in reality the "paradise on earth" is a mere illusion. After all, in his dream, Oblomov was actually an outsider in relation to his ancestral world, and his dream was not an entirely pleasant experience. Perhaps Oblomov realizes that the idyll he has found in Agaf'ja Matveevna's house in the Vyborg-district is what can be reached realistically. In this respect, Oblomov demonstrates a down-to-earth attitude. The Romantic idyll, Oblomovka, is replaced by the Realistic idyll, the house of the widow.

Once Oblomov has appeared in his full glory, the stage is set for the final confrontation between the two incompatible worldviews. The climax is reached when Štol'c pays his last visit. Andrej does not conceal his contempt for Oblomov's world. His attitude toward life, and therefore his perception of the world, is diametrically opposed to that of his friend. This has been clear from the beginning, but only now is it understood by both of them. For the first time, Oblomov is decisive. It is this new Oblomov, a man who has suddenly understood that his world and that of Štol'c cannot go together, who speaks the crucial words:

- Послушай, Андрей! - вдруг прибавил он решительным, небывалым тоном, - не делай напрасных попыток, не уговаривай меня, я останусь здесь.
(495)

- Что ты хочешь делать со мной? С тем миром, куда ты влечешь меня, я расстался навсегда; ты не спаешь не составишь две разорванные половины. Я прирос к этой яме больным местом: попробуй оторвать - будет смерть.
(496)

- Оставь меня совсем [...] забудь.
(497)

["Listen Andrey," he added suddenly in a determined tone Stolz had never heard him use before; "don't waste your time trying to persuade me: I shall stay here!"

"What do you want to do with me? I've broken with the world into which you are dragging me: you cannot weld together two halves that have come apart. I am attached to this hole with the most vulnerable part of my body - if you try to drag me away, I shall die!"

"Please leave me altogether - forget me - -".]

4.0 mobile and immobile heroes

It is evident from the structure of Oblomov's room and his relation to the surrounding space that immobility is a major element of his character and of the type of culture he represents. Indeed, the oppositional pair "static - dynamic" plays an important role in Gončarov's novel. The opposition is basically a spatial one, related both to the characters and the plot.

Лежанье было его нормальным состоянием. (8)
Он беспрестанно в движении. (167)
["Lying was his normal condition" vs. "He was continually on the move".]

The main character's immobility is stressed by the contrast to the dynamism of his friend Štol'c. The latter is associated with restless travelling inside and outside of Russia (cf. 44, 62), whereas Oblomov stays in one type of space, and even almost the same place, throughout the novel. Oblomov is not able to undertake "necessary" journeys like going abroad or visiting his estate, whereas Štol'c and Ol'ga do so easily. In their worldview, borders seem to be altogether missing. In the end, it is Štol'c who undertakes the journey to Oblomovka, Oblomov visits the place only in his dreams.

According to Lotman (1968), a literary character is either a mobile or an immobile hero, depending on his relationship to the structure of literary space and his behaviour in this space[14]. Basing himself on analyses of Tolstoj, Lotman distinguishes:

I. heroes who belong to a *closed*, immobile locus, whom he calls "герои своего места, своего круга, [..] которые, если и перемещаются согласно требованиям сюжета, то несут вместе с собой и свойственный им локус". (Lotman, 1968: 10) [Heroes with their own place, their own surroundings, who, if they move as a result of demands of the plot, carry with them the type of space that is typical for them].

II. heroes of *open* space, who are subdivided into "герои пути" [heroes of the road] and "герои степи" [heroes of the steppe, of open space]. The linear structure of space of the former is connected to a goal. His space in not unlimited, but marked by a distinct point of departure and a point of destination. The "герой степи", on the other hand, moves in a kind of space that is virtually boundless. He is able to cross borders prohibited to the other types of heroes, for these borders do not exist in his space.

Thus, Oblomov resembles the immobile type of hero, the "герой своего места". There is a "mutual presupposition between personage and setting", they complement each other and may seem even "interchangeable, as elements from one semantic field or domain" (Van Baak, 1983: 96). This means that Oblomov can, among other things, be defined by the space that surrounds him. What is typical for that space is also typical for him, such as the apathy of the landscape at Oblomovka or the negligent way things lie about in his room. The narrator himself stresses this connection when he states:

Сам Обломов был полным и естественным отражением и выражением того покоя, довольства и безмятежной тишины.
(486)
[Oblomov was the complete and natural reflection and expression of that repose and calm that reigned all around him.]

Oblomov carries Oblomovka with him wherever he goes - to the house on Gorochovaja street, to the house of the widow, and even to the dača, which he leaves only long after all other visitors have returned home. At the same time, however, he is not deprived of his goal, to realize his dream of returning to Oblomovka and the creating of a family. In his own eyes, he reaches this goal at the end of his life.

Жизнь его сложилась.
(487)
Грезится ему, что он достиг той обетованной земли...
(493)
[He had attained the ideal of his life.
He dreamt that he had reached the promised land...]

This circumstance classifies the "immobile" Oblomov as a "hero of the road" ("герой пути"), whose linear space points to a goal, "Движущийся герой имеет цель" [The moving hero has a goal] (Lotman, 1968: 48). This calls for yet another type of literary character, a hero who does not move physically, but who does strive for a certain goal. He does not attain this goal, however, by the means of movement, shifting in space, but only through mental processes. In an early stage of his life, it forced him to quit his office in order to preserve his dignity, and so he turned his back on bureaucratic St. Petersburg, on its careerism, bad taste and so on.

Considering the two contradictory "conclusions", the typology of Lotman does not apply to Oblomov entirely. Though the classification of literary characters into mobile and immobile can be useful with respect to many literary texts - it may reveal information about the typology of the plot or the structure of the literary space and the typology of the culture modelling that space - it does not work in this particular case.

Štol'c does fit into Lotman's system. He represents the type of "герой степи" whose function it is to cross borders, which are insurmountable for others. As a matter of fact, Štol'c arrives from the "outside". When he enters Oblomov's room he has just returned from a trip abroad. He repeatedly steps into the closed world of his friend and then leaves it again, travels inside and outside Russia, overcomes every difficulty, but never strives for the unattainable. He crosses all the borders Oblomov cannot and does not cross, and he is the one who takes the final hurdle - he asks Ol'ga to become his wife.

Considering the stress on apathy, lack of energy and static position in the space of Oblomov, recurrent allusions to his and Štol'c's "path of life", their destiny, their goal in life, are all the more striking. In fact, the majority of the conversations between the two old friends deals with these matters. In these talks, the word путь and other terms with the same connotation play an important role. A limited number of synonyms is used for the road: дорога, тропа, путь, поприще.

Штольц указывал в дали пути своей и его жизни. Оба давали друг другу торжественные обещания [...] обещания идти разумною и светлою дорогою [...] Обломов сгорал от жажды труда, далекой, но обаятельной цели.
(65)
[Stolz pointed out the distant goals of his own and his friend's life [...] They exchanged solemn promises to follow the path of reason and light [...] Oblomov was aflame with the desire to work and to reach his distant, but fascinating goal.]

Since the terms "mobile" and "immobile" heroes are not adequate, the application of the spatial parameters "static vs. dynamic" seems more satisfactory. The closed, static world of Oblomov can be related to a concentrical world picture in which the archetype of the *house* is dominant. The counterpart of this view is a world in which movement prevails and boundaries are absent, in which space is itinerant, in which the *road* is the key-concept.

These two fundamental ways of perceiving space culturally, are both present in *Oblomov*, without either of them prevailing. These essentially different and therefore conflicting ways of looking at the world set the plot in motion. The suspense of the story derives from the question: will Oblomov move or will he not? The words "теперь или никогда?" turn into a question of life and death, "to be or not to be", as Oblomov himself puts it, a question closely interwoven with other values of Oblomov's lifestyle.

5.0 on metaphorical use of spatial oppositions

While investigating the structure of literary space inhabited by Oblomov and Štol'c, abundant metaphorical use of space came to the fore. Human relations, notably Oblomov's relation to the female characters, are frequently described by means of spatial oppositions. Oblomov's position in the world and in life is also treated metaphorically. These are all examples of what Jurij Lotman has called a transmitting of non-spatial relations through spatial language.

At this point it is necessary to distinguish between two types of metaphors. The first type, the stale metaphor, has frequently lost its power, has turned into a cliché, and is often no longer recognized, because of its very popular use. The image of the "road of life" can be considered as this type. The other, much more original, type, the fresh metaphor, catches the reader's attention, and often casts a new light on things.

In *Oblomov*, the narrator appears to make special use of certain spatial metaphors which inform on the axiological and psychological model of the world. Two spatial oppositions are especially important in organising the world-picture: "high vs. low" and "closed vs. open".

The first parameter, "high - low", "up - down", "top - bottom", i.e. a structuring of the world along a vertical axis, is interpreted traditionally as "good - bad", "right - wrong", "worthy - unworthy" etc. The second important modelling parameter is "closed - open", "inside - outside", which carries the meaning of "unfree - free", "captivity - liberty," "spiritual death - freedom of the mind" respectively. The opposite interpretation of "closed - open" is possible as well. In that case, inside space is associated with safety, whereas the outside world is conceived as dangerous. The possibility that one spatial parameter can obtain more than one meaning again suggests the presence of different worldviews in the novel *Oblomov*.

5.1 High versus Low

The relation between Oblomov and Ol'ga is dominated by the spatial opposition "high - low". This parameter predominantly structures the psychological and moral model of the world. In various cultures, high is interpreted as a superior location, for example the world of the gods on the top of a mountain or in heaven. Similarly low is interpreted negatively. This is also true for *Oblomov*.

> Он смутно понимал, что она выросла и чуть ли не выше его.
> (239)
> Когда я буду лежать на дне этой пропасти, вы все будете, как чистый ангел, летать высоко, и не знаю, захотите ли бросить в нее взгляд.
> (258)
> [He felt vaguely that she had grown up and was almost superior to him.
> When I am lying at the bottom of this abyss you will still be soaring high above like a pure angel, and I doubt whether you will want to cast a glance into it.]

Thus a highly romantic motif is introduced. The beloved is compared to a pure angel, some ethereal being, untouchable and unreachable for the "fallen angel", who is condemned to eternal longing for the pure, his own primeval state[15]. For a moment the image and reality even merge:

> [Обломов] видит, вдали она, как ангел восходит на небеса, идет на гору, так легко опирается ногой, так колеблется ее стан. Он за ней, но она едва касается травы и в самом деле как будто улетает. Он с полугоры начал звать ее. Она подождет его, и только он подойдет сажени на две, она двинется вперед и опять оставит большое пространство между ним и собой, остановится и смеется.
> (285)
> [He saw her walking up a hill, looking like an angel ascending the sky, so light was her step, so graceful her movements. He went after her, but she seemed scarcely to touch the grass with her feet, just as if she were really flying away. She waited for him, but as soon as he came within ten feet of her, she walked on, again leaving a big distance between them, then stopped once more and laughed.]

In this passage, "high" and "low" fuses with the "far" and "near". In Oblomov's eyes Ol'ga stands morally so much higher that the distance between them seems like an unbridgeable gap. The words "propast'" and "bezdna" appear whenever Oblomov talks to Ol'ga about their impossible - for the distance beween them is insurmountable - love. The manner in which Oblomov's relation to Agaf'ja Matveevna is represented is therefore all the more meaningful. He bridges this distance without difficulty, and moves easily and steadily towards his goal. (The use of imperfect tense to stress the motion itself should be noted).

Он сближался с Агафьей Матвеевной - как будто подвигался к огню, от которого становится все теплее и теплее, но которого любить нельзя.
(394)
Итак, он подвигался к ней, как к теплому огню, и однажды подвинулся очень близко, почти до пожара, по крайней мере до вспышки.
(396)
[He was getting closer to Agafya Matveyevna just as one does to a fire which makes one feel warmer and which one cannot love.
And thus he drew nearer to her as to a warm fire, and once he drew very near, so that there was nearly a conflagration or, at any rate, a sudden blaze.]

What is stressed in this extremely pragmatic, almost banal, relation is precisely the closeness and warmth of this simple woman, whereas Ol'ga, the superterrestrial creature of almost divine perfection is unattainable for him. The romantic image is thus substituted by a realistic one. Once, when Ol'ga visits the Vyborg-house, Oblomov is forced to look at his world with different eyes:

- Какая, в самом деле, здесь гадость! [...] И этот ангел спустился в болото, освятил его своим присутствием!
(364)
["How disgusting this place really is!" he said, looking round. "And this angel descended into a swamp and sanctified it with her presence!"]

Štol'c finally adopts this symbolic language:

Если Ольга, этот ангел, не унес тебя на своих крыльях из твоего болота, так я ничего не сделаю. [...] Она хочет, - слышишь? - чтоб ты не умирал совсем, не погребался заживо, и я обещал откапывать тебя из могилы ...
(401)
["If an angel like Olga could not carry you on her wings out of the bog in which you are stuck, I can do nothing. [..] She is anxious - do you hear? - that you should not die altogether, that you should not bury yourself alive, and I promised her to dig you out of your grave".]

Ты - другое дело, Андрей, - возразил Обломов, - у тебя крылья есть: ты не живешь, ты летаешь.
[Штольц:] - У тебя были крылья, да ты отвязал их.
Где они, крылья-то? - уныло говорил Обломов.
(403)
["You are quite a different matter, Andrey!" replied Oblomov. "You have wings: you don't live, you fly."
(Stolz:) "You had wings once, but you took them off."
"Wings? Where are they?" Oblomov said gloomily.]

This dramatic conversation reflects the idea that all men are born with equal capacities. By some unknown, secret, reason[16] Oblomov has lost this heritage, his "wings" of movement and life itself.

5.2. Closed versus Open

The second important modelling parameter is the opposition "closed - open". It is linked to the previous one, "high vs. low", through the motif of the *grave*. This location has simultaneous connotations of a "low" and a "closed" place. Oblomov is, according to his own point of view, compared to the living dead, (living in) a grave, hidden under the surface of the earth.

А между тем он болезненно чувствовал, что в нем зарыто, как в могиле, какое-то хорошее, светлое начало, может быть теперь уже умершее, или лежит оно, как золото в недрах горы, и давно бы пора этому золоту быть ходячей монетой.
Но глубоко и тяжело завален клад дрянью, наносным сором...
(100-1)
[And yet he was painfully aware that something good and fine lay buried in him as in a grave, that it was perhaps already dead or lay hidden like gold in the heart of a mountain, and that it was high time that gold was put into circulation. But the treasure was deeply buried under a heap of rubbish and silt.]

This poetic, very expressive and plastic description of the tragic psychological condition in which the hero finds himself, is loaded with spatial images. The grave, the treasure hidden inside a mountain, piled up with junk recall the "boloto", the swamp. Besides the opposition high - low, another spatial opposition operates, "inside - outside" and "closed - open". The mention of "в недрах", "завалить", "закопать", [the heart, the innermost, to burry] contributes to this impression. Inclusion is interpreted negatively in this passage. It acquires the features of involuntary enclosure, imprisonment. In connection with this negative connotation, the motif of "enemy" is interesting. It is noteworthy that the Russian word "враг" may also designate the devil.

Что-то помешало ему ринутся на поприще жизни и лететь по нему на всех парусах ума и воли. Какой-то тайный враг наложил на него тяжелую руку в начале пути и далеко отбросил от прямого человеческого назначения ...
И уж не выбраться ему, кажется, из глуши и дичи на прямую тропинку. Лес кругом его и в душе чаще и темнее ...
(101)
[Something prevented him from launching out into the ocean of life and devoting all the powers of his mind and will to flying across it under full sail. Some secret enemy seemed to have laid a heavy hand upon him at the very start of his journey and cast him a long way off from the direct purpose of human existence. And it seemed that he would never find his way to the straight path from the wild and impenetrable jungle. The forest grew thicker and darker in his soul and around him.]

The motif of the grave is subsequently developed into the opposition between *Life* and *Death*. According to one of the world-views, inclusion is associated with death. This does not come as a surprise after what has been established in the previous two sections. Several features of the inside world can once again be interpreted as typical for a non-living world. It is eventless, static and timeless.

During his youth at Oblomovka, little Il'juša was deliberately kept inside. At this time everything started to go wrong. The connection between the locked-up child and his premature fading is a connection between something spatially enclosed and death.

101

In the other world-view, however, inclusion is not necessarily interpreted negatively. Consider the following quotation:

С летами волнения и раскаяние являлись реже, и он тихо и постепенно укладывался в простой и широкий гроб остального своего существования, сделанный собственными руками, как старцы пустынные, которые, отворотясь от жизни, копают себе могилу. (488)

[The years passed, he was less and less disturbed by remorse and agitation, and settled quietly and gradually into the plain and spacious coffin he had made for his remaining span of life, like old hermits who, turning away from life, dig their own graves in the desert.]

The image of the grave or coffin remains, but it has to be interpreted in an entirely different manner. Owing to the image of the hermit, death can now be accepted as something valuable. Strange as it may sound, certain elements of Oblomov's character resemble those of a monk in seclusion. This leads me to take the liberty of drawing on certain aspects of medieval christian thought, particularly that of monasticism. In particular the spatial categories which define the image of Oblomov allude to the type of space which models monastic society.

Oblomov has withdrawn from life in society, from the world outside his house, even from that outside his room. Chapter 5 of part I relates the hero's past, how he quit his job and retired - "подал в отставку" - and breaks off relations with acquaintances (57-63). Life in the exterior world means the denial of life itself: "Когда же жить?" - he asks twice (59, 64). The "real" world has betrayed him - "он махнул рукой на обманувшие его или обманутые им надежды" [63] [he lazily dismissed all the youthful hopes that had betrayed him or been betrayed by him] (67) - and therefore he has retreated into another world, one made up in his fantasy, invisible to ordinary humans.

Обломов любил уходить в себя и жить в созданном им мире.
(68)
Никто не знал и не видал этой внутренней жизни Ильи Ильича [...]. О способностях его, об этой внутренней волканической работе пылкой головы, гуманного сердца знал подробно и мог свидетельствовать Штольц.
(70)
[Oblomov liked to withdraw into himself and live in the world of his own creation.
(71)
No one saw or knew this inner life of Oblomov; [...] Only Stolz knew and could testify as to his abilities and the volcanic work that was going on inside his ardent head and humane heart; but Stolz was hardly ever in Petersburg.]

This move away from life outdoors resembles a monk's leaving of the world, his "уход". Some of Dmitrij Lichačev's remarks are especially pertinent to this point:

Когда человек уходит в монастырь, то этот "отход от мира" представляется главным образом как переход к неподвижности, к прекращению всяких переходов, как отказ от событийного течения жизни. Пострижение связано с обетом оставаться в святом месте до гроба.
(Lichacev, 1967: 357-358)
[When a man enters the monastery, he "retreats from the world", a withdrawal that is in the first place understood as a transition from mobility to immobility, a refraining from any form of transition, as a rejection of a life full of occurences. Vowing oneself to God means staying in the holy place until the grave.]

I want to stress that I do not intend to prove a perfect resemblance between Oblomov and a monk. The hero of Gončarov's novel has made no vows, there is no mention of faith or God, let alone that consecration takes place. A number of aspects, however, do support this interpretation. Oblomov obviously needs separation, seclusion and quietness in order to be able to concentrate on what is really meaningful to him, to save his human dignity, which alludes to the saving of the soul, and to guarantee his daydreams about Oblomovka. He rejects the outside world, taken by others to be the "real", living world, very consciously. To him, this world of superficial pleasures and false values (cf. his conversation with Štol'c in part II, chapter 4) is worthless. He even calls the Petersburg bureaucrats "мертвецы" - the dead (179). All these details gain an extra dimension if we consider his solitude as a form of retreat. At the end of his life he does reach a form of inner peace.

The oppositional pair "static - dynamic" can therefore be connected to the opposition between a "dead" and a "living" world. The interpretation, the values connected to each of these worlds, depends on the point of view of the characters and narrator, and the world-view associated with it, which may change from page to page. In the eyes of Štol'c and Ol'ga there is no hope for their friend once he has made his final choice. There is no return from the land of the dead, "Погиб!" [He is dead] Štol'c whispers. He fails to recognize that Oblomov has found happiness, even a certain degree of bliss, in that same, "dead" world. On the one hand there is a complete condemnation - living in a closed world is fatal. On the other hand, Oblomov has the objective of saving his human dignity by means of withdrawal from the Petersburg society and the realization of this goal in a down-to-earth way, by replacing the idyll of his childhood by the realistic idyll, the house of the widow. Thirdly, there is the narrator who does not choose sides. He neither condemns Oblomov nor does he explicitly agree with Štol'c. His message seems to be that both world-views are equally acceptable. The reader can choose for the one or for the other or, like the narrator, he may not choose at all.

6.0 the two world-views

The structure of literary space in *Oblomov* is as follows: all literary space in Gončarov's novel is divided according to different worldviews, namely those of a declining feudal world and those of a rising business culture, as seen against the background of bureaucratic St.Petersburg society. The contrast between the two types of culture is predominantly realized by the opposition between static and dynamic space. These are the two basic structures of the world, with each member of the opposition implementing a different modelling of space.

In the statically conceived world of Oblomov, the organisation of space is based on the opposition "inside - outside", which runs parallel to other spatial oppositions like "closed - open", and is linked to non-spatial notions such as "we - the others", "safe - hostile", "warm - cold", "known - foreign". The meaning attributed to the spatial parameters is an indication of archaic world-pictures lying at the roots of the "feudal" world-view. The border function ascribed to the Volga and Neva rivers is another hint in that direction. Boundaries and barriers marking the line between two territories are of special importance in Oblomov's world. Seen from his viewpoint they are interpreted favourably, as "protection", seen by "outsiders" they have negative meaning.

On the other hand, the dynamic world of the careerman Štol'c is not sensitive to boundaries at all. In connection with this second type of culture, I want to point shortly to an episode which I have left unmentioned until now. What I have in mind is the idyll of Štol'c and Ol'ga's matrimonial life in their house on the Crimea, chapter 8 of part IV. Like Oblomov, they have moved to the periphery - "на южный берег Крыма" [on the southern shore of the Crimea] - and at first sight they seem to have established a same kind of "бытовая идиллия" [a day-to-day idyll] as Oblomov has tried to create in his room on Gorochovaja street, and has finally found in the house of the widow. Their home is also filled with "things" (459-60) and children, but it lacks the boredom and sleepiness typical for the prototype of Oblomovian space.

Только не было дремоты, уныния у них; без скуки, без апатии проводили они дни. (465)
[But there was no drowsiness or depression about them; they spent their days without being bored or apathetic.]

In time, Štol'c has replaced his "nomadic" way of life by a more sedentary one, but the notion of enclosure is still altogether absent from this picture of the world. This can be understood from the fact that the Crimean-location is represented as a harmonious merging of inner and outer sphere. The passage between the two territories - inside and outside of the house - appears as gradual, without marked lines or boundaries (465-6). Štol'c, with his entrepreneurial mentality, is a representative of modern mercantilism or business culture, which is wrestling with ancient feudal culture in this novel. According to the world-view of the former, comfort and rest can be attained only through hard work, and not by heritage.

In *Oblomov*, point of view is crucial, since it is used to contrast the two cultures' world-view on the situation. All these double visions - of Oblomov's room in the centre and his behaviour in it, of the similar situation in the house in the outskirts of town (the "periphery") - can be traced back to the ambivalent picture of Oblomovka in the dream-chapter.

6.1 proper and improper behaviour

From the point of view of St. Petersburg, i.e. bureaucratic, culture, Oblomov's behaviour in space is improper (cf. also Van Baak 1981: 393). It is not acceptable to hide from public life by locking oneself up and finally moving to the outskirts of town. Only during his holiday at the dača does Oblomov behave properly in the eyes of the established culture. But eventually he lacks the flexibility to adjust his behaviour to his environment. A conflicting situation occurs every time he behaves as if he were in Oblomovka. He fails to recognize that his way of life is literally "out of place" in St. Petersburg. This "wrong" behaviour contributes to the conflict which finally leads to the hero's "destruction".

It is not my intention to question the place of *Oblomov* among the works of Russian Realism. Undoubtedly, Gončarov's novel belongs to the so-called "primary style" works of literature. At certain moments, the work even takes on a polemical attitude towards the preceding period of Romanticism, its metaphors and its world-pictures. This is particularly evident in the introductory passages to the Oblomovka-chapter. The description of the landscape (102-4) evokes a literary manifesto in its emphatic way of denying, almost abjuring, the aesthetic code of Romanticism[17].

In this description, many prominent attributes of the traditional Romantic landscape are repudiated and replaced by contrasting elements. The foaming sea turns into a charming river; steep, wild mountains become rolling hills. The structuring of the world along a vertical axis is replaced by a more horizontal modelling of the world. This can be illustrated by the following two quotations, the first from Lermontov's *Geroj našego vremeni* [*A Hero of our Time*], the second a description of Oblomovka.

Казалось, дорога вела на небо, потому что, сколько глаз мог разглядеть, она все поднималась и, наконец, пропала в облаке.
(Lermontov, 1981: 202)
[It seemed as if the road was leading up into the skies, because as far as the eyes could reach it climbed and climbed, and finally got lost in a cloud.]

Небо там, кажется, напротив, ближе жмется к земле.
(103)
[The sky there seems to hug the earth.]

The established image of nature as a dynamic, wild and magnificent force disappears. Space is domesticated and subdued to human scale. Thus, the conception of space as being infinite (Romanticism) is replaced by a finite concept. Instead of being "необозримый, необъятный, недосягаемый" (102-3) [boundless, far and unattainable], the landscape of Oblomovka is measurable, the river has borders, it even runs into a pond. However, Gončarov did not succeed in leaving behind him the romantic code completely. A typical secondary style feature is preserved in his description of nature, in which human properties are attributed to sky, sun and river.

Небо [...] жмется к земле, чтоб обнять ее покрепче, с любовью. [...] Солнце [...] удаляется оттуда не вдруг, точно нехотя, как будто оборачивается назад взглянуть еще раз или два на любимое место и подарить ему осенью, среди ненастья, ясный, теплый день. [..] Река бежит весело, шаля и играя.
(103-4)
[The sky there seems to hug the earth, not in order to fling its thunderbolts at it, but to embrace it more tightly and lovingly; [..] The sun there shines brightly and warmly for about six months of the year and withdraws gradually, as though reluctantly, as though turning back to take another look at the place it loves and to give it a warm, clear day in the autumn, amid the rain and slush. [..] The river runs gaily, sporting and playing.]

On other occasions, the narrator even makes fun of his romantic predecessors. In a fairly ironic tone, he ridicules the traditional images of the moon and the nightingale - the "луна" [the coquette-moon] is replaced by "месяц" [the ordinary moon], and the singing bird substituted by a quail. But again, part of the code that is being denied is preserved.

One metaphor is replaced by another, the use of the simile, as such an attribute of secondary style literature, is not questioned when the "месяц" is compared to a "медный вычищенный таз" (104) [a polished brass basin]. The picture of Oblomovka that emerges eventually has an affinity with the idyllic landscape, which emerges every now and then in the course of literary evolution. This is due to the limited number of settings possible in literature. Each literary period is in fact compelled to make its choices and selections of locations from a finite set of alternatives.

Notwithstanding some clearcut Realistic features in the Oblomovka picture, it still fulfils the role of a romantic, idealized place, somewhere "far away", where the hero hopes to find rest and peace from the troubles of "this world". Oblomov's romantic nature longs for a place where he is not. Like the heroes in the works of Byron, Puškin, Lermontov and partly Bestužev-Marlinskij, Oblomov wants to flee society, to escape the established way of life in the capital. But unlike his predecessors, it is not the exotic and raw South, the Caucasus or the Orient which he longs for. His dreams are projected on a more "realistic" place - his estate. The opposition, typical for the worldpicture of Russian Romanticism, "the capital (Moscow/Petersburg) vs. the Caucasus", is replaced by the opposition "the city vs. the estate" in the period of Realism. The basic opposition "urban vs. rural", however, remains. In "Oblomov" another spatial opposition is activated simultaneously, namely the notions of distance and proximity, "near vs. distant". Oblomov yearns for the distant, not only in space, but also in time. The Oblomovka he dreams of belongs to the past, and he knows it is no longer the same anymore. What he "chooses" in the end is the exact opposite, it is the "near" and "present" of the house in the Vyborg-district that eventually becomes his refuge from the world. The notion of a rural life is now attributed to the Vyborg-district, for the location is depicted in agrarian terms, there are chickens, a rooster and a goat, the yard is watched by a dog (482). Here, in this substitute Oblomovka, Oblomov finds peace in the end. In this respect, he has overcome his own romantic nature. In his acceptance, his resignation, even his reconciliation with the "here and now", Oblomov acts as a Realist.

1. Cf. also Gončarov's own comments on the aesthetics and poetics of his own work, in his article "Lučše pozdno čem nikogda" ["Better late than never"], in: Sobr. Soč. v 8-mi tomach, t. 8, M., 1953, pp. 64-114.

2. Setting: the place plus the social and cultural circumstances; cf. also Van der Eng 1978: 15-17, who, following E. Muir 1928 (quotations in Van der Eng 1978), points at the importance of the setting in the type of novel called the character-novel, to which type *Oblomov* obviously belongs.

3. All quotations according to Gončarov, Sobr. Soč. v 8-mi tomach, 1953, t. IV.

4. English translations are from Gončarov 1954.

5. A.G. Cejtlin, situates the events in *Oblomov* exactly between 1819 (when Oblomov was seven years old) and 1856, cf. Cejtlin 1950: 162-4.

6. A similar spatial intrusion by means of a letter recurs in the ninth - the dream - chapter, cf. 139-40.

7. Apart from marking the boundary between inner and outer space, the door is a crucial part of the house, the territory into which man retreats, where he finds shelter and security. "Дом обеспечивает замкнутое пространство, в котором можно укрыться, однако без двери замкнутое пространство не существует". (Civ'jan, 1978: 70). [The house guarantees an enclosed space, in which man can hide, however, without the door the enclosed space can not exist.]

8. There is an obvious kinship between these literary 'types' and the characters in Gogol's *Mertvye duši* [*Dead Souls*], especially the similarity between the description of Čičikov at the beginning of the novel and the indentically "faceless" Alekseev catches the eye.

9. This fact is summarized in the traditional sentence for retirement: "Podal v otstavku" (57) [He quit his job].

10. Michail Bachtin records the following three, main, features of the idyll:
a. органическая прикрепленность, приращенность жизни и ее событий к месту, к родной стране со всеми ее уголками [...] к родному дому.
b. строгая ограниченность ее основными немногочисленными реальностями жизни.
c. сочетание человеческой жизни с жизнью природы.
(1975: 374-375)
[a. an organic attachment, a growing together of life and its events with the location, with the homeland with all its little corners [...], with the parental home.
b. a strict restriction to the few basical realities of life.
c. the combination of human life with the life of nature.]

11. Cf. M. Ehre's approach of the Štol'c character, M. Ehre 1973: 195-219.

12. Cf. Van Baak 1983: 86 and note 13, 263.

13. In theoretical studies of the semiotics of the town - in particular St. Petersburg - the antithetical pair "centre vs. periphery" is repeatedly mentioned. The most prominent location in the centre is, of course, the Nevskij prospekt, whereas the islands, such as the Vasil'evskij ostrov, Kolomna, or in the case of Gončarov's novel, the Vyborg-district in the North, constitute the "okraina" - the land on the border. Cf. Ju. Lotman 1984: 41. Other articles dealing with this subject are by Toporov 1984 and Lotman & Uspenskij 1982.

14. For subsequent development of his thoughts on this subject cf. i.a. Lotman 1971, chapter 8, and Lotman 1979.

15. The image of the "propast'" (the abyss) can be traced back to the "ovrag" (ravine) in Oblomovka (118). "These images (high-low) are not without a realistic basis in his experience: they are the dreamlike exaggerations of the fearful ravine - supposedly swarming with all sorts of horrors - that little Ilya was not allowed to approach. The region of the unknown and of its undeveloped self, becomes his hell; for bog and abyss are appropriate images of hell". (Lyngstad, 1971: 111)

16. I do not wish to enter into the discussion about what these reasons may be here. There is a long tradition of interpreting "oblomovism", beginning with N.A. Dobroljubov's article "Čto takoe oblomovščina?" ["What is Oblomovism?"] of 1859. Soviet literary critics blamed oblomovism primarily on serfdom and its influence on the Russian gentry (cf. Cejtlin 1950).

17. It should be kept in mind that the dream (chapter 9 of part I), was written and published some ten years earlier (1849). The "need" for the author to distance himself from the Romantic tradition and its influence could very well have been more urgent at that time. This circumstance could account for the strong polemical nature of this chapter in comparison to the rest of the novel.

CHAPTER IV

The structure of space in Sologub's "V tolpe"

1.0 introduction

The disintegration of Realism in Russian literature becomes evident towards the end of the nineteenth century. At the same time, and probably related to this process, there is a clear change in the function of the category of space as one of the narrative blocks in the literary text. As regards the depiction of space, Čechov's "Step'" ["The Steppe"] (1888) serves as a turning point in the development of Russian literature, a development that eventually culminated in the appearance of Andrej Belyj's *Peterburg* of 1913. This novel is an outstanding example of a work of fiction, in which space and spatial details play a dominant role[1].

From a diachronic point of view, the structure of the model of the world undergoes some sort of change along with altering world-views. At the end of the 19th century, the shift in the functioning of the category of space resulted primarily in a more autonomous position of this narrative block. In the previous period of Realism, as well as during Classicism and Romanticism, authors used descriptions of space first of all for the creation of the setting, i.e. as a background for the action and the literary heroes[2]. The role of the block of space was subordinate to the other two blocks of heroes and action. This does not preclude, of course, a semiotic functioning of the categories of space. As I have demonstrated in previous chapters, in both Romanticism and Realism, it can easily be ascertained that space and spatial details or objects (elements of space) occurring in literary works may be understood as cultural, psychological or socio-historical signs. The description of Oblomov's room (e.g. the negligence, the dust on the open book) in relation to the character of its inhabitant, or the wild Caucasian nature, which underscores the passionate nature of Pečorin and other romantic heroes, are examples of this semiotic function.

Realism, in particular in Western Europe, stressed man's dependance on his social milieu. As a result, the description of places and locations was given ample room. Their function, however, was to provide a rational account of man's being and behaviour. This purpose was subverted in the postrealist era.

In various articles on Russian Symbolism and other Post-Realist periods of style[3], primarily Modernism, scholars have pointed out the tendency of literary space to acquire not only a more prominent and autonomous, but also a disruptive role. This latter aspect can be considered in connection with a change in the literary hero at the turn of the century which leads to a "loss of the human character as the underlying framework of the structure" (Flaker, 1979:338). The character becomes someone full of doubt, questions and uncertainty. He is not anymore the confident centre of a world he knows well.

1.1 Sologub's prose

This chapter will focus on the structure of literary space in "V tolpe" ["In the Crowd"], a short story by the decadent symbolist writer Fedor Sologub. Sologub (1863-1927), one of the oldest writers of the generation of Symbolists, is mainly famous for his novel *Melkij bes* [*The Petit Demon*] (1907). His shorter prose writings have been somewhat neglected by literary critics, and have not received the attention and recognition they deserve for their originality, their suggestiveness and powerful emotional appeal. The story "V tolpe" provides an excellent opportunity to take a closer look at the category of space in Russian symbolist literature.

"V tolpe" is one of Sologub's most upsetting stories. It is based on the tragic events that occurred in Moscow in 1896, when hundreds of people were trampled to death in a crowd on the Chodynka field during the festivities in honour of Nicolas II's coronation. Sologub has situated his story in Mstislavl', a provincial town celebrating its seven-hundredth anniversary. The archaic name of Mstislavl'[4] evokes associations with Russia's epic past, and thus gives the events more universal meaning. In addition, "V tolpe" was written and published in 1907, while the memory of the disastrous Russo-Japanese war and the abortive 1905 Revolution was still very much alive. Symbolist writers cherished, even cultivated, premonitions of the Russian monarchy's decline. These events only confirmed apocalyptic predictions. "V tolpe" leaves a shattering impression on the reader, partly because its material was drawn from actual facts. Furthermore, there is a psychological explanation for the strong emotional impact, because the feeling of terror described from the point of view of three children lost in an immense crowd is very recognizable. Sologub's story is about the existential experience of terror.

Sologub often chooses to focus his stories on children[5], and "V tolpe" is no exception. He uses their eyes to describe the crowd and its disastrous excesses. This point of view[6] has a great influence on the reader's emotional perception. "V tolpe" is evidently a symbolic story, for Sologub uses fairy-tale and apocalyptic images to relate the historical events. The story thus acquires a mythological dimension; it describes the universal struggle between the powers of light and darkness.

2.1 the story

On the anniversary of Mstislavl's founding, officials from all over the country and even from abroad are invited to celebrate. Separate festivities for the common people are planned to be held on the municipal meadow, which for unknown reasons bears the ominous name "Opalicha", a name which evokes associations with fire and burning (see below). Puppet theaters and other attractions have been erected on the field. On the day of the anniversary, presents[7] are planned to be distributed to the ordinary people. For this reason, men and women head for Mstislavl' from all over the province.

On the eve of the anniversary, a huge crowd has already gathered on Opalicha. After outlining this general situation, the anonymous, omniscient narrator now focusses on the gymnasium-pupil Leša and his two older sisters, Nadja and Katja. Excited by the festivities and by the anticipation of the next day's presents, the children are caught up in a state of feverish expectation. Afraid to be late in the morning, they beg their parents to let them go to the field after dinner. Though reluctant to let the children spend the night away from home, the parents, profoundly insipid and weak, are unable to refuse permission (Sologub, 1913/14: 93)[8].

As night falls, Leša and his sisters reach the meadow where they plan to sleep. Meanwhile, a huge crowd has gathered, and the children plunge into the mass of people. As the campfires fade one by one, and as the night grows darker and gloomier, they lose themselves in the crowd. Walking without direction and without goal, the field appears infinite to them.

The author describes the children's movements with powerful suggestiveness: they experience increasing terror, wander around, and lose their bearings. The feeling of joyful expectation gradually changes to claustrophobia and agony. Around them the crowd draws closer and closer in a circle, until by morning it is virtually impossible to move about. The children have been transformed from free and independant human beings to mere playthings of an insensible and nameless crowd that determines every movement. The three children witness the disintegration of all human values: they see rape, prostitution and senseless killing, and they soon realise that this crowd will be their death.

By morning, panic breaks out, and the crowd goes mad. At this point the metaphysical dimension of the story reaches its climax. In his description of this final metamorphosis - the people in the crowd remove their masks and reveal themselves as devils - Sologub switches to apocalyptic language. The sun appears in the sky in the form of a dragon. As the most prominent symbol of evil, this Dragon, or Serpent, is the cause of mass hysteria: "Ярый Змий ярил людей" (123) [The raging Serpent enraged the people]. A figure resembling the Antichrist[9] even detaches itself from the crowd and walks on top of live human heads and shoulders, crushing them and smashing them.

In the last chapter, Leša reaches a narrow opening in the fence surrounding the field. He is able to get out, but as he is welcoming his freedom, he is run over by others. Leša dies like his sisters, trampled and crushed by the merciless crowd. But he dies with a smile on his face, for the terror and the nightmare have now come to an end for him.

3.0 some remarks on Symbolism

As in every typical symbolist story, "V tolpe" contains two levels - a realistic and a symbolic one. On the first level, an illusion of reality is created by means of setting, time and events. This is the "бытовая поверхность событий" (the layer of day-to-day events), events can all be motivated "realistically", because the crowd actually crushes the children. On the second level, the reader is confronted with the metaphysical dimension of the story, emphasized by the choice of special images, and by lyrical and emotional language[10].

Essential to the symbolist model of the world is a dualistic world-view. Behind the visible and tangible world lies another, higher reality. This second world is mystical and beyond sensory perception, though suggested to the symbolist poet by signs. This "world beyond" - "потусторонный мир" or "запредельный мир" - is only accessible by way of symbols, and can not be comprehended rationally. These special images or symbols also bring together the two levels of reality, and, therefore, strengthen the awareness of opposites in the symbolist model of the world.

In an attempt to formulate some unifying principles of the heterogeneous symbolist movement in Russia, Georgette Donchin writes:

> Whatever the impact of French influence or of the common romantic background, the main premises of symbolist mysticism - art is irrational, the poet is a seer whose intuition makes him realise the deep correspondences of another world, symbolism is an attempt at revealing the eternal in the ephemeral - were shared by both the Russian and French symbolist poets.
> (1958: 93)

Symbolism has some obvious correspondences to Romanticism. This is connected to the fact that both artistic systems belong to the so called "secondary style" periods of art. Both periods prefer a dualistic worldview, and are oriented towards another world as an alternative for the here and now. However, the essence of symbolist dualism differs from the romantic variety. For the symbolist artist, the "other" world possesses a higher value and is more real than the world of objects around us, whereas the visible world here and now is perceived merely as pseudo-realistic. A synthesis between the two can, however, be attained through the symbol.

In Sologub's semantic system, a number of key-oppositions indicate the presence of such a dualism. These oppositions are: child - adult, man - animal, heaven - earth, day - night, life - death. In every one of Sologub's stories, the reader may encounter at least one of these oppositions, but in "V tolpe" they all occur together. It is noteworthy that some of the oppositions are ambivalent, since they have no absolutely positive or negative meaning. In the opposition "child vs. adult", for instance, the child is not necessarily always beautiful and innocent. In "V tolpe", for example, there are two kinds of children, the charming Udoev-children and the rather repulsive Šutkin-children. The former are fair, modest, quiet, delicate and refined, whereas the latter are tanned, darkhaired, coarse and uncivilised. Even their parental houses reflect this contrast, "tidiness - dilapidation". The unfavourable details connected with the Šutkin chidren suggest that they are already part of the adult world and corrupted by evil. With their provocative conduct and tempting talk, they seduce the Udoev children and lead them astray.

The basic opposition between the existing material world and another, better and more preferable world, comes to the fore in the following quotation from the 5th chapter:

> Ясное бледное небо быстро темнело, и радостно было смотреть на неизменно совершающееся в нем таинство открывающей далекие миры ночи. [...]
> Все стало музыкой на миг, - но отгорел миг, и стали снова предметы и обманы предметного мира. [...]
> И все было звонко и весело, как в сказке и как не бывает в жизни, обычной и серой.
> (103-104)
> [The clear pale sky was darkening quickly, and it was a joy to look at the mystery which was immutably forming in it, opening the distant worlds of the night. [...]
> Everything became music for an instant, and the instant burned away and once more they became the objects and deceptions of the objective world. [...]
> And everything was ringing and gay as in a fairy tale and as it never is in everyday, gray life.]

In the last sentence of the quotation, the antagonism between the two worlds stands out as a crucial tension between "сказка" [fairy-tale] and "жизнь" [life]. Paradoxically, "сказка" thereby acquires the higher status, for "жизнь" is equated to "обманы предметного мира" [the deception of the material world]. The problem of "appearance vs. reality" permeates all of the subsequent narrative. In particular, it makes itself felt through the frequent occurence of the word "казалось", which constantly reminds the reader of the permanent uncertainty, whether he is dealing with "сказка" or with "жизнь".

4.1 the town

The title "V tolpe" suggests the predominance of spatial language in the modelling of the world. In the decadent tradition, the theme of the city and the motif of the crowd are closely linked. In general, the town represents a very strong literary motif in symbolist and modernist literature. A few examples are the "urban" poetry of the symbolists Verhaeren, Brjusov and Blok, or the futurist Majakovskij.

The first chapter portrays an ambivalent picture of the town. In the very first lines it is called "древний и славный" [ancient and renowned], "богатый, промышленный и торговый" (87) [wealthy from industry and trade], whereas later on the tone becomes menacing and gloomy:

В городе немощенном, пыльном, грязном и темном [...] в этом полудиком городе для съехавшихся отовсюду почетных гостей и властей устраивались торжества и пиршества, никому не нужные, и щедро тратили на эту пустую и глупую затею деньги, которых не хватало на школы и больницы.
(88-89).
[In a city that was unpaved, dusty, filthy, and dark - [..] - in this half-wild city, they were arranging totally unnecessary celebrations and banquets for the distinguished guests and dignitaries arriving from all over, and they were spending money generously for this empty and stupid escapade, money that they did not have for schools and hospitals.]

The social criticism of these lines is an exception in the story, for it does not reappear in the subsequent description of events. Its negative tone, however, foreshadows the coming disaster. It also charges the rich and powerful, who remain indifferent toward the poor, with the actual cause of the tragedy (this interpretation is of course restricted to the "realistic" level of the story).

4.2 the journey

The children's journey from their parental home to the Opalicha-field, where the crowd has gathered in expectation of the festivities (chapters 5 and 6), is the first part of the action in the story. Sologub describes the trip in terms of a descent into the depths, and, as we shall see, the Opalicha location even features some of the traditional concepts of hell. The Udoev family's house, as described in chapter 2, is located on a high ground at the very edge of a slope, and commands a lovely view of the lower part of town:

На Никольской площади у самого обрыва стоял домик Удоевых. Над обрывом разбит был сад, и из него открывался великолепный вид на нижние части города, Заречье и Торговый конец, и на окрестности.
С высоты все очищалось и казалось маленьким, красивым и нарядным. Мелкая, грязная Сафат-река отсюда являлась узкой лентой переменчивой окраски.
(91-92)

[On Nikolskaya Square, right by a precipice, stood the Udoev's house. Above the precipice, a garden was laid out, and from it a magnificent view unfolded onto the lower parts of the city, across to the other side of the river and the commercial district, and to the outlying regions.

From that altitude, everything was clear and seemed small, beautiful, and elegant. From there, the shallow, dirty Safat river looked like a narrow ribbon of shifting colors.]

In order to reach the Opalicha-field, the children have to descend the steep slope behind their house and cross the river.

Наконец выбрались из дому. Побежали по крутому съезду к реке. И вдруг, едва спустились, увидели Шуткиных.
(103)
[Finally they managed to get out of the house. They ran along the steep descent to the river. And suddenly, they saw the Shutkins just starting to come down.]

The world in this part of the story is thus modelled according to the oppositions "high - low", "up - down". The opposition between "closed" and "open" space is also felt. From the sheltering, orderly and charming world of the family house - by its very nature an enclosed and protecting location - Leša and his sisters go down into the open, chaotic, dirty and threatening field. Unknowingly, they head for disaster. The parental home can also be understood as the innocent state of the child, with all of its beauty, purity and refinement. In the lower, adult world, ugliness, vulgarity and barbarism reign. The chidren's descent, therefore, symbolises the inevitable transition in human life from childhood to adulthood. The "transitory" age of the Udoev children, fifteen, eighteen and twenty years old respectively (cf.chapter 2) - they stand on the threshold of life - signals the movement from innocence to worldliness.

Seen from above, all "seemed" clean and beautiful to them, the polluted river "appeared" to them as a colourful ribbon. There is the suggestion of the deceitfulness of the material world and the illusion of the presents, both of which attract the children to Opalicha.

As the children are walking down to the field, there are also allusions to the fairy-tale journey or quest. According to V.Ja. Propp (1969 and 1986), who thoroughly investigated this genre, one of its main themes is the journey of the hero, who, driven by desire, leaves his home and family in search of some unknown country or kingdom, from where he will return with precious objects or a beautiful princess after fighting and killing a terrible monster. A comparison between "V tolpe" and the fairy-tale genre reveals many parallels between this symbolist story and the folklore prototype. The children's parental home takes on the traditional function of "исходная ситуация" [point of departure] from the "отцовский дом" [parental home], which they are not allowed to leave at first, a "запрет" [prohibition] (Propp 1969: 29-30). The indifference of the parents (the father) along with a strong desire for the presents motivates the children's eventual departure from home, the "отправка" [departure] (ibid:41). "Одному из членов семьи чего-либо не хватает, ему хочется иметь что-то", (ibid: 37-39;69-71) [one of the family-members longs for something].

114

Царство, в которое попадает герой, отделено от отцовского дома непроходимым лесом, морем, огненной рекой с мостом, где притаился змей, или пропастью, куда герой проваливается или спускается. Это - "тридесятое" или "иное" или "небывалое" царство. В нем царит гордая и властная царевна, в нем обитает змей. Сюда герой приходит за похищенной красавицей, за диковинками, за молодильными яблоками и живущей и целющей водой, дающими вечную юность и здоровье.

(Propp 1986: 281)

[The kingdom which the hero reaches is separated from the parental home by an impenetrable wood, a river of fire with a bridge, where a serpent is hinding, or a ravine, into which the hero falls or descends. It is the "thirtyninth" or "alien" kingdom. In it reigns a proud and almighty queen, and a serpent lives in it. The hero comes here in order to free the abduced princess, and to get rarities, such as the rejuvenating apples, and the water of life and healing, which gives eternal youth and health.]

According to Propp, the genre of the fairy-tale is, in part, based on the cult of the dead and the conceptions of the hereafter in primitive cultures (Propp 1986, i.a. pp. 48-51). Following this theory, the "other" land in fairy-tales can be interpreted as the land of the dead. In order to reach his destination, the fairy-tale hero always has to cross a distinct boundary, which often takes the form of a river (Propp, 1986: 202, 214, 219). The river in "V tolpe", known as Safat reka, separates the safe world of childhood from the other unknown world[11]. The odd name of the river is, again, an allusion to the fairy-tale country or land of the dead:

Сафат-река - сказочная река в народном творчестве, на которой гибнут русские богатыри. Заимств. из апокрифической литературы; от названия Иосафатской равнины [...] на которой якобы Иегова будет судить народы.
(Fasmer 1971)
[The river Safat is a fairy-tale river in folkculture, where the Russian bogatyrs go to die. It is derived from apocryphal literature, and from the plain of Josaphat [...] where, it is believed, Jehova will judge the peoples.]

Apart from the reference to the fairy-tale genre, the name of the river in "V tolpe" calls up associations with the Last Judgement, and therefore with the Apocalypse[12]. These allusions forebode the horrifying events awaiting the children on the other side of Safat reka. The serpent or dragon, the traditional guardian of the entrance to the underground world (Propp 1986: 219), is also an important image in the Apocalypse of St. John. In "V tolpe", this monster appears only at the climax of the story, and the folklore and apocalyptic connotations of death and hell at this stage of the narrative motivate its subsequent appearance.

4.3 in the crowd

The initial opposition between the higher world of the children's home and the lower Opalicha-location continues once the children have reached the crowd in the field. Only a slight alteration transforms it into the archetypic opposition of sky (heaven) and earth. References to the sky above and the earth below are strikingly frequent in the crowd-episode, the main episode of the story, which constitutes its greatest part (chapters 6 through 18).

At the beginning of the main section, the narrator's voice is extremely lyrical when speaking about the nocturnal sky and its contents:

Над городом тихо мерцали звезды, как всегда, такие далекие, такие незаметные для рассеянного взгляда, и такие близкие, когда взглядишься в их голубые околицы.

Ясное бледное небо быстро темнело, и радостно было смотреть на неизменно совершающееся в нем таинство открывающей далекие миры ночи.

В монастыре звонили, - отходила всенощная. Светлые и печальные звуки меделнно разливались по земле. Слушая их, хотелось петь, и плакать, и идти куда-то.

И небо заслушалось, заслушалось медного светлого плача, - нежное умиленое небо. Заслушались, тая, и тихие тучки, заслушались медного гулкого плача, - тихие, легкие тучки.

И воздух струился разнеженно-тепел, как от множества радостных дыханий.

Приникла и к детям умиленная нежность высокого неба и тихо тающих тучек.

(103-104)

[As always, the stars twinkled above the city, so distant, so unnoticeable to the vacant look, and so close when one looks into their sky-blue surroundings.

The clear pale sky was darkening quickly, and it was a joy to look at the mystery which was immutably forming in it, opening the distant worlds of the night.

The bells sounded in the monastery; the evening service was coming to an end. The radiant and sad sounds were slowly spreading over the land. Hearing them, one wanted to sing and cry and to take off for somewhere.

And the heavens listened spellbound, listened spellbound to the radiant weeping of bronze - the tender, touching heavens. And the quiet little clouds, melting away, listened spellbound, they listened spellbound to the resonant weeping of bronze - the quiet little clouds.]

As the atmosphere in the crowd grows increasingly more oppressive and hostile, the opposition between the free open sky above and the sultry earth below is accentuated. The boy Leša then has a very short but very significant dream:

И вдруг вокруг Удоевых сдвинулась толпа. Стало тесно. И сразу показалось, что по земле стелется и ползет к лицу тяжкая духота.

А с темного неба темная и странная струилась прохлада. Хотелось глядеть вверх, на бездонное небо, на прохладные звезды.

Леша привалился к Надиному плечу. Мгновенный сон охватил его ...

... Летит в синем небе, легкий, как вольная птица ...

(114)

[And suddenly a crowd gathered around the Udoevs. It became close. And all at once, it seemed that a heavy stuffiness was spreading and crawling towards their faces.

And a dark and strange coolness flowed from the dark sky. One wanted to look upwards to the fathomless heavens, to the cold stars.

Lesha was leaning on Nadya's shoulder. A momentary dream enveloped him...

... He was flying in the blue sky, light as a free bird...]

At one point, the opposition takes on features of a cosmic struggle between the elements: "казалось, что душный земной воздух борется с небесной прохладой" (116) [it seemed that the suffocating earthly air was struggling with the heavenly coolness]. The negative descriptions of the earth, such as "(между) темной, такой грешной, такой обремененной землей" (121) [the dark earth, so sinful and burdened] all reflect the "realistic" threat it represents, especially when the children are cramped for space and threatened to be run over and trampled to death.

116

Леша почувствовал, что кто-то давит на его плечи. Так тяжко вдавливал в землю. В темную, жестокую землю.
(124)
[Lesha felt that someone was pressing on his shoulders. He pressed into the earth so heavily. Into the dark, cruel earth.]

Eventually the sky betrays Leša. At nighttime it had been the source of fresh air and the object of his dream of freedom. But at daybreak it seems hostile, for it is inaccessible. And what is worse, the sun, which turns out to be the children's greatest enemy, shines from this evil sky:

Леша поднял голову вздохнуть воздухом высокого простора. Но было жарко в высоте.
Небо сияло ясное, торжественное, недостижимо высокое, нежно усеянное перламутрами перистых облаков на западной половине.
Море торжественного света изливалось от только что поднявшегося солнца. И солнце было новое, яркое, величественное и свирепо-равнодушное. Равнодушное навсегда. И все его великолепие сверкало над гулом томления и бреда.
(124).
[Lesha raised his head to breathe in the air of the high open space. But it was hot up there.
The clear, triumphant, unattainably high heavens were shining, tenderly dotted by the mother of pearl of fleecy clouds on their western half.
A sea of triumphant light flowed from the sun which had just risen. And the sun was new, bright, majestic and fiercely indifferent. Forever indifferent. And all of its splendor sparkled above the rumble of the languor and delirium.]

Therefore, it is impossible to attribute either an absolutely favourable or an unfavourable meaning to this member of the opposition between "height" and depth". The sky can be a positive as well as a negative place. This ambiguity is actually a fundamental property of the story. It also accounts, for example, for the ambivalence of emotions, such as "жуткий и сладкий страх" (106) [terrible and sweet terror].

In sum, the structure of space in "V tolpe" is modelled along the axis of verticality. The field, situated at the very bottom, is a menacing and terrible place. Most importantly, this is indicated by its very name, *Opalicha*. This unfriendly name underscores the danger emanating from the Opalicha-location, where the havoc-wreaking crowd has gathered. The word "opalicha" is derived from "опала", "опалять", "опаленье" - to singe, to sear, to scorch, to burn. Opalicha therefore entails notions of heat, flames, and fire, which are traditional attributions of purgatory and inferno[13].

In the second chapter, music seems to emanate from below, from under the ground: "..тяжкие ломовые грохоты доносились наверх едва слышной музыкой подземелья" (92) [..and the heavy thundering of the wagons drifted upward like the barely audible music of the underground]. The depiction of the Opalicha field as an underground world becomes more and more explicit once the children are lost in the crowd. The darkness in the field is called "кромешная тьма" (109) [pitch darkness], which is reminiscent of the outer darkness where the souls of the sinners are condemned to dwell and suffer in eternity.

Захотелось уйти из этого темного и нечистого места. [...]
В темноте творилась для чего-то ненужная, неуместная и потому поганая жизнь.
(112)
[They wanted to get away from this dark and unclean place. [...]
In the darkness, an unnecessary, inappropriate, and therefore foul life was being created.]

Sologub describes the field as nothing less than hell itself. The choice of motifs such as unclean, enchanted space, fire (the campfires lit at nightfall) and the darkness in the field down on the other side of the river underscore this impression. Recurrent mentioning of "жарко" and "душно" also emphasize the infernality of Opalicha. And in this hell, the children suffer the most terrible experience of fear.

4.4 chaos

Toporov (Mify, 1982, II: 582) states that the motif of fear connects the concept of hell with chaos: "Царство смерти, с которым тоже связан страх, нередко описывается как своего рода Хаос" [The kingdom of death, to which fear is also related, is often described as a form of Chaos]. The Opalicha-location, as it is described in chapters 6 through 8, loses some of its most important - its spatial - characteristics. A number of fundamental properties of space, such as order, necessary for orientation, or roads, which enable purposeful movement through space, break down.

Lotman (1968: 30) mentions continuity and coherence as the fundamental conditions for space. Precisely these essential properties are affected in this part of "V tolpe". "Отрывчивость" [fragmentation] , "несвязность" [incoherence] and "разорванность" [disunity] are introduced. For a short time, the world returns to primeval chaos, defined as "неупорядоченность" [disorganisation], "случайность" [chance)] "удаленность от сферы культурного, человеческого, от логоса, разума, слова, и как следствие - ужасность, мрачность" [a world distant from the sphere of culture, from human values, logic, ratio, the word, and as a result: terror and darkness] (Mify, 1982, II: 581).

> Сначала казалось, что идут к какой-то цели, - все ближе к ней, и все было определенно и связно, хотя и тонуло в сладкой жуткости многолюдства.
> Потом вдруг все стало отрывчивым, потеряло связность, и какие-то клочки ненужных и странных впечатлений зароились вокруг...
> Все стало отрывочно и несвязно, и казалось, что предметы, нелепые и ненужные, возникали из ничего. Из глупой и враждебной тьмы возникало неожиданно нелепое.
> (108)
> [In the beginning, it seemed that they were walking toward some kind of goal, - as if they were getting ever closer to it, and everything was defined and coherent, although submerged in the sweet frightfulness of the throng.
> Later everything suddenly became fragmentary, and lost its coherency, and bits and pieces of unnecessary and strange impressions swarmed all around...
> Everything became fragmentary and incoherent and it seemed that absurd and unnecessary objects were springing out of nothing. The absurd rose up unexpectedly from out of the stupid and hostile darkness.]

The "ничего" [nothing], is nothing but the void that appears when all has vanished. It is the ultimate "form" of non-space, of emptiness and chaos. The notion of infinity, which arises from endless walking without direction represents the most important aspect of this "anti-space" during the first part of the crowd-episode. Seen through the eyes of the children inside the crowd, the world becomes a labyrinth, a space structured in circles without marked beginning or end. This kind of space is infinite, an anti-space where meaning can no longer be established, coherence is lost, every movement loses any goal. "Шли вперед, а может быть, в сторону, и поле казалось бесконечным", (108) [They walked forward, and perhaps to the side, and the field seemed endless]. The words "поле казалось бесконечным" [the field seemed endless] refrain like a magic incantation, as the children wander around in circles (pp. 108, 109, 110).

- Колесим вокруг да около, сказал Леша.
(110)
["We're going round in circles," said Lesha.]

Поле оказалось бесконечным, потому что они кружили на небольшом пространстве.
(113)
[The field appeared endless because they were circling around in a small area.]

The structure of space as represented here strongly resembles the labyrinth, traditionally symbolising man's difficult, mysterious road of life. Two types of the labyrinth exist, one with a complicated, yet unequivocal path from entrance to centre, the other with a multitude of false tracks and delusive paths, that either lead back to the entrance or simply in circles. The latter form is the metaphor for an obscure and inscrutable world, in which man is lost forever[14].

The Opalicha-location displays other, alarming peculiarities. In the episode following the children's first confrontation with the infinity of space and the incoherence of everything inside the crowd, they suddenly encounter holes in the ground and run the risk of falling into one of them. In chapter 7, Leša and his sisters are surprised by a trench, an old well, an unforeseen pit, and all sorts of "неровности почвы" (111) [unevennesses of the ground] in a row. The boy actually tumbles down into one of them, and the sight would have been a most amusing one, had it not been for the haunting atmosphere:

Вдруг Леша упал. Ноги мелькнули вверх, головы не видно. Сестры бросились к нему. Помогли выбраться, - оказалось, что он попал руками и головой в какую-то неожиданную яму.
(110)
[Suddenly Lesha fell. His legs flashed upwards, his head was not visible. His sisters rushed to him. They helped to pull him out - it turned out that he had fallen headlong into some kind of unexpected pit.]

Besides the "realistic" motivation of this incident - the complete darkness in the field - the holes demonstrate that in this model of the world one is actually dealing with anti-space. Holes are structured emptiness. The spatial concept of holes is but one step removed from the abyss, empty space in its most extreme form. The abyss means total destruction of space, it is the manifestation of chaos. Lotman (1968: 38) equates space enlarged to a maximum with space reduced to a minimum. Both are impossible to live in: "обе ведут к уничтожению пространства: одна - расширяя его до бездны, другая - сжимая до прорехи" [both lead to the annihilation of space: one by enlarging space untill it becomes a bottomless pit, the other by reducing it to a hole].

4.5 time

Just as the category of space is fragmented, so is time. The experience of time in "V tolpe" is similarly chaotic. As far as time by the clock or conceptual time is concerned, the events related in the story take place in the course of less than twenty-four hours. The children set out at nightfall, the moment of sunset[15], they spend the whole night in the field, and at daybreak they are already dying. However, during the long dark night, the endless walking around in circles creates the impression of eternity. In this night, described in existential terms as "значительная, единственная и последняя" (112) - [significant, unique, and the last one], not only space is perceived as infinite, but time also loses its boundaries. This night of suffering seems never-ending.

At the same time, in this model of the world, a strong notion of uncertainty dominates. The fragmentation of space, "все стало отрывочным, потеряло связность" (108) [everything became fragmentary and incoherent], makes every occurrence in this space unpredictable and unexpected. The high frequency of the word "вдруг" [suddenly] (with variations: "внезапно", "неожиданно"), which occurs no less than 23 times in this short story (cf. also Toporov, 1973: 233-234), illustrates the fragmentation. Through "вдруг" time falls into pieces and continuity - the basic feature of time (and space) - is shattered.

Therefore, in "V tolpe" all sorts of spatial concepts are stripped of their "normal" or at least their "familiar" meaning. Space virtually loses its spatial characteristics. A path that does not lead anywhere is deprived of its "raison d' être" and becomes an anti-path. The children walk in circles, the geometric figure which has neither a beginning nor an end. They are thus unable to establish meaning in a space without coordinates. Of course, the circle may be seen metaphorically as well, representing the absence of a way out, the dead-end and prison-like being of man's dwelling on earth[16]. In this chaotic anti-world, orientation is impossible and movement senseless. As a result, the experience of time is bewildering. Expectations are deceived and total uncertainty becomes the rule. In this world, man is no longer in control of his feelings or his actions. The children fall prey to fear, to the crowd and to chaos. The crowd, showing increasing traces of dehumanisation, takes over action.

This peripetia takes place in chapter 8. The children's initial joyful excitement turns into fear, claustrophobia, panic, and finally agony. This shift is accompanied by a change in behaviour. The centripetal movement now turns into a centrifugal one. The notion of infinity disappears and is replaced by its opposite - cramped space and compression.

Захотелось уйти из этого темного и нечистого места. Но не могли найти дорогу. Опять огни костров путали, ослепляли глаза, являли мрак чернее мрака и делали все непонятным и разорванным.
(112)
[They wanted to get away from this dark and unclean place. But they could not find the way. Again the bonfires' flames confused them, blinding their eyes, displaying a gloom blacker than gloom, and making everything incomprehensible and fragmentary.]

Проходить становилось все труднее, все теснее делалось вокруг. [...] И вдруг вокруг Удоевых сдвинулась толпа. Стало тесно.
(114)
[It was becoming even more difficult to make their way - everything had become more crowded all around.]

Было тесно и душно, хотелось выбраться из толпы, на простор, вздохнуть всей грудью. Но не могли выбраться. Запутались в толпе, темной и безликой, - как челнок запутался в тростнике.
(115)

[It was crowded and stifling, they wanted to get out of the crowd, out to the wide open spaces, to breathe fully.
But they could not get out. They were caught in the dark and faceless crowd - like a canoe caught in the reeds.]

The children, lost in the crowd, resemble the fairy-tale hero lost in the magic forest. Their position also alludes to the fantastic folklore genre, in which the entrance into an enchanted location - "заколдованное место" or "обморочное место"[17] - is believed to be accompanied by a deception of the senses, in particular sight and hearing. The strange sound of the human voices in the darkness and the inability to see hint at this relationship. Once again, disorientation is linked to the experience of chaos, according to which "бесконечность во времени и в пространстве, разъятость вплоть до пустоты или, наоборот, смешанность всех элементов" (Mify, 1982, II: 581) [infinity of time and space, separation up to the point of emptiness, or, on the contrary, the merging of all the elements] are ultimately one and the same. At this point the opposition between unbounded, infinite space and limited space restricted by boundaries is abolished. The two notions are absorbed in the single, all-embracing experience of chaos.

5.0 behaviour

Space also affects and influences man's behaviour. The aimless movement in circles corresponds with a disintegration of values. The Opalicha-location causes the crowd to undergo a complete metamorphosis. In the course of the night in the field, people behave more wildly than animals - not only are they bestial, but also cruel. With the exception of the three Udoev-children, the men and women in the crowd gradually change into monsters deprived of human emotions and values. This behaviour is reminiscent of the werewolf-motif, described in Russian by the more general term "оборотничество" (i.e. a being able to transform itself). The crowd turns into an uncontrollable, wild force, a kind of "стихия" depriving the individuals of their identity and free will.

И поняли дети, что здесь вся толпа насквозь была враждебная, чужая, непонятная и непонимающая.
(111)
[And the children understood that the whole crowd here was hostile, and alien through and through - incomprehensible and uncomprehending.]

Уже нельза было выбирать дорогу, повернуть по воле туда и сюда. Приходилось влечься вместе с толпой, - тяжки и медленны были движения толпы.
Удоевы медленно двигались куда-то. Думали, что идут вперед, потому-что все шли туда же. Но потом вдруг толпа тяжко и медленно пятилась. Или медленно влеклась в сторону, и тогда уже совсем непонятно стало, куда идти, где цель и где выход.
(115)
[It was impossible now to pick out the road, to choose their own direction. They had to drag along together with the crowd, - and the crowd's movements were heavy and slow.
The Udoevs were moving along slowly in some direction. They thought they were going forward because everyone was walking in the same direction. But then suddenly the crowd was heavily and slowly moving backwards. Or it was slowly drawing to the side. And then it became totally incomprehensible in what direction one should go, where the goal was and where the exit was.]

The thought of death occurs in the end:

> В истоме и бреду тяжкие, медленные мысли теснились в сознании детей, в темном сознании задыхающихся, каждая мысль была страхом и тоской. Жестокая надвигалась погибель.
> (121-122)
> [In the lassitude and delirium, grave thoughts crowded into the children's consciousness, into the dark consciousness of those suffocating, and each thought was terror and melancholy. Cruel perdition was drawing near.]

The Šutkin children's rather odd and jealous behaviour, evident right from the very beginning, foreshadows this transformation. Repeatedly, their unpleasant - "нагло и лукаво" - laughter is mentioned: "И почему-то казалось сегодня, что улыбки у них скверные и сами они нечистые" (97) [and today for some reason, it seemed that their smiles were nasty and that they themselves were unclean]. At the end of chapter 5, when the children are on their way down to Opalicha, one of the Šutkin girls is described as follows:

> В слабом отблеске дымных праздничных плошек ее веснучатое лицо и рыжие волосы являлись пламенеющими, и оттого, что ее ноздри трепетали, казалось, что по лицу бежит огонь.
> (105)
> [In the weak reflection of the smoky, festive torches, her freckled face and red hair appeared flaming, and because her nostrils were quivering, it seemed that flames were running across her face.]

They shriek and jump around hysterically and their faces light up. Already they look and behave like little devils. A hellish dehumanisation seizes the crowd as night progresses. When everyone is totally drunk, the crowd loses control, and the people's behaviour becomes completely primitive, revolting and disgusting. The most terrible crimes humans are able to commit, occur in passing. The vulgarity, the promiscuity, the decadence, and finally the knives horrify the children. The crowd no longer appears to be a mass of human beings, but a group of wild and hostile animals:

> Люди зверели и со звериной злобой смотрели на детей.
> (120)
> [The people were now becoming like wild beasts, and they were looking at the children with the malice of wild beasts.]

> Иногда показывались чьи-то странно и страшно знакомые лица. Как все лица в этой озверелой толпе, и они застыли в своем ужасном преображении.
> (123)
> [Sometimes, some strangely and terrifying familiar faces came into sight. Like all the faces in this bestial crowd, they too were frozen in their terrible transfiguration.]

By morning, the terrible metamorphosis reaches its apocalyptic finale. The people take off their masks and show their true demonic nature:

122

Уже как будто не люди, казалось задыхающимся детям, что свирепые демоны угрюмо смотрят и беззвучно хохочут из-за людских сползающих, истлевающих личин.
И дьявольский мучительно длился маскарад. И казалось - не будет конца кипению этого сатанического котла.
(122)
[They were not like people now - to the suffocating children it seemed that fierce demons were looking sullenly and laughing soundlessly from behind the human masks that they were slipping off, rotting.
And the demonic masquerade stretched on excruciatingly. And it seemed that there would be no end to it - there would be no end to the boiling of this satanic cauldron.]

Демонская злоба кипела окрест, в истоме и бреду.
Свирепые, сатанические хари виднелись повсюду.
(123)
[Demonic malice was boiling all around, in the lassitude and delirium.
Fierce, satanic visages were visible everywhere.]

По изкаженным злобой лицам, видно было, что здесь уже не было людей. Дьяволы сорвали свои мгновенные маски и мучительно ликовали.
(126)
[It was obvious by the faces distorted with malice, that there were no people there. The devils had torn off their instantaneous masks and were rejoicing excruciatingly.]

With the devils, the former underground world theme reappears[18], preparing for the climax of the story with the appearance of the Dragon and the Antichrist.

6.0 the way out

The first action the main characters took was to depart from home and to make the subsequent journey down to the field and into the crowd. In the last chapters, the reverse movement is described. The theme of the journey regains importance at this point, as the connecting element of the narrative. The movement through space accounts for the action of the story, in other words, "движение формирует сюжет" [movement forms the plot]. When, at daybreak, Leša seeks to leave the field, he desperately tries to struggle out of the crowd's grasp. Easy as it was to enter the Opalicha-location, it is difficult to leave it. The field has by now turned into a prison, enclosed on all sides by fences and walls. In contrast to the nocturnal experience of infinity and eternity, daytime is linked to the notions of confinement and the sensation of impending death, (i.e. the end of time).

In order to escape death, the children must overcome a last obstacle. In their panic, some people in the crowd crawl on top of other people's head and shoulders. But they still try to get hold of the presents: "Видно было несколько человек, неловко бегущих по плечам и головам к крышам буфетов" (131) [One could see several people awkwardly running across shoulders and heads to the roofs of the refreshment counters].
The crowd is no longer a group of human beings, but an object, passive material: "..и толпа была под ним сплошной, неровной мостовой, тяжко движущимся глетчером" (131) [and the crowd under him was like a solid, uneven bridge, like a heavily moving glacier]. This is the last stage of the process of dehumanisation, when free will has left the body, and only apathy remains. The crowd is now merely a thing, part of the setting, a spatial detail taking on the function of a street. The device of reification, "Verdinglichung", comes to the fore in this picture. It seems as if only the boy Leša - his

sisters are already, or almost, dead from suffocation - has kept his humanity. This impression is, of course, the effect of focalisation, since the reader witnesses the events through the eyes of the child. The focalisation also accounts for the emotional impact of the last scene, when Leša is swept along with the crowd to one of the narrow openings in the fences. There, he goes through an intense experience of claustrophobia: "Здесь было нестерпимо тесно, - Леше казалось, что все его кости сломаны" (133) [It was unbearably crowded there - it seemed to Lesha that all of his bones had been broken]. What should have been the road to freedom and life, is really a road to freedom and death. For Sologub the latter are joint concepts:

Но кончился узкий проход.
За балаганом стало просторно, светло, радостно.
"Сейчас умру", - думал Леша и счастливо засмеялся.
(133)
[But the narrow aisle came to an end.
Beyond the booth it became spacious, light, joyful.
"I'll die right now," thought Lesha, and he began to laugh happily.]

In this finale, the notion of fear and agony has completely vanished. Instead, Leša feels euphoria. His joyful laughter contrasts with the distorted laughter of the Šutkin children, "И кто-то засмеялся грубо и невесело темным в темноте смехом" (107) [And someone began to laugh coarsely and joylessly with dark laughter in the darkness]. On the "realistic" level, Leša's happiness could be explained as relief. But on the metaphysical level, the way Leša dies informs the reader of Sologub's philosophy of life. According to this philosophy, man only reaches real and complete freedom by death (cf. Klejman, 1983: 39, where the author discusses the influence of Schopenhauer on Sologub).

7.0 interpretations

The children's passage through hell is reminiscent of yet another archaic genre, the medieval tales in which innocent or holy persons descend into hell and take upon themselves the sins of those condemned to dwell there. The apocryphal *Choždenie Bogorodicy po mukam* [*The Passage of the Mother of God through Agonies*] is the most famous example of this genre in Russian medieval literature). The idea behind this kind of tales is that only innocent beings, pure and immaculate souls, can redeem the souls of the sinners by taking over their sufferings, an idea which ultimately refers to the Passions of Christ. In "V tolpe" the children are portrayed as pure and innocent beings, and take upon themselves the sins of the world, for which they suffer and finally sacrifice their lives.

On a "realistic" level, the story of "V tolpe" follows three children who perish in a crowd. But on a symbolical level, their journey is really a passage through hell after which they find salvation. During the night in the field, the children move from entrance to exit, however confused this movement may be. Their final movements through the narrow tunnel and the light and joy at the other side symbolise their entrance into paradise.

A more universal interpretation of the children's journey through Opalicha (a place symbolising the corrupted adult world according to Sologub's worldview) deals with the inevitable moment in every human life of reaching adulthood. The children are tempted by this materialistic (symbolised by the presents) world, and are sentenced to dwell among adults for some time. According to Sologub, however, it is preferable to die before falling victim to the evil of this world, an idea he expressed in many of his child-stories. The adult world in "V tolpe" is conceived as a chaotic labyrinth. Like Ikarus, Leša longs for a way out of the labyrinth (witness his dream of flying), and like his distant mythological relative, his dream ends in a fatal, yet blissful crash.

8.0 final remarks

In analysing "V tolpe", I have demonstrated the importance of the modelling function of space (and its correlate time) in this decadent-symbolist story. The spatio-temporal category plays an essential role in creating the haunting atmosphere of the story. Neither the heroes nor the events account for the effect that the story makes on the reader, but rather the connected experiences of time and space that generate the intense feeling of terror and doom do. As a result, individual and universal, cosmic fear merge. Space and spatial details contribute most to this impression.

In this story Sologub has created an anti-world, a chaotic world where everything is turned upside-down. In the establishment of meaning in "V tolpe" several spatial key-oppositions are used such as "high - low" or "closed - open". "Infinity - finiteness" - cf. the circles, the holes (abyss) at first and the subsequent notion of confinement in the crowd - is another opposition crucial for the creation of meaning in this story. An important aspect of the world-picture in "V tolpe" is the fact that the evaluative meaning of the members of the oppositions is ambivalent. In turn, this ambivalence contributes to the notion of chaos, to the impression of a world where nothing is stable but everything is uncertain.

Compared to the preceding periods of Romanticism and Realism, during the symbolist period space acquires a more prominent position among the narrative categories of the text. As a result of the apocalyptic world-view in "V tolpe", space acts as a central destructive force. Space dominates the action and the behaviour of people as expressed in the nature of the dehumanised crowd and of chaos. Psychologisation of the characters in the traditional realist way, among other things by interaction of description and state of the mind (metonymy), is altogether absent. It is replaced by suggestions of feelings, which are communicated via spatial language in recurrent images and leitmotifs. The emancipation of this previously much more subordinate literary category, which previously mainly functioned as a background for the heroes and their action, reached maturity in the subsequent period of Modernism. This development, however, began during the period of Symbolism, as Sologub's story clearly demonstrates.

NOTES

1. In addition, the preference for titles referring to a location is significant.

2. This is what Flaker 1987: 139 calls the "teleologische Bedeutung" of spatial details.

3. Cf. Flaker's suggestions concerning periodisation and designation of post-realist literature in slavic literatures. "Modernism", according to his definition, "means a superimposed denomination for a variety of structures from a period in which realism disintegrated and new stylistic groups appeared" (Flaker, 1979: 337).

4. A very old town with this name does exist. Indeed it lies in the Smolensk district.

5. The theme of the child is a remarkable constant in Sologub's fiction. According to St. Rabinowitz (1980:13), who made a special study of this subject, more than half of his stories written between 1894 and 1914 have child-heroes.

6. The most appropriate term for this peculiar way of narrating, seems to be L. Doležel's "subjective third person narration":
"In general, subjective third person narration gives not only the depiction of 'narrated events', but, simultaneously, also expresses 'internal' reactions of a character. This simultaneity of 'extrospection' and 'introspection' can be considered as the main quality of subjective narration; it is also the source of its effectiveness in the modern psychological novel" (Doležel, 1967: 549). This was applied to Sologub's stories by C. Hansson 1975.

7. Для раздачи народу изготовили подарки. Предполагали давать каждому кружку с городским гербом и узелок (89) [They made gifts to be distributed among the people. They intended to give each person a mug with the town's coat of arms and a small bundle] - a detail based on historical evidence for such cups were indeed planned as presents in 1896.

8. All quotations from the only complete edition of Sologub's works existing at the time: F. Sologub 1913-1914. English translations are from F. Sologub, *"The Kiss of the Unborn" and other stories*, 1977.

9. Stylistically this is underscored by a formulation obviously derived from the Apocalypse: "И слова его были - кошунство, и хула, и скверная брань" (132) [And his words were - blasphemy and abuse, and foul swearing].

10. Sologub's style is essential for its contribution to the effect of the story. The author uses poetic devices in order to evoke the dark mood and threatening atmosphere. Through rhythm, leitmotifs and abundant use of epitheta, he creates a strongly suggestive style. Moments of intense emotionality are stressed by impressionistic one-word sentences or one-sentence paragraphs. For the sake of suggestiveness, the narrator often turns to impersonal (third person singular neuter) formulations such as "было жутко и неловко", "было тесно и душно", "казалось" [It was crowded and stifling, it seemed].

11. Because of the recurrent mention of this river in the first chapters of the story, I assume that the children actually do have to cross it in order to reach their destination. An explicit mention of this crossing is, however, missing.

12. The biblical Revelations of John is the best known apocalyptic text, which presents a catastrophic description of the end of the world and an ultimate promise of the New Jerusalem. Related to the Apocalypse are eschatological notions such as plagues, flood and death. The most prominent apocalyptic images are the Horsemen, the Whore of Babylon, the Sun, the Beast and the Antichrist. Cf. Bethea 1989 on the theme of Apocalypse in Russian fiction.

13. In an earlier story by Sologub, "Zemle zemnoe" (1898) [To the Earth what belongs to the Earth], the name Opalicha occurs in a likewise "unclean" connotation: "Е. рассказывал [...] что в пруду на Опалихе не чисто, живет шишга" [E. told that the pond on Opalicha is bewitched, a shishiga lives there].

14. The walking in circles is similar to the circles in Dante's *Inferno*. Parallels between "V tolpe" and this famous image of hell are obvious, but were not the concern of this study. Common roots in archaic concepts of the underground world account for the similarities between Sologub's Opalicha and Dante's Hell.

15. Cf. Toporov (1973: 240) on the fatefulness or fatality of this hour of the day.

16. This theme of man's confinement on earth is typical of Sologub, cf. his famous lines:
    Мы пленные звери
    Голосим как умеем,
    Глухо заперти двери,
    Мы открыть их не смеем. (1908)
[We are captive animals/We shriek as loud as we can/The doors are firmly locked/We dare not to open them.]

17. Cf. my analysis of space in Gogol's "Nevskij prospekt" where the concept of "obmoročnoe mesto" is introduced, in chapter 2 of part II of this study.

18. The idea behind this passage is, however, also linked to the problem of identity as such and to the question of the true face behind the mask. This was a popular theme during the symbolist period.

CHAPTER V

The structure of space in Platonov's "Kotlovan"

1.0 introduction

Besides Sologub's "V tolpe", Andrej Platonov's (1899-1951) short novel *Kotlovan* [*The Foundation Pit*], written between December 1929 and April 1930, is an outstanding example of a story in which space and time themselves become central topics. In the story, buildings, landscapes, and other spatial elements and motives play a role far beyond that of the simple setting. The spatial structures convey ideological, existential, and emotional values that appear to be crucial for the interpretation of the story. Nature as such stands out as a dominant emotional and lyrical force. Therefore, spatial images and symbols are of primary importance in creating the meaning of the text. Like Platonov's great philosophical novel *Čevengur* (1927) *Kotlovan* could be called a *symbolic* novel[1].

The most striking aspect of *Kotlovan*, apart from the gloomy and depressing impression it makes, is the alienating effect which results from its unusual composition (fragmentary fabula, lack of suspense), the characters' and narrator's peculiar use of language, the often enigmatic images, and the elusiveness of the sometimes absurd world Platonov describes. Furthermore, Platonov's world is of an extremely ambiguous nature. Since this ambiguity affects virtually all levels of meaning of the text, this would make any final statement on the essence of this world impossible. Therefore, all of the interpretations of the story below, need to be put into the perspective of this fundamental ambiguity.

At the same time, *Kotlovan* deals with an all too realistic theme: the collectivisation, and the mass deportation and liquidation it entailed, of the so-called kulaks in Russia at the end of the twenties. The annihilation of the rural community (the village) was made in the name of the superiority of the proletariat (the town). The building of a socialist society, symbolized by the project of the all-proletarian apartment house "общепролетарский дом", are the motives that constitute the historical and socio-economic layer of meaning of the story. On a more abstract, philosophical level, problems such as man's search for the meaning of life, the interrelation between man and nature, man as part of Creation on the one hand and man's existential solitude on this earth on the other, are discussed.

It is obvious that my analysis of the text can not do justice to all of these aspects. I will mention them only in as far as they are related to the central question of my study: the function and meaning of literary space in *Kotlovan*.

Whereas Sologub's "V tolpe" models an apocalyptic picture of the world, Platonov creates what one would call a utopian world model[2]. It must be said that both these notions are often confused (i.a. by E. Tolstaja-Segal 1978). Others, quite rightly, define this story as an *anti-utopia*, thereby stressing the necessity to take the historical circumstances, i.e. the cultural and political context in which Platonov wrote his work and in which it can be understood best into consideration, namely the failing of the revolutionary experiment and its fatal consequences for the country and its people.

In Platonov's short novel, eschatological and utopian projections sometimes take over the reality of the "here and now". To a certain extent, a dualisitc structure of the world lies at the basis of the worldview in *Kotlovan*. However, contrary to what happens in Symbolism, this dualism functions exclusively on the thematic level. As a primary style period, Modernism does not recognize the existence of "another" reality. A division of the world into a sensory perceptible reality and a reality comprehensible for the mind, as was typical for the preceding period of Symbolism, is altogether absent. Processes of the mind, which as such do play a central role in many modernist writings, are understood as part of one, undivided, universe of phenomena, however complicated that universe may seem.

As a result of the "apocalyptic-utopian" thematics, time and space in *Kotlovan* are indissoluble. And, as in the symbolist story by Sologub, time and space play a dominant role in the creation of meaning. As a matter of fact, the idea of utopia combines both of these notions, because it contains both questions of where and when, and juxtaposes "here and now" reality (which to a certain degree can be designated as "свой") with a yet absent, unknown "then and there" (a usually positive "чужой").

Moreover, *Kotlovan* represents a so-called double utopia, as I will prove below. In the first place, the author deals with the ideal of the socialist proletarian state, as embodied in the housing-project. This utopia comes to nothing at the end of the story, for it suffers a crushing defeat when the child Nastja dies. This plot-line belongs to the concrete-historical layer of meaning of *Kotlovan*. It connects the story to the epoch in which it was conceived. On a higher, more abstract level, there is the second plot-line of the labourer Voščev in search of the Truth. This is a timeless human striving, and I propose to call it the "existential utopia" of *Kotlovan*[3].

Initially, both utopias seem to merge. Voščev believes he will find the answer through the diggers of the foundation pit, as the new ideology seems to promise universal happiness for all. In due time, Voščev finds out that communism merely builds castles in the air; it is even incapable of laying the foundation of a real house. After this unmasking, the two utopias part. Voščev realizes that communism is not the answer to everything, and that he will have to look elsewhere. His search continues. This universal utopia, the human ideal of truth and happiness, although out of reach, is even preserved at the end of the story.

As a result of the importance of the spatio-temporal block, and as result of the utopian thematics and the important role of symbolics, certain archaic images and motives are reactivated in *Kotlovan*. A so-called "mythopoetic" picture of the world filters through the actual and existential layers of meaning, (cf. i.a. Toporov 1973, 1982, 1983 and Lotman 1987). Spatial elements such as "the centre" and "the road", known for their key function in archaic and cosmological texts (mythopoetical space), prove to be of crucial importance. Also as a result of their non-spatial connotations, these motives are involved in the structuring of worldviews in *Kotlovan*.

Because he is continuously searching for the meaning of life, the labourer Voščev loses his job in a machine shop:

... он почувствовал сомнение в своей жизни и слабость тела без истины, он не мог дальше трудиться и ступать по дороге, не зная точного устройства всего мира и того, куда надо стремиться.
(53)[4]
[...he felt doubt in his life and weakness of the body without truth; he could not go on working and keep taking step after step down the road without knowing the precise arrangement of the whole world and whither one must strive.][5]

Absorbed by his thoughts, he is no longer sufficiently productive, and is therefore dismissed. After a short period of wanderings, Voščev reaches another town, where he meets some workmen who are digging a foundation pit for a so-called all-proletarian apartment house - "общепролетарский дом" (61) - a communal flat for all workers, which will be erected according to engineer Pruševskij's plans. Voščev joins the collective, a heterogeneous group of socialist leaders and their subordinates. The characters in the story range from kind to extremely unpleasant. The most "human" of all is the warm-hearted Čiklin. He shows compassion for the weak and unhappy, and is also the most zealous and hard-working among the diggers of the pit. Safronov is the prototype of the socialist, and the weak Kozlov turns out to be an informer. The invalid Žačev comments viciously on the events in the story and on other people's deeds, but his hatred against mankind and society is primarily directed at the communist Paškin, who represents the new power by being a typical bureaucrat and very well to do. He has a wife, all the food he can dream of, and lives in a solid brick house (66), whereas the workers are nearly starving in their shabby barracks. It is among these people, representatives of the new ideology, that Voščev hopes to fathom the secret of life. The workmen's way of life, however, is dreary and cheerless, they are emaciated, rather limited human beings.

Хотя они и владели смыслом жизни, что равносильно вечному счастью, однако их лица были угрюмы и худы, а вместо покоя жизни они имели измождение.
(56)
[Although they possessed the meaning of life, which is the equivalent of eternal happiness, nonetheless their faces were gloomy and thin; and instead of the peace of life they had exhaustion.]

Only the prospect of the future house, their hope of a better life, gives them strength and a little happiness. Čiklin finds a little girl, the orphan Nastja - one of the best examples of a symbolic character in this story[6] - who joins the workers' community. She is, as it were, the embodiment of their expectations, and restores hope and a sense of purpose to their drab world.

In the middle of the story, the setting shifts to a nearby village. Most of the characters described in the first part set out for this village in order to help transform it into a collective farm. It is here that the gradual degeneration of the socialist ideal, which finally leads to the destruction of the utopian dream occurs. The murder of Kozlov and Safronov (87) heralds this downfall. By now, winter has come, and Platonov describes collectivisation, cold, hunger and death (p. 92 ff.) in gloomy colours. The atmosphere

131

grows more and more grim. The communists use a bear in order to unmask the peasants (101 ff.), by walking the animal from door to door and using its roar as the signal to arrest the inhabitants of the house before which it happens to be standing. This scene symbolizes the bestial stupidity and blind arbitrariness of what is going on in the country. Eventually, during the so called raft-scene satire passes into horror. The peasants who do not wish to join the collective farm resist the forced expropriation by letting their cattle starve. They are sentenced to liquidation for being class enemies. The communists put them on a raft on the river and send them downstream. This is no doubt the most shocking scene of *Kotlovan*, illustrative of the perversions of the original ideal. Therefore, whereas the scenes situated in the town showed socialism's constructive aspects, the scenes in the village illustrate the ideology's destructive aspects. Once the kolchos is established, the workers return to their foundation pit. The pit, however, only becomes deeper and broader, whereas the building activities themselves are postponed forever. All hope disappears when the child Nastja dies. Her death is the definite end of utopia, "коммунизм - это детское дело" [communism is for children]. Without the child, the future, and therefore life itself, have lost their meaning. Voščev is, once more, overcome by doubt, and looking at her dead body, he no longer sees the purpose of knowing the secret of life[7].

1.2 narrative aspects

The plot of *Kotlovan* is marked by a striking lack of external action and the composition is of a rather fragmentary character. The story consists roughly of two parts. The central action in the first, so-called, "urban" part concentrates on the digging of a foundation pit, whereas the second part focuses on the collectivisation of a village. The characters convey some sense of continuity, since most of the actants of the first part reappear in the second. Another link between both parts is of a more thematic nature, for the events all refer to the historical, economical, (even cultural) reality of those days - at the time Platonov wrote *Kotlovan* gigantic, multifunctional building projects were actually being carried out. The famous "House on the Embankment" (Dom na naberežnoj) in Moscow is to a certain extent a realization of the utopian model. In the same period, Stalin's agricultural reforms caused a systematic decimation of the peasantry.

The story seems to come full circle when the peasants from the village come to town to help finish the foundation pit, and the digging continues. As far as the physical action is concerned, there is a return to the point of departure on the last pages[8]. As for the mental action, this is only partly true: Voščev is still looking for his truth, and has not gotten any closer to it than he was when we first met him. The only real occurrence is Nastja's death and the implicit death of the workers' utopia. Therefore, we only deal with a cyclical construction typical of the utopian genre to a certain extent. The impression of fragmentation derives above all from the chain of more or less autonomous episodes and independent descriptions which are not held together by a distinct plot-line. Continuity, in this case, derives from a number of recurrent images and motifs[9].

At first, the characters of the story make a rather superficial impression. Upon first encounter, they seem to be merely flat characters, figures without a profound psychological image. They are almost without exception only referred to by their family name, and as a result seem to lack individuality. On the other hand, each character makes his own baffling statements, typical Platonovian remarks that could be interpreted as a special type of aphoristic "answers" to the continuous questions about the meaning of life. If it were necessary to distinguish a hero in the traditional sense of the word, it would be Voščev, who is the only person present throughout the story, the mind that filters most of the important impressions. Čiklin and Pruševskij are other central characters because, like Voščev, the author/narrator seems to identify himself with them and obviously sympathizes with them.

However, the most typical feature of Platonov's prose is above all his peculiar language, strange metaphors, and lingual deviations:

"Игра на овеществление переносного значения, на столкновение буквального, прямого, исконного, этимологического значения и образно-символического.
(Gavrilova, 1990: 173)
[The play of materialising the metaphorical meaning, of the collision of the symbolic meaning of an image with the litteral, direct, primary and etymological meaning.]

In a most stimulating article on *Kotlovan*, Jurij Levin describes Platonov's often intentionally incorrect, bad grammar, as "ненормативное использование валентности слова" [the use of word-valency not according to the norm] (Levin, 1990: 115). This unconventional linguistic usage can be ascribed to the omniscient narrator and to the characters of the story. Levin (1990: 124) characterizes the narrator as a kind of popular philosopher, "народный философ-самоучка", which would explain not only the idiosyncratic language, but also sudden jumps of thought and unexpected associations. The language of the characters is also rather unconventional. The characters in *Kotlovan* come to life as a result of this, and also as a result of several stream of consciousness passages (that replace the narrator's role of psychologisation in a typically modernist way).

The utterances and thoughts of the seeker of truth, Voščev, seem full of hidden, and deeper meanings and are often moving by their sheer naiveness and directness:

- Не убывают ли люди в чувстве своей жизни, когда прибывают постройки? - не решался верить Вощев. - Дом человек построит, а сам расстроится. Кто жить тогда будет? - сомневался Вощев на ходу.
(55)
["Do not people lose in their feeling for their own life when construction projects gain?" Voshchev hesitated to believe. "A human being puts together a building - and comes apart himself. And who then is going to exist?" Voshchev mulled over his doubts as he walked on.]

The speech of the other characters can likewise be profound, and testifies to a special insight into life and to a special feeling for the surrounding world:

[Voščev:] - Некуда жить, вот и думаешь в голову.
(65)
["There is nowhere for life to go, so then one thinks in one's head".]

[Čiklin:] - Мы все живем на пустом месте, разве у тебя спокойно на душе?
(69)
["We are all living in an empty world - do you really have peace in your soul?"]

Persiflage of the Soviet jargon and socialist slogans take a special position in Platonov's linguistic usage:

[Safronov:] - Поставим вопрос: откуда взялся русский народ? И ответим: из буржуазной мелочи! Он бы и ещё откуда-нибудь родился, да больше места не было. А потому мы должны бросить каждого в рассол социализма, чтоб с него слезла шкура капитализма и сердце обратило внимание на жар жизни вокруг костра классовой борьбы и произошел бы энтузиасм!...

(77)

["Let us put the question; where did the Russian people originate from? And let us reply: from out of bourgeois smallfry! The Russian people might have been born from somewhere else, but there was no other place. And therefore we must hurl everyone into the brine of socialism so that the hide of capitalism will come off them easily and so their hearts will pay attention to the heat of life around the bonfire of the class struggle, and so enthusiasm should take place!..."]

2.0 the setting

Platonov's consciousness was determined by the mass scale and both the *impersonal* and *depersonalizing* character of what was happening. His novels depict not a hero against a background but rather that background itself devouring a hero. And that's why his surrealism, in its turn, is impersonal, folkloric, and, to a certain degree, akin to ancient - or for that matter any - mythology, which in all fairness, should be regarded as the classical form of surrealism.
(J.Brodsky, 1986: 289-290) (Emphasis mine-KHL)

The action in Kotlovan takes place in two locations: the proletarian setting of the town and the setting of the peasantry in the village community. All locations remain nameless, not only the town, and the village, but also other locations, such as, "в далеком центральном городе"(65) [a distant central city]. Which town or village is concerned remains a question, a fact which applies to the province as well. Against the background of Platonov's biography, it is possible to discern that this anonymous place is the Voronež-region with its flat steppes, the typical landscape of the Russian province. The precise geography is, however, only of minor importance for the story itself. The omission of actual topografical details could even be understood as an indication of a hidden, broader meaning, of a symbolic or philosophical (even existential) dimension.

Platonov's descriptions of the surrounding world are strikingly vague and indeterminate, and this accounts for the impression of abstractness, even generality and universality of the setting:

Из неизвестного места подул ветер.
(51)
[The wind began to blow from an unknown place.]

...но полевой свет тишины и вянущий запах сна приблизились сюда из общего пространства и стояли нетронутыми в воздухе.
(55)
[...yet the quiet of the light of the open field and the fading smell of hay crept in here from out of general space.]

Пашкин глянул вдаль - в равнины и овраги; где-нибудь там ветры начинаются, происходят холодные тучи.
(63)
[Pashkin looked off into the distance - to the plains and the ravines; somewhere there the winds are commencing, cold clouds are originating.]

Вощев, прибывши на подводе из неизвестных мест, тронул лощадь, чтобы ехать обратно в то пространство, где он был.
(86)
[Voshchev, who had arrived on the cart from unknown places, started up the horse so as to ride back into the space in which he had been.]

Basing himself on grammatical evidence from the text (i.e. on Platonov's language), Jurij Levin qualifies *Kotlovan* as an existentialist work of literature in his 1990 article, and ascertains a continuous "shift from empiricism towards existence" - [движение от эмпирии к экзистенции], "from phenomenon (the concrete) towards essence (the abstract)" - [от явления (конкретного) к сущности ("абстрактному")] (Levin 1990: 120-1). This holds true for several aspects of the story, and, among other things, for the category of space:

Локус, в котором пребывает данный человек, животное, растение, это не просто данное конкретное место, а или весь мир, или нечто обобщенное-природное.
(ibid.: 123)
[The locus, in which a certain person, animal or plant finds himself, is not merely the actual, given place, but also either the whole world, or something overall-naturelike.]

According to Levin, Platonov's language also influences the relationship between the characters and their surroundings:

Бытовое движение в конкретном окружении вдруг выводит в широкий мир, во вселенную: подчеркивается одновременно и включенность человека в мировую жизнь (метафизическая укорененность человека в мире), и его экзистенциальная "брошенность" в мир, одиночество, сиротство.
(119)
[The day-to-day movement through the actual surroundings all of a sudden leads into the open, vast world, into cosmos: what is stressed is man's involvement in life on earth (his metaphysical roots on earth) and his simultaneous existential "being cast" into the world, his loneliness, orphancy.]

Indeterminate space seems to correspond to the anonymity of the people who "live" in this elusive setting, or, as Platonov expresses it, who "exist" there. Voščev's encounter of the foundation pit diggers is, e.g., described as follows:

Но спящий лежал замертво [...] - каждый существовал без всякого излишка жизни [...]
Вчерашные спящие живыми стояли над ним [...]
- Ты зачем здесь ходишь и существуешь ? [...]
- Я здесь не существую, - [...] Я только думая здесь [...].
(56)
[But the sleeper lay there like dead [...] - everyone existed without any superfluity of life [...].
Those who had been sleeping the previous night stood over him [...].
- "Why do you come here and exist?" [...]
- "I am not existing here, - [...] "I am only thinking here".]

Platonov's references to time are as vague as his spatial indications. The passing of time in *Kotlovan* is described only indirectly through observations of the changing seasons, in terms of the different appearances of nature. Time is, as it were, merged into space:

В начале осени Вощев почувствовал долготу времени и сидел в жилище, окруженный темнотой усталых вечеров.
(77)
[At the beginning of autumn Voshchev felt the longness of time and sat there in the living quarters, surrounded by the darkness of tired evenings.]

День был мутный, неопределенный, будто время не продолжалось дальше - в такие дни дремлют растения и животные, а люди поминают родителей. Прушевский тихо глядел на всю туманную старость природы....
(81)
[The day was cloudy, indeterminate, just as if the time would not continue much longer - on days like this plants and animals doze, and people recollect their parents. Prushevsky looked quietly upon the entire foggy old age of nature...]

Time is described in similarly vague terms. It also acquires existentialist dimensions when a particular moment becomes a universal happening. This is accompanied by personification (animation) of nature, such as images of "tired evenings", or "the old age of nature".

It is remarkable that spatial and temporal vagueness, and to a certain extent vagueness of action as well, are interwoven with the description of Soviet reality. This specific combination is one of the peculiarities of Platonov's poetics, and one of the most striking and fascinating aspects of his prose. Even though the text does not indicate a specific time, it is possible to locate the occurrences approximately at the end of the 1920-s, or to be even more precise, 1929-30 (the beginning of the collectivisation), a date which corresponds to the period of time during which Platonov wrote *Kotlovan*[10].

2.1 closed and open space

The foundation pit is not only the setting of the first part of *Kotlovan*, it is also the symbol for the socialist theme, the building of a new society, and, more generally, for the utopian theme of the story, the building of the ideal society. What is more, the foundation pit entails a whole cluster of spatial images, of which the house and the town are the most prominent examples. A second type of space, which is active throughout the entire story and which is also very obviously symbolic, already appears in the first paragraphs. The background to the action in *Kotlovan* is dominated by open space, extensive plains and distances.

As Voščev leaves the machine shop (closed space) at the beginning of the story, he experiences the indeterminate infinity of the night, and also a sense of liberation from the unfamiliar distances in front of him:

Вощев захватил свой мешок и отправился в ночь. Вопрошающее небо светило над Вощевым мучительной силой звезд ...
(51)
[...]
..и Вощев очутился в пространстве, где был перед ним лишь горизонт и ощущение ветра в склонившееся лицо.
(52)

[Voshchev picked up his bag and went off into the night. Up above Voshchev the questioning heavens shone with the poignant strength of the stars ....
[...]
and Voshchev found himself out in space, where before him lay only the horizon and the sensation of the wind in his face which was bent forward.]

At the end of the story, he leaves a house again for the sake of the open, free air. Here he makes a deliberate choice for boundless space:

Вощев отворил дверь Оргдома в пространство и узнал желание жить в эту разгороженную даль, где сердце может биться не только от одного холодного воздуха, но и от истинной радости одоления всего смутного вещества земли.
(117)
[Voshchev opened wide the Org-House door and recognized the desire to live away out in that unfenced-in distance, where the heart could beat not only from the cold air but also from the honest gladness of overcoming the whole dull substance of the soil.]

Similar motifs of open space - simply designated as "space"- "пространство" (84, 86, 90, 92), "distance" - "даль"(63, 83, 88), "plain" - "равнина" (58) or even "horizon" - "горизонт" (52, 83) recur throughout the novel. As a consequence, the significance of this type of space for the interpretation of the world-picture in Kotlovan takes on importance, especially against the background of the primary image - the foundation pit itself.

This open, dynamic and unbounded space, which I propose to call *itinerant space*, following Toporov (1982) and Van Baak (1983), contrasts with the enclosed space of the foundation pit. This pit has the potential, and is a kind of prefiguration of the future apartment house, which is a walled-in, closed space par excellence, a typically static archetype, and the central image of *radial space*. These two fundamental ways of perceiving space culturally lie at the basis of two different cultural worldviews, the nomadic worldview on the one hand, and the rural and urban models of the world, with their shared concentric world-view, on the other hand. Each of the two world-views has its own representative archetypes. Radial space - the spatial organisation of sedentary man, of agricultural and subsequently urban society - is connected to the image of the "house", and also to its extention, the "town" or "city". Nomadic man, on the other hand, experiences space primarily in the form of the "road", or possibly, the "steppe" (the desert, the ocean), the archetypes of itinerant space. From the outset, and throughout the novel, this confrontation of two different world-views with their contrasting sets of cultural values - two contrasting evaluations of space - is the central structuring and plot-forming principle. The opposition between itinerant and radial space will serve as a point of departure for all further interpretations of *Kotlovan* in this analysis[11].

2.2 closed, static, concentric space

The construction and setting of houses, like buildings in general, can generate strong ideological and attitudinal connotations.
(Van Baak 1990: 4)[12]

Russian Modernism is without doubt a cultural period which is very sensitive to symbols and archetypes. This is a result of the reactivation of mythological structures in modernist literature (cf. a.o. Meletinskij 1976). One of these images, or archetypes, is, according to

Lotman, "the house", cf. his analysis (1986) of the novel *Master i Margerita* by Michail Bulgakov. In the introductory remarks to this article, Lotman describes how an opposition like, "home - forest", which derives typologcally from the primordial opposition "order - chaos", subsequently evolved via folklore genres such as the fairy-tale and the heroic epos into 19-th and 20-th century literary themes. Van Baak (1983, 1990) discusses the image of the house and its non-spatial connotations of meaning, such as shelter, safety, warmth, comfort, cosiness and food, and correlates it with a sedentary type of culture with its concentrical worldstructure.

The foundation pit, the all-proletarian apartment house and the town are exponents of "sedentary culture". Each of these spatial elements possesses either a closed, enclosed or concentrical structure, features which are typical of the "radial space" of urban societies. The most prominent spatial motive in *Kotlovan*, to which the title also refers, is the foundation pit with its implicit reference to the apartment house for the workmen. Although the house is conspicuous by its absence - at the end of the story the construction work has not even started - it could very well be called the central hero of *Kotlovan*, comparable to Becket's Godot. The house exists only in conversations, plans and dreams of the other characters, who have, each in his own way, set their hopes and their expectations of a better life on it. These projections, among other things, give the story its utopian flavour.

If the foundation pit is the embodiment of these projections, it is also a house "in statu nascendi". On page 85, the pit is referred to as "маточное место" (the English translation would be "the mother excavation", but "mother's lap" would also be appropriate), which derives from the word "матка" [womb] - a clear hint at the symbolic meaning of this place. Eric Naiman (1987) discusses the symbolism of such an "empty space", which he calls "a void with a dual potential" (191) and which, he believes, belongs to the important spatial motifs in Platonov's oeuvre:

> If left unfilled it may become a grave and the pit of Hell. Filled, it becomes a womb symbolizing future paradise and transforms an image of death into one of life.
> (Naiman 1987: 191)

In other words, the foundation pit in *Kotlovan* is a typically ambivalent image, connecting opposite notions such as "digging vs. building" (a downward vs. an upward movement), "house of the living vs. house of the dead" (womb vs tomb). To a certain degree, the pit - with its promise of the dwellinghouse for all - is already associated with notions like "home vs. homelessness"/ "shelter vs. shelterlessness", a famous Platonovian theme, which plays a key role in *Kotlovan* as well. As long as the foundation pit is not complete, the building can not start, and people will be without a home.

The image of the digging workmen, omnipresent in the first part of the story, returns on the last pages. The last act even depicts Čiklin full of grief over the death of Nastja, desperately starting to dig. At first he digs at random, somewhere inside the already existing excavation, an act which irrevocably recalls associations of the pit with death and the grave. But in the end, Čiklin digs a special grave for Nastja, he digs it for 15 hours, in order to make it as deep and protective as possible.

В полдень Чиклин начал копать для Насти специальную могилу. Он рыл ее пятнадцать часов подряд, чтоб она была глубока и в нее не сумел бы проникнуть ни червь, ни корень растения, ни тепло, ни холод, и чтоб ребенка никогда не беспокоил шум жизни с повехности земли.
(120)
[At noon Chiklin began to dig a special grave for Nastya. He dug it fifteen hours in a row so it would be deep and so that neither worms, nor their roots, nor warmth, nor cold would be able to penetrate it, so the child would never ever be troubled by the clamor of life on the earth's surface.]

Here the pit is being transformed into a real grave. In this final passage, the grave takes over the functions of the house as a place of shelter. This fact is stressed by the workers' wish to make the grave as solid and protective as possible. It is more than a grave. Čiklin makes Nastja a house of death.

The association of the pit with death, the tomb and the world underground - the pit left unfilled - recalls of Dostoevskij's novels *Zapiski iz mertvogo doma* [*Notes from the House of Dead*] and *Zapiski iz podpolja* [*Notes from the Underground*]. The latter has an especially strong symbolic potential, cf. Lotman on this subject: "In Dostoevsky the mythological archetype merges with Gogol's tradition: the hero who lives in the 'underground', in coffin-like rooms which are themselves places of death, has to pass through the 'house of the dead' and, 'trampling down death with death', to be reborn and resurrected" (1990: 185). In the case of Platonov, there is no explicit salvation in the Christian sense of the word, but Nastja's name, deriving from Anastasija, which means Resurrection and reminds one of the Risen Lord, hints in the direction of hope. And Platonov's workmen could be regarded as a kind of underworld people - "подпольные люди" - for they live in a constant state of subconsciousness.

Все мастеровые молчали против Вощева: их лица были равнодушны и скучны, редкая, заранее утомленная мысль освещала их терпеливые глаза.
(56)
[All the workmen were silent against Voshchev; their faces were indifferent and bored, and a sparse thought exhausted ahead of time illuminated their long-suffering eyes.]

The house exists preeminently in the expectations of the workmen, who assign the usual values to it, such as shelter and protection. At the same time, however, allusions to death emerge through words like "pokoj" [peace, rest] with its association of "večnyj pokoj" [eternal peace], and "chranit'sja" [to preserve], through which the house is implicitly compared to a coffin. The house, therefore, becomes an extremely ambiguous image in these passages.

Будущий человек найдет себе покой в этом прочном доме.
(58)
Здесь будет дом, в нем будут храниться люди от невзгоды и бросать крошки из окон живущим снаружи птицам.
(61)
[The future human being would find his peace in this firmly built building.]
[Here there would be a building, in it people would be preserved from adversity and would throw crumbs from the windows to the birds living outside.]

In the second quotation, the protective inside world of the house provides not only shelter, but also food, thus gaining the features of a real home (house and hearth), of which the creatures outside, the birds, are deprived. The bird is, as a matter of fact, the animal which symbolizes the state of shelterlessness par excellence. Platonov's world is an inhospitable, barren and desolate place, dominated by hardships, hunger and loneliness. As long as the house is still unbuilt, the workmen are lodged in a barn, where they sleep on the floor, huddled up against each other to stay warm (55, 69). The deserted factory, where Nastja's mother has taken refuge to die in peace, is the most desolate place in the book (75-76). Both locations, the barn and the old factory, are temporary lodgings, transit places, impersonally indicated as "жилище", "помещение", "убежище" [dwelling, accomodation, shelter] and not as a home of lasting value. Only the new elite, most of all the partyboss Paškin, live in real houses. To a certain extent, this also counts for the "intellectual" Pruševskij, but at a certain moment he chooses to sleep with the workmen in order to feel less lonely.

One character in *Kotlovan* is explicitly associated with the interior (domesticated) world of the house-to-be more than any other. The men work for the child Nastja, the embodiment of hope and future, more than for their own sake. They believe that even if they will not live to see the house materialized, the child will. But Nastja does not only symbolize the future society and the virtuality of a better life, she is also a girl, and therefore a representative of the female principle. (She and her mother are the only female characters of interest in *Kotlovan*). Under the influence of psychoanalysis and feminist literary criticism, it has become fashionable to interpret in potential sexual connotations of space, such as the interpretation of closed space as the female principle, representing order, fertility, the womb (darkness, dampness, warmth), but also lack of initiative, inertia, passiveness[13]. This entails, as a logical consequence, the opposite association of the exterior, open and boundless space, of chaos and dynamics, as predominantly male. From this point of view, in this story Nastja would be interpreted as a victim of the destructive (chaotic) male principle. Thus, the male type of space takes on a negative connotation. I reject the "feminist" approach because of its categorical evaluation of space, such as the favourable versus the unfavourable (+ vs. -) view of the male in relation to the female principle. In my opinion, the description of the conflict between the open and the closed models of the world, of sedentary vs. nomadic (static vs. dynamic) world orders does not do justice to the complexity of the story at hand, nor to that of other works of literature in terms of a "male vs. female" antagonism. As far as *Kotlovan* is concerned, such an interpretation is unsatisfactory, because outside space is not at all a negative, let alone a destructive force in this story. On the contrary, open and free space, nature and the cosmos as a whole, can be interpreted not only as valuable, but even as a source of inspiration, as I will demonstrate in the next section.

It is interesting that the type of space under discussion has a distinct concentric shape. The opposition "centre vs. periphery" has an important structurating and meaning generating function. This spatial parameter is known for its organising potential, especially in Creation stories[14] - the so called cosmogonic myths (космогонические мифы). *Kotlovan* is connected to this type of narrative, not only on a structural, but also on a thematic level.

Как пространство, так и время для мифопоэтического сознания не гомогенны. Высшей ценностью (максимум сакральности) обладает та точка в пространстве и времени, где совершился акт творения, т.е. "центр мира" и "в начале", т.е. самое время творения. (Mify, 1982, t. II: 6)

[To the mythopoetic mind, space as well as time are not homogeneous. The highest value in space and in time is accorded to the place where the act of Creation took place, i.e. "the centre of the world" and "in the beginning", i.e. the time of Creation itself.]

Therefore, it is noteworthy that Platonov explicitly situates his town in the middle of the land, "погибший город стоит среди равнины нашей страны" (19) [a doomed city stands in the midst of our country's plain]. In view of the complete anonymity of space in this story, the central position is of crucial importance as a point of orientation. Also other passages underline the mythic dimensions of the town and of its new buildings. In the centre of the town, for example, all sorts of new buildings are erected, which means that the act of creation is located in the middle of the centre, cf.:

Он увидел середину города и строящиеся устройства его [...] Вощев наблюдал строительство неизвестной ему башни.
(55)
[Only now did he see the centre of the city and structures in the process of construction [...] Voshchev watched for a long time the construction of the tower wich was unfamiliar to him.]

The all-proletarian apartment house, on the other hand, is planned for the outskirts of the town (p. 55). This indicates the special (separate) status of this project among the utopian plans which are reviewed in *Kotlovan*. In the eyes of engineer Pruševskij, who is responsible for the design, this apartment house is merely a transitory house. Only the next generation will accomplish the "real" house for all. In other words, his expectations reach higher than those of the simple workers, for he considers the proletarian house merely as a step towards the ultimate house, which takes on mythical-utopian features. It is to be erected in the middle of the earth, and house the workers of all the world:

Через десять или двадцать лет другой инженер построит в середине мира башню, куда войдут на вечное, счастливое поселение трудящиеся всей земли.
(61)
[In ten or twenty years' time another engineer would build a tower at the center of the world into which the workers of the whole world would move for eternal, joyous residence.]

Whereas the town in part I of *Kotlovan* stands in the middle of the country, this tower - башня - will arise in the middle of the earth. With the increasingly utopian dimension, there is also a growing of the mythopoetic content. It is noteworthy that this futuristic building no longer resembles a house, but is specified as a tower, a clear reference to another, well-known megalomaniac building project in human history (or, for that matter, in mythological times), the Tower of Babel. Both images merge on a symbolic level: the Russian Revolution. The building of the all-proletarian house in *Kotlovan*, can be interpreted in a way similar to the Babylonian building of a tower, as a deed of pride, and a "rebellion against God".

According to the mythopoetic worldview, the vertical spatial orientation is another important organizing principle. It is based on the "world tree", which, according to cosmogony, grows in the middle of the earth and joins heaven, the dwelling place of the gods, the earth and the subterranean realm of the dead (Mify 1982, I: 398-406). The houses and towers in *Kotlovan* - the representatives of a new world order - can be regarded as modern descendants (cultural-historical variants, transformations) of this primordial tree. The action of the story (at least in the first part) is a downward movement

- in the direction of the underworld - since it focuses on the digging of a foundation pit. Again this calls up associations with darkness, death and chaos are evoked.

In the second part of *Kotlovan*, the section about the establishment of the collective farm, the opposition of "interior vs. exterior" space plays a role as well, although less prominently than in the urban part of the story.

Вблизи была старая деревня; всеобщая ветхость бедности покрывала ее - и старческие, терпеливые плетни, и придорожные, склонившиеся в тишине деревья, имели одинаковый вид грусти. Во всех избах деревни был свет, но снаружи их никто не находился.
(86)
[Nearby was an old village; the universal decrepitude of poverty was all over it - and the ancient, enduring, wattle fences, and the roadside trees which were bent over in the solitude had an identical appearance of sadness. In all the village cabins there was light, but there was no one outside them.]

The hut, or "izba", is above all, a representative of the old world order. The village makes the woeful impression of total delapidation, not only the huts, but also their owners, who are more dead than alive in their homes. Even nature is in a state of decay (autumn and winter are the seasons accompanying the events in the village). Humans and cattle die in great numbers (a fact that is connected not only to the collectivisation, but also to the famine which struck the country in the same disastrous year 1929-30). In one of the episodes, the workers find a peasant, who, although still alive, has been lying on a table for days. (According to Russian tradition, the body of the deceased was placed on a table until the funeral). Another peasant is found in his own coffin, simply lying in expectation of death (93). Again, references to death and the house of the dead occur. What was once a house for the living has become a house for the dead.

The huts' other connotations depend on the ideological point of view. According to the communists, the old houses are unhygienic breeding places, and also strongholds of bourgeois values, such as family life and private ownership. An important feature of the izba is its enclosure - "огороженный дворовый капитализм" (94) [fenced-off barnyard capitalism]. It was considered preferable fpr the people to leave their homes more frequently:

Активист еще давно пустил устную директиву о соблюдении санитарности в народной жизни, для чего люди должны все время находиться на улице, а не задыхаться в семейных избах.
(90)
[The activist had long since issued an oral directive on the observation of sanitation in the life of the people, for which people were required to be out on the street all the time, and not suffocating in their family huts.]

Since in this episode people have to leave their homes for political reasons, the evaluation of open space is not unequivocal. Again, the ambiguity of Platonov's world comes to the fore. The so-called Organisational Yard, "Организационный двор", is the embodiment of the new worldorder in the village. It is a house which serves many purposes, but not for living. It is also the residence of the activist (the leader of the collective farm). Political meetings are held there, but it also serves as a political prison for the kulaks. This multifunctional building is stripped of all the functions of a real home (protection, hospitality) and, like the foundation pit for the all-proletarian apartment house, it stands at the edge of the collective farm.

Several images of the harshness of the world outside stress the fact that inside-space has lost its protective function. These images of the outside world, however, do not create an impression of hostility. On the contrary, outdoor space seems to take over functions of the home, such as protection and a place of rest:

Снаружи в то время все гуще падал холодный снег; земля от снега стала смирней.
(98)
[Outdoors at this same time the cold snow kept falling ever more densely; the earth itself became the more relaxed as a result of the snow.]

Снег падал на холодную землю, собираясь остаться в зиму; мирный покров застелил на сон грядущий всю видимую землю.
(99)
[The snow was falling upon the cold ground, ready to stay there the whole winter; the peaceful covering was bedding down for sleep the entire visible earth.]

Once more, Platonov confronts the reader with an ambiguous evaluation of space, and therefore with the world as he sees it. In these descriptions of the winter landscape, the outside world is deprived of the impression of shelterlessness. The winter world, on the contrary, creates an intense feeling of security and peace. And it is noteworthy that this new type of emotions does not belong to human beings, but to the earth as a whole. No longer closed, inside space, with its ideological, and socio-historical connotations, space now seems to have no limits or boundaries, like the cosmos itself. This type of space has actually been present from the outset of the story and will be discussed separately in the following section.

2.3 open, dynamic space

On the first page of the story, Voščev leaves the machine shop where he works and goes out into the world. Thus, from the very beginning, the relationship between one of the central characters and the surrounding world is characterized as "being on the road". As he sets out, his goal is uncertain and vague, as obscure as the the truth he seeks.

Вощев не знал, куда его влечет.
(51)
[Voshchev did not know whither he was drawn.]

Вощев захватил мещок и отправился в ночь.
(51)
[Voshchev picked up his bag and went off into the night.]

Его пеший путь лежал среди лета (...) и Вощев очутился в пространстве, где был перед ним лишь горизонт и ощущение ветра в слконившееся лицо.
(52)
[His way afoot lay in the middle of the summer; (...)and Voshchev found himself out in space, where before him lay only the horizon and the sensation of the wind in his face which was bent forward.]

The various descriptions of the landscape again create a rather ambiguous impression of open space. On the one hand, there is the idea of an intimate relation between man and nature, on the other, the feeling of man lost in a void. Levin (1990: 122) draws attention to this peculiarity of space in *Kotlovan*: "Оно (пространство) объединяет все живущее, но одновременно может быть неуютным, чужим, холодным" [It (space) unites all the living, but at the same time it may be cheerless, alien, cold]. This type of space transcends the dimension of pure landscape, or of merely the outdoor setting of the actions of the characters. It is a type of space that represents at once the whole world, the earth, cosmos and in certain cases even life itself:

На выкошенном пустыре пахло умершей травой и сыростью обнаженных мест, отчего яснее чувствовалась общая грусть жизни и тоска тщетности.
(58)
[On the mowed empty lots it smelled of dead grass and the dampness of exposed places, from which the common sadness of life and the melancholy of futility were felt more clearly.]

А отчего, Никит, поле так скучно лежит? Неужели внутри всего света тоска, а только в нас одних пятилетний план?
(68)

[And why is it, Nikit, that the field lies there so bored? Can it really be that inside the whole world there is only longing, that only we alone possess a five year plan?]

Уныло и жарко начинался долгий день. Солнце, как слепота, находилось равнодушно над низовою бедностью земли. Но другого места для жизни не было дано.
(71)
[Wearily and hot began the long day; the sun, like blindness, hung there in place indifferently above the lowly palidness of the earth; but there was no other place alloted to life.]

These and other similar descriptions of the infinite and deserted landscape are either expressions of the emotional bonds between man and nature, the common sadness of life - общая грусть жизни, or they are expressions of man's solitude on earth, it became hostile and desert-like on earth - пустынно и чуждо на свете (90). However, both situations arouse the same kind of feelings. Open space affects the people in it, for it seems to act upon the characters with heavy melancholy feelings. The Russian language expresses this through a rich vocabulary: toska, ravnodušie, skuka and grust' are the dominating emotions. But even nature itself seems full of melancholy and longing, as if nature and humans alike are subjected to one and the same universal principle of life.

In open space, in free nature, the workers seem less limited than in their barracks. Nature seems to hide some of the mysteries of life, but it does not reveal its secrets:

Вощев взял на квартире вещи в мешок и вышел наружу, чтобы на воздухе лучше понять свое будущее. Но воздух был пуст, неподвижные деревья бережно держали жару в листьях, и скучно лежала пыль на безлюдной дороге - в природе было такое положение.
(51)
[Voshchev took his things in a sack from his apartment and went out into the open air, the better to comprehend his future. But the air was empty, the unmoving trees thrifly preserved the heat within their leaves, and the dust lay there bored on the unpopulated roadway - such was the situation in nature.]

Он отошел из середины города на конец его. Пока он двигался туда наступила безлюдная ночь; лишь вода и ветер населяли вдали этот мрак и природу, и одни птицы сумели воспеть грусть этого великого вещества, потому что они летали сверху и им было легче.
(55)
[He left the center of the city for its end. While he moved on an unpopulated night descended; only the water and the wind inhabited this darkness and this nature in the distance, and only the birds were capable of singing the grief of this great substance because they flew above and for them it was easier.]

Он осмотрелся вокруг - всюду над пространством стоял пар живого дыханья, создавая сонную, душную незримость; устало длилось терпенье на свете, точно все живущее находилось где-то посредине времени и своего движения: начало его всеми забыто и конец неизвестен, осталось лишь направление. И Вощев ушел в одну открытую дорогу.
(84)
[He looked about - everywhere over space hung the steam of living breathing, creating a sleepy, choking invisibility; endurance went wearily on and on in the world just as if everything living was somewhere between time and its own movement; its beginning had been forgotten by all and its end was unknown, the only thing remaining was direction. And Voshchev departed down the one open road.]

It is noteworthy that the spatial images in these quotations are clearly connected to ideas about time - the future, the night, beginning and end, (cf. also Levin 1990: 131 ff. on this subject). Time seems mere space in movement - "движение", "направление" [movement, direction]. Time, and in particular its most indeterminate variant, eternity, is an obstacle on Voščev's road to happiness and ultimate knowledge:

Вощев, опершись о гробы спиной, глядел с телеги вверх - на звездное собрание и в мертвую массовую муть Млечного Пути. Он ожидал , когда же там будет вынесена резолюция о прекращении вечности времени, об искуплении томительности жизни.
(86)
[Voshchev, leaning back against a coffin, looked up from the cart to the dead mass of the mist of the Milky Way. He was waiting for the day when up there a resolution would be promulgated on the cessation of the eternity of time, on atonement for the weariness of life.]

This preoccupation with the phenomenon of time as a reality of our planet and a fact of life, and also as the eternal counterpart of space, is connected to the central theme of the story, the theme of utopianism. Images of open space, the void as well as the free space are full of expectation, contemplation, waiting, abeyance. It would be erroneous to understand these notions as static images, for this type of space is also full of movement. This is the result of the image of the road, the central structurating element of open space. The road is the motor of open space, which I therefore propose to call dynamic space. Finally, all these ideas relate to the theme of utopia, a theme which directs all attention towards the distant horizon and future itself.

Whereas static society, with its emphasis on closed spatial structures, projects its utopian expectations on a nonexistent, but ever so concrete and pragmatic, apartment house, the utopian idea of open space is immaterial. It possesses not only an ideological, but also a philosophical dimension. Voščev's quest, his search for truth goes far beyond the workmen's dream. His irrational longing for knowledge and answers is timeless, it is a recognizable mental activity, even a spiritual necessity of the human mind. The pursuit of this dream is set in open space, on the open road, in an abstract and empty landscape - the literal meaning of utopia is "no-place" - that is sometimes as indeterminate as the substance of the ideal.

The motifs of nature in *Kotlovan* have several functions. In the first place, nature is one of the correlates in the ideological and cultural antagonism between culture and nature. This is one of the thematic lines which elaborates the opposition between the nomadic world-view (itinerant, open space) and the sedentary world-view (radial space, the town, the house). From the sedentary point of view, man is the master of the earth on which he has imposed his will. The episodes about the construction of the house, seen mainly through the eyes of the architect (pp.55 and 58) exemplify this idea best. But man as an integral part of Creation, an entirely different idea, turns out to be of equal importance in the thematic constellation of *Kotlovan*. There is a constant interaction between man and the world that surrounds him. Images of open space, nature and cosmos seem the most appropriate means to express this idea. Moreover, on close reading, one will find certain spatial elements emerge with which the characters (and narrator) seem to identify themselves in a special way. Such recurrent images are, among other things, the birds, the stars, the wind, the sun, emptiness, smoke, steam, fog. Two of these images are of particular importance in connection with Voščev and with the type of space and world-view he represents: the images of the birds and the wind, images which are, in themselves, not unequivocal. For example, in the following quotation the words "грусть" [grief], and "расставание" [departure] are used, and the birds are also clearly associated with death. The images of the wind and the birds not only symbolize his wandering and his shelterlessness, but also his freedom and independence, his unknown origin and his movement without a clear goal.

Лишь вода и ветер населяли этот мрак и природу, и одни птицы сумели воспеть грусть этого великого вещества, потому что они летали сверху и им было легче.
(55)
[Only the water and the wind inhabited this darkness and this nature in the distance, and only the birds were capable of singing of the grief of this great substance because they flew above and for them it was easier.]

На том месте собрались грачи для отлета в теплую даль, хотя время их расставания со здешней землей еще не наступало. Еще ранее отлета грачей Елисей видел исчезновение ласточек, и тогда он хотел было стать легким, малосознательным телом птицы, но теперь он уже не думал, чтобы обратиться в грача, потому что думать не мог.
(88)
[On that place the rooks had assembled in order to migrate to warm faraway lands, even though it was not yet the right time for their departure for the land hereabout. Even before the departure of the rooks Yelisei had seen the swallows disappear, and at that time he had wanted to turn into the light, untroubled body of a bird, but now he no longer thought about becoming a rook, because now he no longer could think.]

The image of the stars in the sky stresses the immensity of the firmament and man's smallness in its face. Images of emptiness inspire both freedom and cosmic fear:

Велика и прохладна была ночь над ним, бескорыстно светили звезды над снежной чистотою земли, и широко раздавались удары молотобойца, точно медведь застыдился спать под этими ожидающими звездами и отвечал им чем мог.
(109)

[Great and chill was the night above him, the stars shone down unselfishly upon the snowy cleanliness of the earth, and the striker-bear's blows resounded widely, just as if he were ashamed of sleeping beneath these expectant stars, and was replying to them the only way he could.]

Снежный ветер утих; неясная луна выявилась на дальнем небе, порожненном от вихрей и туч, на небе, которое было так пустынно, что допускало вечную свободу, и так жутко, что для свободы нужна была дружба.
(106)
[The snowy wind fell quiet; the dim moon appeared on the distant sky, made empty by the stormwind and the clouds - on a sky which was so deserted it could envision eternal freedom and which at the same time was so terrible that for freedom friendship was necessary.]

Platonov's message seems to be that the only remedy against cosmic loneliness is the deserted sky and human warmth. Friendship is the answer to human melancholy and to the sufferings of the whole universe and is represented by the selfless stars.

The typical Platonovian theme of shelterlessness and the idea of man cast into the world, "мысль бесприютности людей, брошенности их в мире", is used to describe both types of space, although its function and importance differs for each of them. From the point of view of sedentary culture, it is most tragic to be without a home. A homeless person is deprived of the most valuable thing in the world, and unprotected against the hostile, dangerous outside world, he is actually lost. According to the nomadic way of life and perception of the world and space in particular, a person is the better off without a home. The positive evaluation of "shelterlessness" represents a more favourable interpretation, such as "escape", "independence", and "liberty". Houses and other material belongings are seen as mere ballast, hindering movement and travelling. After all, in *Kotlovan*, none of the characters possess a real home. In the end not a single character acquires a home, because the apartment house is not completed. The condition of man "cast into the world" is thus maintained as the ultimate existential condition of man in *Kotlovan*. This idea could even be regarded as the connecting link between the two worldviews at hand - as a universal "condition humaine". The people on this earth are deprived of a home, for they have nowhere to go, no refuge. The effect of this condition differs from person to person. The weak suffer the most - the child Nastja perishes from cold and deprivation. The vagabond-type Voščev, on the other hand, seems to suffocate mentally in interior space. He needs to be out in the open, on the free and endless road, feeling one with the wind and the stars, in order to fullfil his vocation of a seeker of the truth.

In the second part, the tale of the collective farm, there are several descriptions of open space, among them the following strikingly elegiac memories of an old peasant:

Его тоскливому уму представлялась деревня во ржи, и над нею носился ветер и тихо крутил деревянную мельницу, размалывающую насущный, мирный хлеб. Он жил так в недавнее время, чувствуя сытость в желудке и семейное счастье в душе; и сколько годов он ни смотрел из деревни вдаль и в будущее, он видел на конце равнины лишь слияние неба с землею, а над собою имел достаточный свет солнца и звезд.
(80)

[His homesick mind would picture the village all in rye with a wind blowing over the fields quietly and turning the wooden windmill grinding the peaceful grain for the daily bread. He had been living like that just a short time before, with the feeling of fullness in his stomach and family happiness in his soul; and no matter for how many years he had looked from out of the village into the distance and the future, he had seen at the end of the plain only the merging of heaven and earth, and up above he had had sufficient sunlight and stars.]

Without the faintest irony, the peasant sings the praise of old-fashioned ideals, of family life and satiation (famine and torn apart families were everyday reality in 1929-30). These values, however, are not associated with the closed space of a home, but with images of freedom, wind, distances, the sun and the stars. Instead of the pursuit of utopian dreams, he proposes life in peace and harmony with nature. This alternative culminates in the picture of the merging of heaven and earth, from which all oppositions (as the source of restlessness and discord) have disappeared. For a moment the narrator creates the illusion of the "pre-utopian", Arcadian way of life, the human situation before man started to ask questions and was therefore expelled from Paradise and sentenced to eternal restless wandering over the Earth.

In sum, the dynamic, open type of space is not structured as clearly as the concentrically ordered space of sedentary culture. The most prominent feature of boundless space is probably the lack of distinct parameters - "its beginning had been forgotten by all and its end was unknown". Space and time are both indeterminate, infinite and eternal. This accounts for the impression of vagueness out in the open, and for the fact that orientation is difficult in this type of space. This also explains Voščev's uncertain path with its blurred goal. Endless space and time are a heavy burden for man "cast into the world", but his burning questions leave him no alternative.

3.0 "static versus dynamic" utopia

The two world-views (the two types of culture) do not only represent two completely different ways of organizing and evaluating space, but the utopian dreams associated with them are also heterogeneous. According to the typology of the two world-views, I propose to speak about a static and a dynamic utopia, with the engineer Pruševskij and the hero Voščev as their respective representatives. The minds of these two "central" characters, the labourer and the architect, filter a number of important events, and also a number of impressions of the space that surrounds them. In the end, however, Voščev remains the sole true hero of the story, for his utopia is the more fundamental one of the two.

3.1 static utopia

Besides the ideal of the all-proletarian apartment house, there is a second spatially concentrical and closed utopia, a utopia with apocalyptical dimensions[15]. While he is on one of his walks, Pruševskij, who has a special relation with utopian plans and buildings because he is the project's designer, notices a marvelous city on the horizon:

В свои прогулки он уходил далеко, в одиночестве. Однажды он остановисля на холме, в стороне от города и дороги. День был мутный, неопределенный, будто время не продолжалось дальше - в такие дни дремлют растения и животные, а люди поминают родителей. Прушевский тихо глядел на всю туманную старость природы и видел на конце ее белые спокойные здания, светящиеся больше, чем было света в воздухе. Он не знал имени тому законченному строительству и назначению его, хотя можно было понять, что те дальние здания устроены не только для пользы, но и для радости. Прушевский с удивлением привыкшего к печали человека наблюдал точную нежность и охлажденную, сомкнутую силу отдаленных монументов. Он еще не видел такой веры и свободы в сложенных камнях и не знал самосветящегося закона для серого цвета своей родины. Как остров, стоял среди остального новостроящегося мира этот белый сюжет сооружений и успокоенно светился. Но не все было бело в тех зданиях - в иных местах они имели синий, желтый и зеленый цвета, что придавало им нарочную красоту детского изображения. «Когда же это выстроено?» - с огорчением сказал Прушевский. Ему уютней было чувствовать скорбь на земной потухшей звезде; чужое и дальнее счастье возбуждало в нем стыд и тревогу - он бы хотел, не сознавая, чтобы вечно строящийся и недостроенный мир был похож на его разрушенную жизнь.

Он еще раз пристально посмотрел на тот новый город, не желая ни забыть его, ни ошибиться, но здания стояли по-прежнему ясными, точно вокруг них была не муть родного воздуха, а прохладная прозрачность.

(81)

[On his walks he used to go far, all by himself. Once he stopped on a hill, off to the side from the city and highway. The day was cloudy, indeterminate, just as if the time would not continue much longer - on days like this plants and animals doze, and people recollect their parents. Prushevsky looked quietly upon the entire foggy old age of nature and saw at its end white peaceful buildings, shining more brightly than there was light in the air. He did not know the name of this completed construction nor its purpose, though one could understand that those distant buildings were built not merely for use, but also for gladness. Prushevsky, who had become accustomed, to his astonishment, to the sadness of man, observed the precise tenderness and the cool contained strength of the distant monuments. He had never yet seen such faith and freedom embodied in masonry and was unfamiliar with the law of incandescence of the gray color of his motherland. Like an island this white vision of buildings stood there in the midst of the rest of the newly building world gleaming peacefully. But not everything was white in those buildings - in other places they had dark blue, yellow and green color which gave them the intentional beauty of a child's portrayal. "When was this built?" Prushevsky asked with chagrin. For him it was more comfortable to feel grief on this earthly, extinguished star; alien and distant happiness aroused shame and alarm in him. He would have wished, without admitting it, for the eternal building and never ever completed world to be like his own demolished life.

He looked fixedly upon this new city once more, wishing neither to forget it, nor to be mistaken, but the buildings stood there just as clear as before, just as if around them there had been not the fogginess of the native air but instead cool transparency.]

In this fascinating fragment, the all-proletarian apartment house is unmasked as a mere fake-utopia. The white city is an alternative to the socialist idea of the commune, and is veiled in Christian symbols[16]. The image of this white, luminous and radiant city recalls the biblical New Jerusalem from the Apocalypse, which stands out from earthly cities by its heavenly gleam. The allusion to the New Jerusalem brings to mind the association of the apartment house (and the socialist experiment as a whole) with the construction of the Tower of Babel: in the Revelations of John the building of the "New Jerusalem" is preceded by the "Downfall of Babylon".

Pruševskij compares the white city to an alien and distant island, which lends it utopian features as well. Traditionally, ideal societies were located on an island, or in other isolated places, like a distant planet or a country surrounded by walls, in order to guarantee the continuity of utopia and to protect them against influences from the outside which would cause changes, and risk the end of the perfect system[17].

Pruševskij notices that the distant buildings are not only there for practical reasons, and this could be understood as an indirect criticism of the socialist principle of utility. These edifices possess a kind of additional value, for they seem to promise joy, however, a joy that is not of this world and not accessible to him. In this imperfect and incomplete world (symbolized by the unbuilt apartment house, and the reference to Pruševskij's ruined life), this city is a model of completeness.

There is another remarkable detail about this image. The ideal city is not situated in a vague and distant future, but in the present reality, and the view is even crystalclear, in spite of the fog. The last line removes any doubt that this could be a vision or fata morgana. It is manifest, here and now reality, although, paradoxically, it seems impossible to reach, it is like an island, and it is alien. Furthermore, the white city is a manifestation of enclosed, concentrical space, but set explicitly in open space. Free nature is described as cloudy, even as an "indeterminate" day. Thus, two types of space seem to merge during the "vision", or at least the opposition between an open and a closed structure of the world is temporarily abolished. Could it be that the "faith and freedom" of the distant monuments is an embodiment of the "truth", of the dynamic utopia which Voščev pursues?

3.2 dynamic Utopia

Voščev leads the life of a drifter. Constantly on the move, he hopes to find peace at heart, for his soul is troubled by many unanswered questions. He is a "странник" - an idealistic Russian wanderer[18], and although the motives of the road, the distance and the horizon, characterize him throughout the story, he does not at all know were he is going, he just follows the road, and his goal is uncertain. According to Lotman's categories (1968: 10 ff.), Voščev can be classified as a "hero of the steppe" rather than as a "hero of the road", although the traditional psychological categories do not seem to apply well to Platonov's heroes. Voščev, for example, is neither crossing insurmountable boundaries, nor is there any real "growth of knowledge". The key to Voščev's quest seems to lie in the word "сущность" - the essence of things/life. All the other characters, including the central hero, raise fundamental issues, "ultimate questions", questions one would sooner expect of a philosopher or scholar than of simple workmen:

> Но вскоре он почувствовал сомнение в своей жизни и слабость тела без истины, он не мог дальше трудиться и ступать по дороге, не зная точного устройства всего мира и того, куда надо стремиться.
> (53)
> [He felt doubt in his life and weakness of the body without truth; he could not go on working and keep taking step after step down the road without knowing the precise arrangement of the whole world and whither one must strive.]

Now and then (83-84, 90, 119), the narrator makes ironic allusions to the socialist doctrine when describing Voščev's thoughts and feelings. But it is always clear that he seeks a higher truth than the Bolsheviks have to offer. At a certain point he realizes that no good will come from the foundation pit diggers. Disappointed, he decides to leave and lead the life of a simple man:

- Говорили, что все на свете знаете, - сказал Вощев, - а сами только землю роете и спите! Лучше я от вас уйду - буду ходить по колхозам побираться: все равно мне без истины стыдно жить.
(69)
["You said that you knew everything in the world", said Voshchev, "and for a fact all you do is dig in the earth and sleep! I would do better to leave you: I will go and wander about collective farms; for no matter what without truth I am ashamed to live".]

Thus, Voščev becomes a distant relative of the Romantic hero, who refuses to comply with the masses, and who prefers solitude. This is also the theme of the conflict between the individual and the group. In *Kotlovan*, it also stands for the conflict between privacy and the collective way of life in the commune of the all-proletarian apartment house, a way of life which became all too real in the entire socialist world's communal flats.

At the beginning of the story, Voščev is, as it were, expelled from the collective (the place where he was making a living), but on several occasions he apparently prefers leaving rather than staying. He is, almost unwillingly (cf. the references to his mechanical behaviour), attracted by the distant, unknown horizon:

Один Вощев стоял слабым и безрадостным, механически наблюдая даль; [...]
Отдалившись несколько, Вощев тихим шагом скрылся в поле и там прилег [...]
Позже он нашел след гробов, увлеченных двумя мужиками за горизонт в свой край [...] Быть может, там была тишина дворовых теплых мест или стояло на ветру дорог бедняцкое колхозное сиротство с кучей мертвого инвентаря посреди. Вощев пошел туда походкой механически выбывшего человека.
(83)
[Only Voshchev stood there weak and cheerless among them, staring mechanically off into the distance; [...]
Going off away by himself Voshchev, with slow steps, he disappeared out in the open field [...]
Later on he found the trail of the coffins which had been hauled by the two peasants over the horizon to their own country [...] Perhaps there existed there the quiet of warm farmyard places, or perhaps there was to be found there in the wind of the roads the collective farm orphanhood of

the poor peasants with a pile of dead inventory in the middle. Voshchev proceeded on his way there at the pace of a person automatically detached.]

The organizing parameter of this bipartitioned world is the opposition between "proximity - distance", or simply "here - there". In *Kotlovan* time is structured similarly, according to the opposition "proximity - distance", cf.:

По вечерам Вощев лежал с открытыми глазами и тосковал о будущем, когда все станет общеизвестным и помещенным в скупое чувство счастья.
(74)
[Evenings Voshchev lay there with open eyes and longed for a future when everything would become universally known and a place would be found for it in the meager feeling of happiness.]

Voščev's ideal is inaccessible, neither in space nor in time, and its essence is unknown. In spite of this, he goes on searching for it. This is why I propose to designate this ideal, this dream, as a dynamic utopia, as opposed to the static concept of the house. This utopia is dynamic because of the archetype of the road, the path man must walk in order to reach his goal in life. But this utopia is also dynamic by itself, for it refuses to be caught in words, it can only be grasped by "intuition". Its essence is illusive, maybe even an illusion, as all utopias ultimately are.

ᐧThe spatial structure of *Kotlovan* contains conflicting world-views on two levels. In the first place, there is a dualistic world-view which results from the utopian theme. The world of today, in appearance as well as in organisation, is imperfect and opposed to either an ideal future society or an idyllic past. There is also a typological opposition "svoj - čužoj" on the ideological level, where a collision takes place between ideal and reality, and between dream and deed. Simultaneously, a second typological conflict is embodied in the clash between the sedentary and the nomadic way of life, with their contrasting evaluations of space. Platonov describes the confrontation of these two cultures, and their different interpretations of utopia. This collision has a different result for each of them. The socialist ideal collapses with the burial of Nastja, when the pit - the potential paradise - becomes a tomb. In *Kotlovan*, Platonov demonstrates the defeat of one utopia and the indecisive outcome of the other. But even though Voščev does not find his answers, his search for the truth continues. The existential utopia survives.

From the point of view of literary evolution and the concomitant shifting functions of the narrative blocks, space gains unprecedented importance in this modernist story. It dominates the strucure of the text on several levels. On the stylistic level, Platonov's language is permeated by spatial images and expressions. On the thematic level, spatial language reveals the existentialist problems which Platonov discusses. In the person of Voščev, man finds himself alone with Creation and the Cosmos. Space's archetypical dimension is clearly revealed in the central image of the House. To a certain extent the House even plays the role of literary hero. Furthermore, the category of action is suppressed in favour of descriptions and, to a certain extent, substituted by a sequence of fragmented narrative situations. This is a clear case of dominance of spatial language, and typical of modern art. On the symbolic level, space as such dominates through recurrent images and leitmotifs. The majority is of spatial nature.

As a result of spatial language loaded with archaic images and mythological motives, Platonov's story transcends the level of Soviet-reality, and ultimately rests on a higher, more universal level of meaning. This explains the lasting fascination of this distressing novel.

NOTES

1. Eric Naiman calls Čevengur "the ultimate symbolic novel". "Episodes of the plot are motivated by concerns not of character development but of symbolic progression" (1987: 205).

2. D.M.Bethea who makes a distinction between Apokalypse and utopia in *The Shape of Apocalypse in Modern Russian Fiction*, cf. his Preface: "The important difference between 'apocalypse' and 'utopia', between a divinely inspired conclusion to history leading to an atemporal ideal (the New Jerusalem) and a humanely engineered conclusion to history leading to a secular paradise (one model being the classless society), becomes an issue only in the work of Platonov" (XVI).

3. I admit that this is a rather unconventional usage of the term "utopia", which traditionally refers to more or less concrete designs for the ideal organization of future society, often in combination with semi-scientific and pseudo-religious pretentions. I have taken the liberty to apply the word "utopia" to an all but specific plan, but to a mere "idea", taking into consideration that eventually all real utopias share a general pretention of possessing the monopoly on wisdom and truth, and an answer to all the questions of life, which would guarantee happiness and freedom for all. This ideological aspect of utopias generally makes up the essence of Voščev's quest, which I have therefore chosen to designate as "utopia".

4. Quotation according to the edition of "Kotlovan" in *Novyj mir*, 6, 1987. All subsequent page numbers refer to this edition.

5. Andrei Platonov *The Foundation Pit, Kotlovan*, a bi-lingual edition, English translation by Thomas P.Whitney, Ann Arbor 1973.

6. Secondary literature on "Kotlovan" has repeatedly noted the symbolic meaning of the name Anastasija (of which Nastja is a diminutive) - resurrection - in connection with the workmen's hope for a better and more dignified existence. A. Aleksandrov's interpretation of the character Nastja and her mother is also of interest in this respect. According to his reading, the mother is the symbol of old (holy) Russia, now dying, abandoned and forgotten by all. The daughter symbolizes the new, Soviet Russia, but the harshness and brutality of the new way of life is too much for her, cf. Aleksandrov, 1977: 140.

7. There are several, even contradictory interpretations of the end of "Kotlovan". Some critics even regard it as a positive ending, since the workmen continue digging, which implies that they are still hoping, cf. i.a. E.Markšteijn, 1980: 268-9.

8. "Most stories about utopian dreams and journeys finish in the same bed, the same circle of listeners, the same port or aerodrome where they started", Striedter 1983: 195-6. This device serves as a narrative motivation for the description of a utopia.

9. Cf. E.Markštejn (1980: 263): "Платонов мыслит образами, он нанизывает образы и мотивы, не заинтриговывая читателя фабулой, а как бы доверяя ему умственно расшифровывать их". [Platonov's way of thought is in images, he applies layer upon layer of images and motives, not bothering the reader with the intrigue of fabula, but entrusting him with the mental deciphering of those images.]

10. Basing himself on certain notorious details from the political history of the country, Michail Geller locates the events in "Kotlovan" precisely between December 27th 1929, the day Stalin issued his decree on the liquidation of the kulaks, and March 2nd 1930, when Stalin's famous article "Golovokruženie ot uspechov" ["Dizzy with successes"] appeared, (Geller 1982: 253).

11. This can also be understood in the light of the development of the utopian genre: "The utopian novel as a genre in its variety and tradition always combined the description of strictly organized, more or less static societies in isolated "cities" (Polis, Metropolis, Cosmopolis) with more or less fantastic and adventurous, dynamic "journeys". What changed historically was the growing emphasis on the second, more dynamic

aspect. The description of utopia became a journey to and through utopia" (Striedter, 1983: 189).

12. This pilotstudy, entitled "The House in Russian Avantgarde Prose: Chronotope and Archetype", inspired and stimulated some of my ideas on the house-motive in *Kotlovan*.

13. Cf. Teresa de Lauretis' criticism of Lotman's 1979 article "The Origin of the Plot in the Light of Typology" in her 1984 article "Desire in Narrative".

14. Van Baak (1990: 2-3) points out the correlation between the house motif in Russian avantgarde prose and cosmogony, cf. also: Mify, 1982, II: 6-9.

15. "Platonov represents the collision of the Christian apocalyptic and Marxist utopian models of meaning", Bethea 1989: 147.

16. Aleksandrov 1977 gives an interesting interpretation of this episode. He believes that Platonov is actually describing cathedrals. The Aesopian language was needed for reasons of censorship (Aleksandrov, 1977: 143).

17. The city Pruševskij witnessess also resembles another utopian dream from Russian literature. In Černyševskij's socialist novel *Čto delat'?* [*What is to be done?*], Vera Pavlovna has several utopian dreams one of which refers to a magnificent city with immense buildings made of aluminium, described as a place of prosperity and happiness for all who live there.

18. "Platonov's hero is typically a wanderer and an orphan, whose quest is to find his homeland (rodina) or to create a new one" (E.Naiman, 1987: 190-1). Bethea speaks of "дураки, the simple folk and peripatetic visionaries who are the post-1917 equivalet of the traditional Russian truth-seeker (странник) and fool-in-Christ (юродивый)" (Bethea, 1989: 158).

Part III

Conclusions

1.0 literary space

The dual principle of continuity and change, which characterises the literary system throughout its historical and artistic development, is also an important feature of literary space. In the course of the present study, I have designated these two poles as an occurence of archetypes on the one hand, and semiotisation based on interpretation on the other. In my opinion, the expression and function of space is based on these two pillars.

The question raised at the beginning of this thesis, whether the way in which literary space conveys meaning, by modelling world pictures, undergoes functional changes throughout literary evolution, must therefore be answered in twofold.

An integration of the semiotic theories on literary space and the thinking about literary evolution according to Formalist tradition contributes to a better understanding of the function of this narrative category in texts which belong to different periods of literary history.

Although archetypes are not exclusively of a spatial nature (the categories of the hero and the plot can also be archetypes or archetypical situations: good vs. evil, poor man vs. rich man, the falling in love, murder, birth and death of the hero etc.) the narrative category of space seems to have a special link with the literary past. But semiosis, a process to a great extent dependent on the cultural context of author, reader and work of art, remains ambivalent.

The, so-called, constant elements may be devided into two categories: a) archetypes, i.e. literary motifs with a more or less standard meaning, unmodified throughout cultural and literary evolution; b) spatial oppositions, the indispensable, and immutable structural elements with which literature models the world. However, the semantisation and interpretation of these spatial oppositions does change. They vary from one period to the next, but also, within the same period, from one work or author to the other. In the same way, the function of space varies synchronically as well as diachronically. The significance of space among the narrative categories may range from total triviality to a means of expression of primary importance.

2.0 spatial invariants

In all the texts that have been analysed, disregarding the period to which they belong, I have encountered ancient, primordial images of space and achronic categories of thought, spatial images whose meaning is rooted in the mythopoetic tradition (Toporov). Such recurrent, permanent literary motifs seem to have a more or less stable significance throughout cultural and literary history. Various scholars have focused on this characteristic aspect of literature.

157

Vladimir Propp, in his book *Istoričeskie korni volšebnoj skazki* [The historical roots of the fairy-tale] [1986 (1946)], establishes links between traditional fairy-tale motifs and structures and historical reality, notably their relation to much older cultural traditions, such as the ritual, initiation rites and the cult of the dead. Archaic motifs, among which spatial images such as the journey or quest of the hero, or the crossing of a boundary, may reappear in modern literature and may be recognised as modern offsprings of this folklore genre. By pointing out the chronotopical aspect of literature, which involves primarily the time-space category of the text, Michail Bachtin drew special attention to the stable properties of this form of literary expression.

Lotman also has repeatedly paid attention to what he calls the reactivation of mythological images in modern literature. Smirnov (1977) designates these spatial images as achronic forms of thought which each stylistic period and each individual writer transforms into actual narrative categories.

However, it is the merit of Toporov in particular to have established links between modern literature and the picture of the world according to mythological (pre-scientific) thinking. For instance, in his extremely detailed analysis of Dostoevskij's novel *Crime and Punishment* (1973) he reveals the archaic structures of the text. As Toporov demonstrates in his analysis, such schemes appear to function in modern literature on various levels. They may affect the categories of time and space, causality, or the use of numbers. Furthermore, Toporov's contributions to the encyclopedia of mythology (*Mify narodov mira*) (1982) provides information which is valuable for the analysis of modern literature as well.

During the symbolist and modernist periods, there is a clear preference for this kind of images, whereas Romanticists as well as Realists draw from the arsenal of archaic motifs on a more modest scale. This may be related to the growing importance of the function of space as a narrative category towards the end of Realism.

Archetypes can be regarded as visualisations of subconscious images of the mind, as the concretisation of processes that are themselves more or less abstract. They have similar functions whenever and wherever they occur in a work of literature, as the representatives of individual or collective reflections of hope, fear, promise, prohibition, shelter or threat, etc. In this respect, the meaning of archetypes such as the wood, the river, the border, the house, or the mountaintop is stable and universal, and always understood by intuition. This does not imply, however, that all spatial motifs can automatically be considered as archetypes. This is only the case when they have a modelling function, thereby contributing to the establishment of the world-picture of a text. On other occasions, a location or setting may have the single function of providing the background for the narrative, without topological and other abstract (non-spatial) connotations. This is especially the case in Realism, such as the forest in many of Turgenev's hunter's stories, or the park in *Oblomov*, or the houses in Tolstoj's *Anna Karenina*.

The second element responsible for the literary continuity of spatial aspects, are spatial oppositions. The orientational parameters are the permanent elements of the spatial structure of literary texts from all periods. Verticality, horizontality, proximity, distance, interiority, exteriority, crossing, centrality, height and depth, etc. are the dimensions with which each writer models the world and conveys meaning by transforming them into concrete spatial relations in an actual work of art. The oppositions as such, however, are stable and universal.

2.1 Mcyri

The "generality" of the location and the "abstractness" of the setting in "Mcyri" (the wood and the river are unnamed), take on archetypical features, as does the whole landscape. The world outside, Nature, may be identified as Paradise itself, as the Garden of Eden. The description of the dark wood in terms of an enchanted, frightening, forest - "večnyj les", described as "animated" space (a thousand eyes - animation of course typical of the romantic description of the landscape), suggests archetypicity of this location. It is the personification of all the subconscious fears of the hero. Like the forest in the fairy-tale, the wood is impenetrable. But, unlike the fairy-tale hero, the mcyri is unable to cross this archetypical boundary in order to reach his goal, the "wuthering heigths" of the Caucasus, which represents the hero's aspirations for higher things.

2.2 Nevskij prospekt

In "Nevskij prospekt" the archetypical features of literary space are found first of all in the images of "unclean", threatening, space. A "demonic" interpretation of specific regions, or parts of the earth, is a typical feature of mythopoetic space - the north in the case of this story is seen as a realm of evil spirits, identified with the land of the dead (Meletinskij). In my analysis, I have proposed to interpret the strange "behaviour" of certain locations, during certain hours of the day, from this perspective. The role of the stairs which lead one of the heroes to the dwelling of his beloved, may to a certain extent be understood as akin to the image of the ladder, referring to a vertical spatial orientation, in which a link is established between the realm of the gods and the dwelling of man, as an archetypical opposition between heaven and earth.

2.3 Oblomov

In *Oblomov*, the strong impact of myth and mythological thinking on the hero's behaviour is primarily brought about in the form of what I have called the Oblomovka-myth. This Oblomovka resembles Arcadia. However, all sorts of taboo-locations - typical of the mythopoetic spatial structure - such as the forest and swamp, where space merges with danger and fear, may be found there too. The way the central hero experiences the world, the way in which he faces the surrounding world (important modelling opposition: "inside - outside") is determined by the worldview typical of archaic societies. Myth, and its specific spatial structures, exercise strong psychological power over the central character of this novel. The kinship between "byt" (day-to-day reality) and myth is embodied in the "bytovoe prostranstvo" of Oblomovka, Oblomov's room on Gorochovaja street and subsequently in the house of the widow. These locations and their specific meaning in the story may be seen as offsprings of mythopoetic space. Furthermore, the image of the river has obvious archetypical features and a mythological border-function. This image occurs twice, in the world-structure of the inhabitants of Oblomovka and in Oblomov's own perception of the surrounding world, when he loses the ability to travel into town.

2.4 V tolpe

In "V tolpe", the depiction of chaos is closely aligned with the mythopoetic concept of space and spatial organisation. A central issue in this story is the description of the disintegration of all values, the regression from order back to chaos. In order to generate the apocalyptic mood of his story - and to enable "universal", "general", "existential" interpretation of events - Sologub makes use of archaic images such as the sun, the dragon, the labyrinth, to describe a struggle between the powers of light and darkness, in itself a prominent archetypical theme, for which the key-opposition between heaven and hell - top and bottom - is a crucial one.

2.5 Kotlovan

The utopian picture of the world in *Kotlovan* can to a certain extent be called the mythological antipode of the idyll. The use of archetypical images (the town, the house, the tower) and abstract spatial oppositions "centre - periphery" gives the story its existentialist dimension, and is therefore crucial for the creation of meaning in this story. Cosmogonic myths lie at the basis of this (anti-)utopia, and consequently the spatial oppositions "centre - periphery" and "heaven - earth - underground world" are of importance. Apart from the archetypical horizontal and vertical structuration of space in *Kotlovan* the novel is an outstanding example of a story in which the archetypical opposition between "radial" and "itinerant" space is effectuated.

3.0 ambivalence of meaning

Die Ambivalenz der Semiose ist das Wertkorrelat der Sinnfreiheit. Wo der Zeichenprozesz werthaft eindeutig festgelegt wird, geht auch die Freiheit der Interpretation verloren. Wo aber das Zeichengeschehen in seinem Wert völlig unbestimmt bleibt, läszt es die Sinnanarchie nicht zur Ausbildung einer prägnanten Sinnstruktur kommen.
(Grübel 1982: 119)

The second basic feature of the literary text is the shifting evaluative connotation of spatial parameters. Lotman repeatedly pointed out the relative nature of the interpretation of spatial oppositions, which results from the connection between this interpretation, or evaluation, and the typology of the culture. To this I would like to add that the interpretation also depends on the point of view of the narrator and characters within the text. Therefore, similar spatial structures may differ strongly in meaning, and may carry different, even opposite messages according to the context. To avoid arbitrary interpretations, a logical and consistent method of analysis is necessary. An important feature of such an analysis is the systematic discussion of the topological oppositions in the text, taking into account subtle distinctions of point of view.

3.1 Mcyri

The structure of space in "Mcyri" is characterised by the complexity of the Caucasus-location in Russian romantic literature. Furthermore, the interpretation of the typical romantic opposition "svoj - čužoj", and "I - the other", depends on the point of view of the focalisator in question, be it the hero, narrator, or cultural context (contemporary readers, or the anonymous moral authory represented in the epigraph). Moreover, this point of view tends to module. The ambivalent attitude towards notions as "freedom vs. confinement" is inherent to the complexity and ambiguity of the Caucasus in Russian romantic perception. The contrasting world-views of the two cultural systems that are being juxtaposed in "Mcyri" and the ensuing contrasting organisations of space, a closed monastic society and the free space of the mountaintribes, are differently evaluated. And the evaluation of the key-oppositions "inside - outside" and "high - low" shift in the course of the narration, which is in accordance with the psychological development of the mcyri.

3.2 Nevskij prospekt

In the extremely ambivalent story "Nevskij prospekt", the world is turned upside down, and things are never quite what they seem . The comic and tragic occur at the same time, and as a result of a carnivalesque world-view, with its logic of opposites, a spatial metamorphosis takes place, which results in a world where everything is deception and nothing is really what it seems. The ambiguity also affects the literary historical position of the story, as it is an exponent of the romantic-realist intermediate genre of "phantastic realism", which at certain moments leads to inconclusiveness of styles.

3.3 Oblomov

In the case of the rather large narrative text, such as the realist novel *Oblomov*, ambivalence of semiotisation is primarily brought about by the use of different and changing points of view - that of Oblomov, Štol'c and the narrator, the shifting focalisation throughout the novel. Therefore, focalisation is a central issue in my analysis of the structure and interpretation of space in this novel. The narration starts with focalisation by one party, then shifts to another point of view, resulting in what I have designated as "dialectics" or "polyphony" of spaces. The problem of focalisation is particularly important with respect to the so-called dream-chapter. Overlooking this aspect may lead to superficial and erroneous interpretations of this crucial episode.

Another important factor in the novel is the shifting (evaluative) attitude of the central character itself, which occurs after the episode at the summer house, when he is urged to move from the centre of the town to its outskirts, to which he is very strongly unfavourably disposed in the beginning. This initial negative attitude, however, becomes more positive, and eventually brings him peace of mind. It also explains the position of Oblomov during his final confrontation with Štol'c at the end of the book. Careful examination of this narrative aspect, the focalisation of space, may therefore reveal crucial information about the meaning of the story and its interpretation.

3.4 V tolpe

As in "Nevskij prospekt", a comparable metamorphosis of space occurs in "V tolpe". In both stories, the world is turned upside-down, leading to ambivalence of evaluation, double meaning, contradiction, even inconclusiveness, and the intrusion of chaos, which destroys meaning. In romantic literature this is a demonic force, which encroaches from outer space. In symbolism, on the other hand, it is the immanent absurdity of the world itself that is pictured in apocalyptic terms. The awareness of opposites as a result of the bipartite structuration of the world ("reality vs. non-reality") is inherent to the symbolist world-view, and ambivalence appears to be a central issue in the interpretation of Sologub's story. It affects the (positive vs. negative) evaluation of the key-oppositions, and explains the ambivalence of emotions of the heroes.

3.5 Kotlovan

The fundamental ambiguity in Kotlovan rules out an unequivocal evaluation of images and situations in a similar way. Non-spatial connotations depend on (ideological) points of view - i.e. communist or existentialist. Opposition between inside and outside space (the house and open nature) is evaluated differently, depending on the ideological point of view. One of the central Platonovian themes, shelterlessness, does not have an absolutely negative meaning at all. On the contrary, it expresses important favourable values as well - independance and freedom of the mind and soul.

4.0 the evolution of space in Russian literature

A typological model of evolution must always take into account the arbitrariness of criterias and also the phenomenon of dominance which is inherent to the literary system as such. Typological criterias, literary sub-codes in Smirnov's terminology, that have proven recurrent in the course of this investigation of literary space, were primarily those concerning the presence of "dvoemirie", "verticality" or "horizontality" as the dominant structure of the world, "dynamic" and "static" visions of the world, the presence of metaphoric and metonymic descriptions.

Literary evolution, as I have come to understand it, is a shift in dominance between these codes, as well as the various constitutive elements of the text and their functions, and not a process of disappearance and exclusion. Smirnov's 1977 transformation theory also hints at this overlapping and intermingling of style-codes from different periods, cf. his statement about the different speed of transformation between the various levels of the text (1977: 22).

The different speed of evolution of the various transformations taking place on different levels of the system from one literary period to the next may therefore explain the phenomenon of inconclusiveness of styles and also inconclusiveness of world-views. In this research, only one particular aspect of the literary system has been considered: the category of space. It appears that not one of the criterias for typological classification or sub-codes is exclusively reserved for one of the two styletypes. However, this needs not imply the condemnation of Smirnov's model. The concept of "primary" and "secondary" styles, as Lichačev (1973) intended it, remains intact as the designation of two basic styletypes with two fundamentally different attitudes toward the world and reality: 1) a "simple" view, according to which the world of the text is seen as a continuation of extra-literary reality; 2) an "encoded" world-view, dominated by semiotisation of reality. It is a useful model for discerning the general among the individual. However, it can never explain the peculiarities of a unique work of art sufficiently.

4.1 Romantic space

A strong and distinct bipolar structure of the world - dvoemirie - may be called typical of the romantic style, in as far as it is one of the dominating organisational parameters of romantic space and the romantic world-view in general. In "Nevskij prospekt" it takes the form of a confrontation between a rational, and, to a certain extent, even realist world (topographical realism, first impulses for psychologisation) and a demonic-fantastic world. In "Mcyri" this dvoemirie is active on several levels: the typically romantic, inwardly torn hero, in an almost cliché-like bipartite world. The link between the romantic hero and the romantic conflict on the one hand, and the structure of romantic space on the other, is, i.a., expressed in the selfdefinition of the romantic outsider - "ja-čužoj" - and the compulsory crossing, or attempt at crossing, of the boundary between the two worlds that are being juxtaposed.

The structure of space along the axis of verticality appears in both "Nevskij prospekt" and "Mcyri", expressing the fundamental irreconcilability between the two worlds.

However, both stories may be read from a realist perspective as well. We find such a reading, for instance, in much Soviet criticism. That such a reading is still possible also hints at the transitory position in literary evolution of these two stories.

4.2 Realist space

In *Oblomov*, I detected another confrontation of two distinct worldviews. One could argue that these are views of "equal" status - a fading feudal world, typified by an archaic attitude towards life and reality, and rising commercialism clash in the persons of the two central characters.

Contrary to the characters of Romanticism, the opposition can be attenuated and even abolished. At certain points, Oblomov's dream and reality become one, notably in the "diffusion" of spaces between Oblomovka and his actual home in the outskirts of Petersburg. I have argued that in this respect Oblomov, the romantic, becomes a realist. The end of the novel may be interpreted also from the point of view of the lifting of oppositions, when Štol'c succeeds in pulling Oblomovka out of its apathy by building a railway, a symbol par excellence of movement and change.

Metonymic descriptions of space are essential in this realist novel. In as much as the rooms and landscapes relate to the hero's mental state, spatial descriptions have the function of informing the reader about the psychology of the characters. These are moments of interaction between psychic condition and spatial description. However, this does not preclude metaphorical episodes as well, situations in which the spatial metaphors (such as the image of the grave, and the treasure hidden down below under the surface, unseen) hint at the symbolical interpretation of the hero's hidden inner life. Such similes provide the reader with a deeper insight in the hero's psychology.

The use of the traditional romantic metaphors of fallen angels, and the fading hothouse plant, the "polemical", "anti-romantic", description of the "realist" landscape, and descriptions of so called "domesticated" space (in contrast to the wild and passionate romantic nature) are indications of the partly transitory position of this novel in literary evolution.

More generally speaking, space in Realist literature often has the sole function of providing the rational background for the events, in the form of a socio-geographical setting. This is, for instance, the case in the novels of Tolstoj and Turgenjev. Abundance of details, objects in rooms, plants and animals in open nature create the illusion of verisimilitude that is crucial during this literary period.

4.3 Symbolist space and Modernist space

From the analyses in this study it has become evident that the function of space as a literary category undergoes a considerable and unprecedented shift towards the end of Realism. Space, and for that matter also time, no longer merely constitute the framework of the narrative. They become active, influential powers of equal status as the heroes and the plot. In some texts of this period, the literary character and his actions are even subordinated to the power of space. In its most extreme form, this results in a "personification of things" (Drozda 1987: 159) and "anthropomorphisation of space" (Koschmal 1980 and 1987). At the end of Realism, there is a loss of hierarchy on all levels of the artistic structure. The category of space gains importance, also as a result of its modelling capacities. Time and space are seen to reflect the new perceptions of reality, man's bewilderment and estrangement during this particularly tormenting period in history and in art.

The significance of events (actions) and persons is described less often against the background of specific historical, social or psychological circumstances, as in the preceding period of Realism (and to a certain extent of Romanticism). Instead, events are presented as fatal occurrences of a sometimes universal meaning (Drozda 1987: 157), which implies a form of literary space with very specific, especially chaotic, features.

A "forerunner" of this emancipatory process of literary space can be found in the fantastic, and grotesque genre. This also accounts for some parallels between, e.g., "Nevsky prospekt" and "V tolpe", such as enchanted space and chaos of meaning. We see here the influence of the mythopoetic tradition, which, generally speaking, has a powerful modelling function in modernist literature. In "V tolpe" the hostility of surrounding space, which seeks to destroy the literary characters, is an example of this animation of space. Modernist literature frequently elaborates this theme, with the city and its attributes (streets, houses, squares, crowds), or nature with its cosmic phenomena (sun, moon, stars, cold, heat, etc.) as the personifications of such hostile space.

As far as the thematisation of space and time in post-Realist literature is concerned, no essential difference can be found between the functioning of this category in Symbolist and Modernist texts. The way in which space and time figure in Symbolism and subsequently in Modernism is innovative and norm breaking compared to the preceding two periods of Romanticism and Realism. However, if we are to follow Smirnov's typological scheme of primary and secondary styles, these periods belong to different style categories.

Sologub's story possesses a powerful metaphysical dimension. The world of symbols dominates day-to-day reality. This leads to a fundamental "dvoemirie", according to which everything perceptible gains meaning and significance only in relation to the "other", "higher" level of existence. The axis of verticality is one of the ways in which this idea is structured in space.

Kotlovan lacks this metaphysical dimension. On another level, there is a confrontation of two worldviews. The "nomadic" and "sedentary" ways of life, and the respective interpretations of space connected with them, takes over what were traditionally the central functions of action and characterisation.

Other examples of Russian modernist literature in which space acquires a more prominent position are the novels *Peterburg* by Andrej Belyj and Isaak Babel's cycle *Konarmija*. Van Baak has analysed the important role of space and spatial language in this latter work extensively. The complexity of space in modernist literature reaches a peak in this work of Belyj. Here, several types of space merge: St. Petersburg as a theme in Russian literary tradition (reminiscences to the works of Puškin, Gogol, Dostoevskij) combined with the city as a historical and geographical reality (a point on the map of Russia); the world of aristocracy versus proletarian and revolutionary St. Petersburg (embodied by the various personages and the places where they live); and the city as an ideological and cultural meeting point of East and West. Space can be called the central hero of this novel.

Bibliography

Aleksandrov, A.
1970   "O povesti 'Kotlovan' A. Platonova", in: *Grani*, 1970: 77, pp. 134-143.

Aster, E. von
1980   *Geschichte der Philosophie*, Stuttgart

Austin, P.M.
1984   "The Exotic Prisoner in Russian Romanticism", in: *Russian Literature*, XVI-III, pp. 217-275.

Van Baak, J.J.
1981   "Zamjatin's 'Cave', on Troglodyte versus Urban Culture, Myth and the Semiotics of Literary Space", in: *Russian Literature* X-4, pp. 381-422.
1983   *The Place of Space in Narration*, Amsterdam.
1983a   "On Space in Russian Literature, a Diachronic Problem", in: *Dutch Contributions to the Ninth International Congress of Slavists*, pp. 25-40, Amsterdam.
1984   "Continuity and Change: Some Remarks on World Pictures in Russian Literature", in: *Signs of Friendship To Honour A.G.F.van Holk*, pp. 365-376, Amsterdam.
1987   "Avangardistskij obraz mira i postroenie konflikta", in: *Russian Literature* XXI, pp. 1-10.
1988   "Visions of the North: Remarks on Russian Literary World Pictures", in: *Dutch Contributions to the Tenth International Congress of Slavists*, pp. 19-43, Amsterdam.
1989   "On the 'Inconclusiveness' of World-Pictures in Russian Avant-Garde Prose", in: *Aspects of modern Russian and Czech Literature*, pp. 22-30, Columbus.
1990   "The House in Russian Avantgarde Prose: Chronotope and Archetype", in: *Essays in Poetics*, 15-1, pp. 1-16.

Bachelard, G
1957   *La poétique de l'espace*, Paris.

Bachtin, M.
1965   *Tvorčestvo Fransua Rable i narodnaja kul'tura srednevekov'ja i renessansa*, Moskva.
1975   "Formy vremeni i chronotopa v romane. Očerki po istoričeskoj poètike", in: *Voprosy literatury i èstetiki*, pp. 234-407, Moskva.
1975a   "Rable i Gogol', iskusstvo slova i narodnaja smechovaja kul'tura", in: *Voprosy literatury i èstetiki*, pp. 484-495, Moskva.

Bethea, D.M.
1989   *The Shape of Apocalypse in Modern Russian Fiction*, Princeton, New
        Jersey.

Brodsky, J.
1986   "Catastrophes in the Air", in: *Less than One*, pp. 268-304, New York.

Burkhart, D.
1987   "Mythoide Verfahren der Welt-Generierung in Andrej Belyjs Roman
        'Peterburg'", in: *Wiener Slawistischer Almanach*, Sonderband 20,
        pp. 169-192.

Butor, M.
1964   "Philosophie de l'ameublement", in: *Répertoire* II, pp. 51-60.

Byrns, R.
1975/6 "Gogol' and the Feminine Myth", in: *Etudes Slaves et Est-Européennes*,
        vols.XX-XXI, pp. 44-61.

Cassirer, E.
1975   "Mythischer, ästhetischer and theoretischer Raum", in: *Landschaft und
        Raum in der Erzählkunst*, Hrg. A. Ritter, pp. 17-35, Darmstadt.
1977   *Philosophie der symbolischen Formen, 2. Teil: Das Mythische Denken*,
        Darmstadt.

Cejtlin, A.G.
1950   *I.A. Gončarov*, Moskva.

Civ'jan, T.V.
1978   "Dom v fol'klornoj modeli mira (na materiale balkanskich zagadok)", in:
        Trudy po znakovym sistemam X, pp. 65-86.

Doležel, L.
1967   "The Typology of the Narrator: Point of View in Fiction", in:
        To Honor Roman Jakobson, The Hague.

Donchin, G.
1958   *The Influence of French Symbolism on Russian Poetry*, The Hague.

Döring, I.R. i Smirnov, I.P.
1980   "Realizm: diachroničeskij podchod", in: *Russian Literature*, VIII, pp. 1-39.

Drozda, M.
1987   "Mifologizm Leonida Andreeva", in: *Wiener Slawistischer Almanach*,
        Sonderband 20, pp. 157-168.

Ehre, M.
1973   *Oblomov and his Creator*, Princeton, New Jersey.

Ejchenbaum, B.
1987   *O literature*, Moskva.

Eliade, M.
1985   *Das Heilige und das Profane*, Frankfurt am Main.

Eng, J. van der
1978   "On Descriptive Narrative Poetics", in: *On the Theory of Descriptive Poetics: Anton P. Chekhov as Story-Teller and Playwright*, pp. 9-99, Lisse.
1984   "Ästhetische Dominante und Fiktionalisierung, Wahrheitsanspruch und Intensivierung der Information, Author und Leser", in: *Text, Symbol, Weltmodell. Johannes Holthusen zum 60. Geburtstag*, pp. 111-131, München.

Erlich, V.
1955   *Russian Formalism. History - Doctrine*, The Hague.

Fasmer, M.
1971   *Etimologičeskij slovar' russkogo jazyka*, Moskva.

Flaker, A.
1979   "Symbolism or Modernism in Slavic Literatures?", in: *Russian Literature* VII (4), pp. 329-349.
1987   "Die Strasse: ein neuer Mythos der Avantgarde (Majakovskij, Chlebnikov, Krleža)", in: *Wiener Slawistischer Almanach*, Sonderband 20, pp. 139-156.

Frank, J.
1963   "Spatial Form in Modern Literature", in: *The Widening Gyre*, pp. 3-63, Bloomington & London.

Gavrilova, E.N.
1990   "Andrej Platonov i Pavel Filonov, o poètike povesti 'Kotlovan'", in: *Literaturnaja učeba*, kn.I, pp. 164-173.

Geller, M.
1982   *Andrej Platonov v poiskach sčast'ja*, Paris.

Gippius, V.
1924   *Gogol'*, Leningrad.

Gogol, N.
1964   "Nevsky Prospekt", in: *The Collected Tales and Plays of Nikolai Gogol*, Ed., Introd. and notes Leonard J.Kent, New York.
1976-1979   *Sobranie sočinenij v semi tomach*, Moskva.

Gončarov, I.A.
1953   *Sobranie sočinenij v 8-mi tomach*, Moskva.
1954   *Oblomov*, Translated and with an Introduction by David Magarshack,
        Penguin Books, London.

Grübel, R.
1982   "Methode, Wertbegriff und Wertung in der Kunsttheorie des Leningrader
        Bachtin-Kreises", in: *Beschreiben, Interpretieren, Werten: Das
        Wertungsproblem in der Literatur aus der Sicht unterschiedlicher
        Methoden*, Herg. B. Lenz und B. Schulte-Middelich, pp. 95-134, München.

Grygar, M.
1982   "The Role of Personality in Literary Development" in: *The Structure of the
        Literary Process*, Studies dedicated to the Memory of Felix Vodička,
        pp. 187-211, Amsterdam/Philadelphia.

Gukovskij, G.A.
1959   *Realizm Gogolja*, Moskva-Leningrad.

Hamon, Ph.
1972   "Qu'est-ce-qu'une description?", in: *Poétique*, No. 12, 465-485.

Hansen-Löve, A.A.
1978   *Der Russische Formalismus*, Wien.
1980   "Semantik   der   Evolution   und   Evolution   der   Semantik.   Ein
        Forschungsbericht zu I.P. Smirnov's Modell einer diachronen Semiotik",
        in: *Wiener Slawistischer Almanach*, 6, pp. 131-190.

Hansson, C.
1975   *Fedor Sologub as a Short-Story Writer* (Stylistic Analysis), Stockholm.

Ivanov, V.V. i Toporov,V.N.
1965   *Slavjanskie jazykovye modelirujuščie semiotičeskie sistemy* (Drevnij
        period), Moskva.

Jakobson, R. and M. Halle
1956   "The Metaphoric and Metonymic Poles", in: *Fundamentals of Language*,
        pp. 76-82, The Hague.

Jakobson, R.
1960   "Closing Statement: Linguistics and Poetics", in: *Style and Language*, ed.
        Thomas A. Sebeok, pp. 350-377, Cambridge, Mass.
1981   "The Dominant", in: *Selected Writings III, Poetry of Grammar and
        Grammar of Poetry*, ed. Stephen Rudy, pp. 751-756, The Hague/Paris/New
        York.

Jauss, R.
1967   *Literaturgeschichte als Provokation der Literaturwissenschaft*, Konstanz.

Klejman, L.
1983   *Rannjaja proza Fedora Sologuba*, Ann Arbor.

Koschmal, W.
1980   "Semantisierung von Raum und Zeit", in: *Poetica* 12, 3-4, pp. 397-420.
1987   "Zur mythischen Modellierung von Raum und Zeit bei Andrej Belyj und Bruno Schultz", in: *Wiener Slawistischer Almanach*, Sonderband 20, pp. 193-214.

Lachmann, R.
1990   *Gedächtnis und Literatur, Intertextualität in der russischen Moderne*, Frankfurt am Main.

Lakoff and Johnson
1980   *Metaphors We Live By*, Chicago and Boston.

Lauretis, de T.
1984   "Desire in Narrative", in: *Alice doesn't, Feminism, Semiotics, Cinema*, pp. 103-157, Indiana Univ. Press, Bloomington.

Lermontov, M.Ju.
1965   *The Demon and other Poems*, Transl. Eugene M. Kayden, Introd. Sir Maurice Bowra, Yellow Springs, Ohio.
1981   *Sobranie sočinenij v četyrech tomach*, tom 4, Leningrad.
1989   *Polnoe sobranie stichotvorenij v dvuch tomach*, Biblioteka poèta, bol'šaja serija, Leningrad.

Levin, Ju.I.
1990   "Ot sintaksisa k smyslu i dalee ('Kotlovan' A. Platonova)", in: *Semiotika i informatika*, vyp. 30, pp. 115-148.

Lichačev, D.S.
1967   *Poètika drevnerusskoj literatury*, Leningrad.
1973   "Velikie stili i stil' barokko", in: *Razvitie russkoj literatury X-XVII vv. Epochi i stili*, pp. 172-183, Leningrad.

Lotman, Ju.M.
1964   *Lekcii po struktural'noj poètike. Vvedenie, teoria sticha*, Brown University Slavic Reprint 1968, Providence.
1968   "Problema chudožestvennogo prostranstva v proze Gogolja", in: *Trudy po russkoj i slavjanskoj filologii XI, Literaturovedenie*, pp. 5-50.
1971   *Struktura chudožestvennogo teksta*, Brown University Slavic Reprint, Providence.
1976   "Gogol' and the Correlation of 'The Culture of Humor' with the Comic and Serious in the Russian National Tradition", in: *Semiotics and Structuralism*, ed. H. Baran, pp. 297-300, New York.
1979   "The Origin of the Plot in the Light of Typology", in: *Poetics Today I*, 1/2, 161-184.

1984   "Simvolika Peterburga i problemy semiotiki goroda", in: *Trudy po znakovym sistemam XVIII*, pp. 30-45.

1986   "Ot redakcii. K probleme prostranstvennoj semiotiki", in: *Trudy po znakovym sistemam XIX*, pp. 3-6.

1986   "Zametki o chudožestvennom prostranstve", ibid., pp. 25-43.

1987   "O sjužetnom prostranstve russkogo romana XIX stoletija", in: *Trudy po znakovym sistemam XX*, pp. 102-114.

1990   *Universe of the Mind. A Semiotic Theory of Culture*, London-New York.

Lotman, Ju.M. and Uspenskij B.A.

1977   "Rol' dual'nych modelej v dinamike russkoj kul'tury (do konca XVIII veka)", in: *Trudy po russkoj i slavjanskoj filologii, XXVIII Literaturovedenie*, pp. 3-36.

Lyngstad, A. and S.

1971   *Ivan Gončarov*, New York.

Maksimov, D.

1959   *Poèzija Lermontova*, Leningrad.

Mann, Ju.V.

1976   *Poètika russkogo romantizma*, Moskva.

1978   *Poètika Gogolja*, Moskva.

Markštejn, E.

1980   "Dom i kotlovan, ili mnimaja realizacija utopii (Čitaja Andreja Platonova)", in: *Rossija/Russia*, Studi i ricerche a cura di Vittorio Strada, 4, pp. 245-269..

Medvedev, P.

1978   *The Formal Method in Literary Scholarship*, London.

Meletinskij, E.A.

1976   *Poètika mifa*, Moskva.

Mersereau, J.Jr.

1971   "Toward a Normative Definition of Russian Realism", in: *California Slavic Studies*, VI, pp. 131-143.

1973   "Normative Distinctions of Russian Romanticism and Realism", in: *American Contributions to the 7th International Congress of Slavists*, Warsaw, 1973, vol.II, ed. V.Terras, pp. 393-417, The Hague/Paris.

Mify

1982   *Mify narodov mira v dvuch tomach*, ed. S.A. Tokarev, Moskva

Minc, Z.G.

1974   "Ponjatie teksta i simvolistskaja èstetika", in: *Materialy vsesojuznogo simpozijuma po vtoričnym modelirujuščim sistemam*, I (5), pp. 134-141.

Mukařovský, J.
1978   "The Aesthetic Norm", in: *Structure, Sign and Function, Selected Essays*, Transl. and Ed. by Peter Steiner, pp. 49-57, New Haven/London.

Naiman, E.
1987   "The Thematic Mythology of Andrej Platonov", in: *Russian Literature*, XXI-II, pp. 189-216.

Nekljudov, S.Ju.
1972   "Vremja i prostranstvo v byline", in: *Slavjanskij fol'klor*, Moskva.

Nilsson, N.A.
1975   "Gogol's 'The Overcoat' and the Topography of Petersburg", in: *Scando-Slavica*, 21, 5-19.

Peace, R.
1981   *The Enigma of Gogol*, Cambridge, MA.

Platonov, A.
1973   *The Foundation Pit, Kotlovan*, a Bi-lingual Edition, English Translation by Thomas P. Whitney, Preface by Joseph Brodsky, Ann Arbor, 1973.
1987   "Kotlovan", in: *Novyj mir*, 6, pp. 50-124.

Propp, V.Ja.
1969   *Morfologija skazki*, Moskva.
1986   *Istoričeskie korni volšebnoj skazki*, Leningrad.

Rabinowitz, S.
1980   *Sologub's Literary Children: Keys to a Symbolist's Prose*, Columbus, Ohio.

Šklovskij, V.
1916   "Iskusstvo kak priëm", in: Striedter 1969, pp. 4-34.

Smirnov, I.P.
1977   *Chudožestvennyj smysl i èvoljucija poètičeskich sistem*, Moskva.

Sologub, F.
1913-1914 *Sobranie sčinenij v XX-i tomach*, St.Peterburg.
1977   "In the Crowd", in: *"The Kiss of the Unborn" and other stories*, Transl. and Introd. Murl G. Barker, Knoxville, Tennessee.

Striedter, J.
1969   *Texte der Russische Formalisten I*, München.
1975   *Texte der Russische Formalisten II*, München.
1983   "Three Postrevolutionary Russian Utopian Novels", in: *The Russian Novel from Pushkin to Pasternak*, ed. by John Garrard, pp. 177-203, New Haven and London.
1989   *Russian Formalism and Czech Strucuralism Reconsidered*, Boston.

Tolstaja-Segal, E.
1978   "Naturfilosofskie temy v tvorčestve Platonova 20-ch-30-ch gg.", in: *Slavica Hierosolymitana II*.

Toporov, V.N.
1973   "O strukture romana Dostoevskogo v svjazi s archaičnymi schemami mifologičeskogo myšlenija, in: *Strukture of Texts and Semiotics of Culture*, ed.J.van der Eng and M.Grygar, pp. 225-302, The Hague Paris.
1983   "Prostranstvo i tekst", in: *Tekst: semantika i struktura*, pp. 227-284, Moskva.
1984   "Peterburg i Peterburgskij tekst russkoj literatury", in: *Trudy po znakovym sistemam XVIII*, pp. 4-29.

Tschiževskij, D.
1968   *Vergleichende Geschichte der Slawischen Literatur*, Berlin

Tynjanov, Ju.
1924   "Literaturnyj fakt", in: Striedter 1969, pp. 392-430.
1927   "O literaturnoj èvoljucii", in: Striedter 1969, pp. 432-460

Tynjanov, Ju. i Jakobson, R.
1928   "Problemy izučenija literatury i jazyka", in: Striedter 1972, pp. 387-392.

Uspenskij, B.A.
1970   *Poètika kompozicii. Struktura chudožestvennogo teksta i tipologija kompozicionnoj formy*, Moskva.

Wörringer, W.
1908   *Abstraktion und Einfühlung*, München.

Žirmunskij, V.
1962   "O poèzii klassičeskoj i romantičeskoj", in: *Voprosy literatury*, The Hague.
1970   *Bajron i Puškin*, Nachdruck, München. (1924)

Zolotusskij, I.P.
1979   *Gogol'*, Moskva.